COMMENTARY
ON GALATIANS

RAGNAR BRING

Translated by Eric Wahlstrom

MUHLENBERG PRESS

PHILADELPHIA

PREFACE

It has sometimes been assumed that an interpretation of the New Testament writings should be concerned only with scientific expositions of the Greek text from a philological point of view together with some comparisons drawn from the study of the history of religions. Some, on the other hand, believe that the interpretation should have a popular character so that attention can be given to the value of the Bible for edification. Consequently it has been held that the purely scientific commentaries belong to the philologists. To people who are not experts these commentaries have often appeared difficult to use and understand, and devoid of general interest.

If this point of view were to prevail, one aspect of the scientific interpretation of the New Testament would be neglected, viz., the orderly presentation of the whole content of thought and the context of ideas found in these writings.

In order to understand the biblical texts it is undoubtedly necessary to study them from the point of view of vocabulary, style, and history of religion, but a theological study of the content and lines of thought is also necessary. These different approaches do not exclude but must complement one another. The main question which we undertake to answer in this commentary is: What did Paul think and intend to say in this letter? For various reasons the discussion of philology and style has had to be eliminated or pushed into the background. These questions have been taken up only in certain important passages where different textual readings have a bearing on the understanding of the thought. A general discussion of the Greek text has not been included.

It is now generally agreed that Paul is the author of the Letter to the Galatians. It is one of the most important documents from which to learn about Paul and his theology.

In order to understand many of the statements in this letter it is frequently necessary to refer to other letters of Paul. We do not need to discuss the authenticity of these other letters. Such discussion belongs to the interpretation of those letters, and furthermore it is immaterial to our purpose to discuss opinions held about the authorship of such letters as Ephesians and Colossians. These letters are so permeated by Paul's thought that they may be used freely to elucidate passages in Galatians. This letter is very brief. Paul deals only with what the Galatians needed to have explained. Sometimes the development of a thought is so brief that it needs to be clarified by comparison with similar thoughts in other letters. In this way the uncertainty of the meaning in some passages may be at least partially removed. The letter was of course written to congregations which Paul had visited several times and where he had already preached the gospel. He presents here the very foundation of that gospel and the proper reception of it. Moreover, Paul's presentation is made with a constant open or concealed polemic against "the Judaizers" who have perverted the gospel and caused confusion among the Galatians.

In the series of interpretations of the New Testament of which this commentary is a part the use of footnotes has been omitted. It is not possible therefore to indicate all the sources used, nor can they be mentioned in this preface. Besides the great German, English, and French commentaries I refer only to the earlier works in this series, the commentary on Romans by A. Nygren, and the commentary on the letters to the Corinthians by H. Odeberg. The author is greatly indebted to Prof. J. Munck for his works on Paul, and also to Profs. A. Wifstrand, E. Starfelt and H. Ljungman.

This book is dedicated to my wife who during many years has been of immense help to me. Without her help this book could not have appeared in the form it has now assumed.

Lund, May 1958. RAGNAR BRING.

CONTENTS

Contents

INTRODUCTION

I. Brief Introductory Paragraphs on the Letter to the Galatians

1. The significance of the letter in the history of theology

Even though the Letter to the Galatians has been interpreted and evaluated differently in the course of time, it has been of considerable importance in the history of theology. Its theological significance entitles it to a place among the "great" letters of the New Testament. This has especially been recognized since the Reformation. During the Middle Ages the letter was interpreted mostly on the basis of the commentaries of the ancient fathers, but these did not present it as of special significance. The Reformers, on the other hand, saw in it a vigorous summary of the whole Christian message of salvation. Luther treasured it very highly (Cf. *WA TR* 1, 146). He delivered two famous series of lectures on the letter, 1516-17 and 1531 (*WA* 2, 436-618, and *WA* 40$^\text{I}$, 1-688; 40$^\text{II}$, 1-184). Calvin, too, wrote a commentary on Galatians.

About the middle of the nineteenth century the Letter to the Galatians became central in the discussion of the New Testament due to the critical studies of the Tübingen School (F. Ch. Baur, *Paulus,* [1845]). Under the influence of Hegel's philosophy of history this school claimed to discover a decisive contradiction between Paul and the original apostles in Jerusalem. The activity of the Judaizers in Galatia was related to the apostles in Jerusalem who were regarded as rejecting the preaching of Paul. In our day these theses have been subjected to considerable criticism from various points of view. Some of these ideas have now generally been abandoned, and J. Munck in his great work, *Paulus und die Heilsgeschichte,* has subjected this school to some radical criticism.

In liberal theology Galatians has been presented as the document which proclaims *freedom* from all law. Albert Schweitzer finds in Galatians the best example of a mystical doctrine of salvation liberated from Jewish influences. But even those who do not accept Schweitzer's emphasis on mysticism have held that *freedom* is the central theme of the letter, and yet they have not shown clearly the unique character of Paul's conception of freedom.

From a historical point of view Galatians is an especially important document for our understanding of how the early church differentiated itself from Judaism. We will demonstrate later, however, that this differentiation did not imply an emancipation from the Old Testament and its law. Here in Galatians especially Paul anchors his theology to the Old Testament, though he interprets it in a new way in the light of the revelation given to him. But his proclamation had encountered opposition. The occasion of the letter was evidently that "Judaizers" wanted to combine a Jewish interpretation of the Old Testament with faith in Jesus. Since they had criticized Paul's message, the letter constitutes his answer to what he regarded as their perversion of the gospel.

Although Paul did not repudiate the Old Testament, but held that he stood in perfect agreement with it, his rejection of the Judaizers meant that the church could not become a Jewish sect. The church became independent of Judaism but retained the Old Testament as its sacred Scriptures.

2. The recipients of the letter

Galatia was the name of a district in the center of Asia Minor, but it was also the name of a Roman province which included additional portions of Asia Minor. The ethnic province of Galatia had received its name from the people of Gaul who had settled there before the coming of the Romans. In 25 B.C. the Romans reorganized the administration of Asia Minor and made a larger province by adding portions of other territories to the old ethnic province and calling this new administrative unit Galatia. It is this situation which makes it uncertain whether the letter was addressed to the people in the old ethnic province of Galatia (the North-Galatian theory), or to the people in the southern part of the Roman province of Galatia. If all the people in the Roman province could be called "Galatians," the letter might have been addressed to the people in that part of the province which Paul visited on his first missionary journey, i.e., portions of the old provinces of Lycaonia and Pisidia. Paul had founded churches in this part (Acts 13:14ff; 14:1ff.), and had visited them again on his second missionary journey (Acts 16:1ff.). The opinion that

4

the letter was written to these congregations (the South-Galatian theory) has been quite generally held in modern times. The Galatian country is mentioned in Acts 16:6, but this seems to be the district in the center of Asia Minor, the *ethnic* province of Galatia. According to Acts 18:23 Paul visited "the Galatian country" also on the third missionary journey and strengthened the disciples.

For our understanding of the actual content of the letter it is relatively unimportant whether we accept the one or the other of these theories. It seems that the South-Galatian theory, although it was generally accepted for many years, is now being abandoned by many scholars. It has been pointed out that it would be strange for Paul to call the people in the southern part of the Roman province (Lycaonia and Pisidia) "Galatians" (cf. 3:1). Since this question is not decisive for the understanding of the letter, we need not discuss it further. If we attach too much importance to these and other historical questions, the theological interpretation and the attempt to understand the content of the letter might tend to be neglected.

It must be admitted, however, that the acceptance of one or the other of these theories has a bearing on the date of the letter. The South-Galatian theory would permit an earlier date, even as early as A.D. 50 or 51. But even though the letter was probably written some years later, as seems more likely, the date has no decisive significance for our understanding of the content.

If we assume that the letter was addressed to congregations founded by Paul in the center of Asia Minor (the North-Galatian theory), it would have been written during Paul's third missionary journey, either during or after his long ministry in Ephesus (Acts 19:1—20:1).

Acts 16:6 does not say specifically that Paul founded congregations in Galatia, nor does it mention the sickness (Gal. 4:13f.) which was the reason for his visit among the Galatians. But Acts is not a complete record of Paul's ministry, and the omission of the details of the first visit does not prove that Paul did not establish congregations in the Galatian country when he was forced to spend some time there. According to Acts 18:23 he visited them again and encouraged the brethren.

3. The occasion of the letter

The occasion for the letter was the disturbing reports which Paul had received from the congregations. We could say that the matter concerned the interpretation of the gospel and its relation to the Scriptures of the old covenant. After Paul had met Christ on the Damascus road, he had learned to understand these Scriptures in a new sense. The law had been fulfilled in Christ. In Christ he had met a revelation of the God who had spoken and acted in the Old Testament. He saw these Scriptures in a new light, and as a result his preaching presented a new interpretation of the word of the Old Testament. According to Paul both the Law and the Prophets pointed forward to Christ, and in Him their words received their explanation and fulfilment. Their inner meaning and purpose became clear through the act of God in Christ. We will discuss Paul's conception of Scripture in another place. Here we may simply state that to him the gospel was firmly grounded in the Old Testament, so that he could constantly refer his hearers to this fundamental document of revelation. But his interpretation was different from that represented by the Jews in the places where he had preached the gospel.

The so-called Judaizers had arrived in Galatia. Their intention was to change the gospel into a variation of the Jewish proclamation in the sense that faith in Christ as the Messiah would be added to salvation by observance of the law, which was the condition of salvation among the Jews. Consequently they made circumcision a condition for participation in salvation. The law, at least in certain parts, had to be observed. They claimed the authority of the Jerusalem apostles for their views. Paul himself, they said, must have received the gospel from these apostles. He could present only what he had received by instruction and tradition, but he had transmitted this tradition in an incomplete and misleading form. The preaching of the Judaizers had evidently been quite persuasive. They appeared to have Scripture on their side. By their emphasis on the necessity of observing the law their preaching appeared very attractive, as any teaching does which claims to represent a strict ethical ideal.

Paul recognized at once that this involved a complete perversion of the gospel and a denial of its power and essential meaning. He writes to the Galatians as to people who are in danger of falling away from the gospel and returning to their earlier religious practices. When Paul visited them, the Galatians had rejoiced in the reception of the gospel, but now they had become confused and lost sight of its meaning. They had been seduced by the preaching of the Judaizers. Circumcision seems to have become the central point. The way in which they made circumcision a condition for membership in the church and for participation in salvation and righteousness meant that they obscured and in reality denied the gospel.

4. The general character of the letter

The letter to the Galatians deals with Christ and the law. But the letter is not written as a calm, dogmatic exposition of a general theme. It has a definite purpose which characterizes the whole letter. Since the occasion was that the congregations were led astray from faith in Christ as proclaimed by Paul and were persuaded to adopt the interpretation of the Judaizers, it is clear that the letter would have been quite different had it been intended as an interpretative presentation of the meaning of the Christian faith. Both the style and the tone have been influenced by the occasion, and the content too has been selected with this situation in view. The reason why Paul recounts certain episodes in his life is that he wants to explain his relationship to the gospel and to the original apostles, and He refutes the claim that his message was dependent upon these apostles, and that therefore an authentic knowledge of the meaning of the Christian faith could be found only with them.

The presentation here of Paul's own life is not an autobiography or a historical record. It is a part of his eager attempt to explain the actual significance of his apostleship and of the gospel entrusted to him as an apostle. What Paul wants to show by reminding them of a part of his life is the divine character of the message he proclaimed. The letter is written with intense feeling but as an objective and factual exposition of faith in Christ in opposition to the Jewish conception of righteousness. It is written to congregations which were drifting toward what Paul considered a false faith, to disciples who without realizing it were on the point of falling away from the gospel. It is obvious that the Judaizers had presented their message as genuinely Christian, but it was nevertheless a perversion of the whole Christian faith. Since the Judaizers were unable to harmonize Paul's preaching with their own presentation of the way of salvation, they had to persuade the Galatians that Paul did not have the same authority as the older apostles. Obviously they claimed that these apostles represented a different theology from that of Paul. Paul was thus forced to introduce his exposition by giving an account of the basis and reality of his own authority and also to explain his relationship to Peter.

Both the introduction and the conclusion of the letter are characterized by Paul's zeal in presenting his message and defending its truth. The whole form of the letter from beginning to end reveals the seriousness of the message which Paul now addresses to the Galatians. The polemical tone does not obscure the positive presentation; it serves rather to make it more intensive and clear. Although Paul expresses himself very briefly, so briefly that at times it is difficult to understand his allusions, the fundamental ideas are vividly expressed and reveal clearly the structure of his thought.

II. Preliminary Consideration of the Relationship of the Pauline Gospel to the Law and Scripture

1. Freedom from the law

Galatians pits freedom against bondage. But it is not just any kind of freedom or just any kind of bondage. It is that freedom which belongs together with faith and the Spirit. The bondage is bondage under righteousness by the law.

It is usually said that the theme of Galatians is freedom from the law. It is supposed to contain a settlement of the question of the Jewish law and a proclamation of complete freedom from this law. Sometimes this has been understood as an emancipation from all law. Certain expressions may seem to indicate that this could be the correct interpretation. We must, however, exercise some caution here, because the question at issue is not the common, popular conception of the meaning of freedom from the law.

As in all the letters of Paul, freedom is freedom from bondage under law, sin, and death; but this is not the same as license to do whatever one may desire. It must not be used so as to give an "opportunity for the flesh" (Gal. 5:13). The positive content of this freedom is a relationship to Christ which also may be designated as bondage or slavery. The liberation is freedom from the necessity of seeking one's own righteousness; but it is also freedom to serve in love (Gal. 5:14). Here on earth that freedom is realized in a constant conflict between "the flesh" and the Spirit, between "the old man" and "the new." Being a slave of Christ (cf. I Cor. 6:19; 7:22; 9:17) is not bondage under external constraint, for the Christian does the will of God from the heart (cf. Eph. 6:6). He is freed from the slavery of sin in order to become a servant of righteousness (Rom. 6:17, 22). No one lives to please himself (Rom. 15:1ff.). But although life in Christ might be called bondage, it is of a nature entirely different from that of slavery under law and sin. Bondage to Christ is connected with joy and peace, and the condition is likened to that of the son who becomes of age and enters upon his rich inheritance.

9

The use of this rich inheritance, however, is a willing service in which the flesh is not given an opportunity, but in which man has found his true Lord in him who is his Creator and Father (Gal. 4:6).

We must guard carefully against the temptation to interpret Paul's words about the freedom from the law as if he meant that the law and the Old Testament were ended in the sense that their words no longer have any meaning or validity.

The Pauline concept of "law" (*nomos*) goes back to the Hebrew *Torah,* which also means scripture or instruction. The idea that Galatians seeks to liberate the gospel from the Old Testament Scriptures is entirely mistaken. It is intended rather to clarify the truth of the faith by showing that the *Scriptures* clearly testify to the righteousness by faith but reject the righteousness based on the law. His argument is intended to prove that the former is proclaimed in Scripture, and that according to Scripture the latter stands under a curse. Faith means freedom from the necessity of seeking righteousness by the law. The curse has been removed through the cross of Christ, and in him the Scriptures have been fulfilled. Christ is "the end of the law" (Rom. 10:4), the goal (*telos*) toward which everything moves; and in his cross the condemnation and the righteousness based on law have been swept away.

What the Scriptures and the law have proclaimed has now, according to Paul, been realized in Christ. This does not simply mean that the promise of a coming Messiah has now been fulfilled in and through Jesus Christ, but rather that the Messiah-Christ has come to *fulfil the Old Testament promises of righteousness and blessedness.* The law was intended to serve righteousness, but it could not produce it. It promised blessedness to the one who fulfilled the demand for righteousness, but it could not produce obedience. The task given to it, therefore, was to condemn. But in Christ the law was fulfilled, and the promise was fulfilled as well.

The freedom the letter speaks of is not a freedom from the will of God as expressed in the law, but rather a realization of his will. This is what took place in and through Christ. He *was* God's righteousness incarnate; he represented it and realized it in his life, death, and resurrection. In him the new life had come through which "the just requirement of the law" (Rom. 8:4) was fulfilled. He was the end of the law, its goal and consummation. Only in him could righteousness be received and actualized. Because

He lives in him, man can now live a real and true life in righteousness. In and through Christ he participates in the new life, the new reality, which He brought. This participation is by faith. *The fruits of faith* are therefore on a level different from that of *the works of the law*. The latter were works done by man's own efforts, by his "free will." They were the result of a conception of the law which obscured its deepest meaning because it was hidden from human wisdom. These works did not correspond to the whole demand of the law and of God's will. Instead they led men in a wrong direction. But the fruits of faith came out of that reality which has come in Christ and which manifests itself in man through the power of the Spirit. It is true that what Christ has brought will not be manifested fully and completely until his return; but the powers of the Spirit and the righteousness by faith which belong qualitatively to the coming age are already present in the lives of believers. But the knowledge of Christ is found only as a treasure in an earthen vessel.

The freedom of which Paul speaks in Galatians therefore is the freedom secured in and through the righteousness given through Christ, in which the law's demand for righteousness has been fulfilled. Only here is there freedom from the burden imposed by the law. To reject the demands of the law without accepting the righteousness of Christ would be to accept an illusion, because man would then make himself free from *one* form of bondage only to fall into another. Unless he has been set free through Christ, every man lives in bondage to the flesh whose works Paul describes in Gal. 5:19ff.

In order to guard against a wrong conception of freedom we might assert that Paul's thought is the direct opposite of the popular understanding of it: it is always his zeal *for* the law (properly understood) that compels him to speak. It is precisely the law that is opposed to human righteousness by the law. His opponents were ostensibly interested in obedience to the law. But to Paul who had been trained in the rabbinical tradition their zeal must have appeared totally misdirected. They wanted to combine faith in Christ with an observance of the law in certain respects. As a disciple of the rabbis he must have despised their imperfect and dilettante observance. Their position was not acceptable to a strict Pharisee, and it completely destroyed faith in Christ.

The question was therefore: *how* is the law to be observed

11

completely, and *how* is it fulfilled? Through revelation Paul had received an entirely new conception. Since Paul had met the risen Christ, the law had taken on a deeper meaning and all its words and commandments had to be given a new interpretation. God himself had provided this new interpretation, which was both a new exposition of what had been said in Scripture, and a new creation which provided new possibilities for faith and life. To be "of the law" meant *to contend against* the deepest meaning and purpose of the law. Now new light had been shed on the old precepts, and something new had been created which permitted a new interpretation of every word. Now a way had been prepared for attaining the righteousness of which the law spoke; a way which had not been found before. Once this new way had been prepared, it became possible to understand Scripture in a completely new way. What had been written was not changed, but it appeared in a new light so that it was now possible to understand its real meaning.

Christ had fulfilled the law. He represented the righteousness demanded by the law. Those who really walked in the Spirit lived a life in which the law's demand for righteousness had been satisfied. We can say, therefore, that it was his zeal *for* the law that drove Paul into this struggle, but the law in a *new* form and in a new sense as an expression of the revelation of the living God. This struggle has been interpreted in a false and superficial way as an attempt to emancipate Christians from the Old Testament. But to seek for righteousness through "the works of the law" is for Paul the very opposite of the real and profound meaning of the law.

2. The law and the Scriptures

Paul obviously regarded the Old Testament as a holy document in which God had revealed his truth and made known his will. It was this element in his preaching which made him susceptible to such attacks as he met here in Galatia. The common and most obvious interpretation of these Scriptures did not go in the direction which Paul proclaimed.

When Paul advocates a new interpretation of the Old Testament Scriptures, different from that of contemporary Judaism, it is not at all implied that he wants to set these Scriptures aside. On the contrary, it is because he regards these Scriptures as divine revelation that he interprets them in this way. According to Paul God speaks and works continually. What he has spoken and done must therefore be understood in connection with his continuing revelation. This has now come in Christ through his death and resurrection. Only through the work of Christ have the Scriptures been fulfilled.

"Law" meant for Paul especially the content of the five books of Moses; but in a larger sense it could also designate the whole Old Testament and its message of God's will and work. The common Hebrew name of the Scriptures and the law was *Torah,* which really means instruction and designates the revelation of God given through Moses. This revelation was to be found both in written and oral form. The rabbis continually developed new additions, commentaries, and instructions relating to the practical life. In its rabbinical form this tradition took the place of the inspired interpretation of God's will by the ancient prophets. According to the Gospel record Jesus emphatically rejected this tradition, and set his own authority over against it. His will was an expression of God's will. He could point out that the rabbinical precepts came into conflict with God's original commandment (Mark 7:6-13; Matt. 15:1-9). He himself represented the will of the living God in its full clarity and perfection. This was not a given and fixed set of instructions through which one might achieve righteousness. According to the ancient church God's will and the meaning of Scripture could be understood only through the Spirit. According to the ancient confession Christ represented God's will in his life and work. He was himself the new *Torah* which fulfilled the old.

The word *Torah* is translated by *nomos* in the Septuagint. Paul uses this word. But the Greek word has a more specifically forensic and juridical connotation than the Hebrew *Torah.* Since Paul can use the Greek word in the light of the Hebrew background, the Hebrew connotation may at times appear even more strongly in his usage than in the Septuagint. The word *nomos* does not have the exclusively juridical sense in Paul which it has in Greek writings, or which the word law has in English (cf. W. D. Davies, *Paul and Rabbinical Judaism,* p. 149). But it is a difficult problem to see how the requirements of the law are to be understood and applied after it has become clear that righteousness is given through Christ.

Paul regarded the holy Scriptures as something which cannot

13

be broken. In one sense they were "inspired" and a record of God's revelation. But this did not mean that they had to be interpreted according to the Jewish tradition. The Jewish interpretation and commentary on the words of Scripture and the law, and the multiplication of the precepts of the law in a rationalistic and casuistic fashion characteristic of the work of the scribes were foreign to Paul. To him God was always a living and active Power. When he had met Christ, he had received from God a new light in regard to the meaning of the words in the Old Testament writings. The words were not changed and were not rendered invalid, but the understanding of them was completely new.

God himself had in the work of Christ supplied the key to the understanding of Scripture. By so doing he did not cancel the earlier word, but shed new light on it and caused it to be understood from a new point of view and in a new context. Only in this new light could its inner meaning and real message be disclosed.

Paul emphasizes that it was through a revelation that he received the gospel he preached. It is reasonable to assume that at the same time he had received a new understanding of the significance of the Old Testament Scriptures. Thus the mystery of God's will had been revealed to him (Eph. 1:9). The veil which to this day lies over the mind of the Jews when the Old Testament is read (II Cor. 3.13 ff.) was removed from Paul's eyes; it was taken away in Christ. Now from the gospel, fully revealed in Christ, there went forth a light that all would be bound to see, unless the god of this world blinded their senses to it.

The revelation through which Paul thus saw the light "in the face of Christ" was given by the God of creation who once had said: "Let light shine out of darkness" (II Cor. 4:6). He had seen the glory foreshadowed in Scripture, and the meaning of Scripture had become clear to him in this light. Paul could therefore refer in his teaching and arguments to the Scriptures of the old covenant, but these could no longer be interpreted according to Jewish principles, but only in the light of the revelation given in Christ.

Paul may have found a suggestion for such an understanding of Scripture through his intimate knowledge of the rabbinical principle that the Scriptures contain a deeper meaning. It was not an uncommon idea in the ancient world that a religious document might have a deeper and secret meaning. The rabbis maintained this firmly and had developed this principle to a great extent. This may have provided a formal possibility for Paul to interpret the Scriptures of the old covenant in a new way.

Nevertheless, his interpretation still differed from that of the rabbis as well as from that of the Gnostics. Paul had a definite point of reference: faith in Christ. In the light of that faith he understood Scripture. Through the work of Christ the Scriptures were fulfilled, and the meaning and purpose of the law became clear. Thus an expansive and capricious allegorical interpretation which has no central point of reference was effectively excluded. When Paul uses an allegorical interpretation (cf. the exposition of Gal. 4:21-31), he does so for a definite purpose. He applies the fundamental idea of God's election, which he found everywhere in Scripture, to the interpretation of a familiar story; but he gives it at the same time a deeper meaning and refers it to God's continual election in and through Christ.

The membership in the congregations founded by Paul was probably predominantly Gentile. But in his missionary work Paul seems to have turned first to the Jews living in the city and to have appeared in their synagogues. His preaching of the gospel and the interpretation he made of the Scriptures in general and of the law and circumcision in particular seem to have aroused bitter opposition among the Jews. In the congregations he founded in spite of all opposition there were no doubt both Jews and some of those Gentile "God-fearers" who had been closely associated with the synagogue, but the majority of the members were very likely Gentiles. All the members were instructed in the sacred Scriptures, which all accepted as the word of the God Paul proclaimed. Paul could therefore refer in his letters to what had been written in these Scriptures. It was axiomatic with Paul that the event of Christ was the fulfilment of what had been written in the Old Testament. When he reminds the Corinthians of what he had proclaimed as of first importance, he emphasizes that Christ died for our sins *according to the Scriptures* and that he was raised *according to the Scriptures* (I Cor. 15:3).

It may appear strange that Paul contends against circumcision and righteousness by the law while at the same time he appeals to the Old Testament as an obvious authority. He does so even in dealing with congregations whose members were mostly Gentiles. We must remember, however, that Paul regarded these Scriptures, i.e., approximately what we call the Old Testament, "the writings of the old covenant" (II Cor. 3:14), as the document in which God had spoken and had given the promise of the Christ. Consequently all his converts must be instructed in the content of these Scriptures, and Paul evidently did so from the very beginning. The event of Christ was the continuation and culmination of the content of the Old Testament. There was an inseparable connection between the old covenant and the gospel of Christ. Just as the revelation of Christ provided an interpretation of the Scriptures, so the Scriptures corroborated the truth of faith in Christ. God had revealed his mysteries in the Old Testament writings, but only now could these be rightly understood.

It was a cardinal doctrine in the ancient church that Moses and the prophets had pointed forward to and prepared for the new age in Christ. It is therefore unthinkable that Paul should have opposed what was written in the Old Testament. That word could not be set aside, but it must be rightly interpreted and applied in the light of the revelation in Christ. This may seem strange to us since Paul's interpretation of the Old Testament does not agree ostensibly with a rational and historical exegesis. But Paul does not ask such historical questions as we do. For him God is the living and only God who speaks now, and thus by his revelation shows the meaning of what he has previously spoken. Scripture represents the voice of the holy and hidden God who now in Christ has fully revealed himself and provided a clear interpretation and fulfilment of his previous revelation. The event of Christ not only shed light on the earlier events and the words spoken by God through his servants, it was also a continuation of God's activity. Everything pointed forward to the goal which alone could give meaning, clarity, and consistency to the whole. Now the word in the Old Testament had received its final form. Christ is the *telos* of the law also in the sense that everything spoken through the Law and the Prophets ultimately has reference to him.

It is therefore perfectly logical for Paul to refer to the Old Testament for illustrations and proofs of what he proclaims. The key to Scripture had been given to him in the revelation of Christ. He could reinterpret the Old Testament and at the same time appeal to it for corroboration of his message. We must always remember that the common conviction of the early Christians was that the event of Christ fulfilled all that was spoken in the Law of Moses, the Prophets, and the Psalms (cf. Luke 24:25ff., 44ff.). The work of Christ was a completion of what had taken place in the Old Testament. Jesus told the Jews: "You search the scriptures, because you think that in them you have eternal life; and it is they that bear witness to me" (John 5:39). It is also recorded that the risen Christ, "beginning with Moses and all the prophets, . . . interpreted to them in all the scriptures the things concerning himself," and that "he opened their minds to understand the scriptures" (Luke 24:27. Cf. 24:44ff.). Jesus constantly referred to the law and the Scriptures. He directed the scribes and those who asked him questions first of all to the law, which must not be distorted by false interpretation and practice, but was to be rightly understood and fulfilled. According to the Gospel of Matthew he also referred to Scripture just before his passion (Matt. 26: 31, 54).

It is clear, therefore, that the primitive church transformed the understanding of the Old Testament. The writings of the Old Testament, which became the Bible of the ancient church, received a new interpretation and use quite different from that prevalent in the synagogues. There may have been variations in the interpretation of the Old Testament in the church, and Paul's view of it may have been somewhat peculiar to him. But all agreed that the God of the Old Testament was active in Christ, had raised him from the dead and through him made available the powers of the new age. It was he who poured out the Spirit and fulfilled the promises. The Christians continually accused the Jews of failing to heed the Scriptures. This is stated several times in Acts. Thus Peter quotes the Prophets and the Psalms in connection with the event of Pentecost. Stephen chides the Jews because they had received the law through the mediation of angels but have not kept it (Acts 7:53). It was their disobedience of the law that had led them to kill Christ. We must always keep clearly before us this conception of Scripture and the law, or else we will fail to understand what Paul's gospel of salvation apart from the law really meant. It is easy to modernize Paul's conception of the law in relation to his doctrine of justification in a completely false manner. It must be clearly undertsood how consistently Paul held to his fundamental starting point, which we may express in these words: "For all the promises of God find their Yes in him" (II Cor. 1:20).

The Introductory Greeting (1:1-5)

In contrast to the brief greetings generally found in the letters of antiquity Paul has included not only his name but also his title, thus giving a special character to his letter. He is not writing as an individual Christian to fellow Christians, nor is the letter a pastoral greeting of encouragement and exhortation by one of the many Christian preachers. He is an *apostle,* chosen by God and called by a revelation of Christ himself, who now exercises his function and speaks with the full authority of his commission. His is the office of the gospel, and he speaks to the Galatians as the servant of the gospel. The message which he sends them is not one which they may heed or not, depending on whether they find it good, edifying, and pleasant. It is the word of the authorized ambassador of Christ who has the right and the duty to instruct them in the faith on behalf of Christ. It is this man who now must present to them the divine truth which has been revealed to him. Neither the Galatians nor any other congregation has chosen him as an apostle. He represents the gospel of Christ by divine commission and authority.

The address is very brief: "Paul . . . to the churches of Galatia." In spite of all the failings of the Corinthians Paul addresses them as "the church of God which is at Corinth, to those sanctified in Christ Jesus, called to be saints" (I Cor. 1:2). The second letter begins with a similar statement. The greeting in Romans is directed to "all God's beloved in Rome, who are called to be saints." Other letters are addressed to "the saints in Christ Jesus" (Phil. 1:1; cf. Col. 1:1; Eph. 1:1). The greeting in Galatians is brief because Paul immediately administers a sharp rebuke to the readers (vs.6).

The introductory greeting is magnificent in tone and form. The phrases appear almost as liturgical formulae in majestic rhythm. The greeting is characterized not only by personal power and certainty of faith; it is presented as a greeting which does not come from an individual person but from one who is God's messenger and has authority as a representative of Christ.

Galatians is not simply an "epistle," a tract, or a general theological treatise; it is a letter addressed to definite persons. But it is not a letter from a private person who writes about his own

ideas. It is a highly authoritative document which nevertheless is
concerned with a concrete situation in which a proclamation contrary to Paul's gospel is undermining the faith of the Galatians.

It is remarkable that Paul from the beginning gives the letter
an official character as a document issued by an authorized representative of God and Christ, but that he nevertheless frequently
addresses the readers in a personal manner.

Already in the greeting Paul designates himself as an *apostle*.
He speaks as an authorized representative, not as a private person.
He also defines the peculiar nature of his apostolic office. The
opposition and criticisms which have been levelled against his
preaching by the Judaizers cause him to put a great emphasis on
the divine character of his apostleship.

The nature of the apostolic office has been the object of many
critical studies in recent years. It has been pointed out that the
apostolic office is related to the contemporary Jewish institution of
a *shaliach,* the practice of dispatching *sheluchim* (Aramaic,
shelichin), i.e., special envoys authorized to act on behalf of the
sender. The word *shaliach,* like the Greek word *apostolos,* means
one who is sent, and, in a stricter sense, an authorized agent. Such
sheluchim were common in later Judaism, and the word apostle
corresponds most closely to this concept. The unique thing about
the *shaliach* was his legal status; within his commission he was
able to act with the same authority as the one who had sent him.

The New Testament does not precisely define the apostolic office.
The twelve disciples whom Jesus selected during his ministry are
called apostles. Among them Peter seems to have occupied a
leading place. In the coming messianic kingdom the Twelve were
to judge the twelve tribes of Israel. This use of the word is especially prominent in Luke and the Acts. In other New Testament
writings the word seems to be used in the general sense of a
messenger, and sometimes also specifically of those who had
received from the risen Lord the commission of preaching the
gospel as witnesses of his resurrection. Peter seems to have been
the first of those who had received this special function. In the
view of the ancient church he had been given a special commission.
Traces of this tradition appear in John 21:15ff. and elsewhere.

Paul too knew that he had met the risen Lord (I Cor. 15:8).
He asserts that he is just as much an apostle as anyone else (cf.
I Cor. 9:1f.). His experience had been identical to that which
distinguished an apostle, and he himself had performed the mighty

deeds of an apostle (cf. II Cor. 12:12). Indeed his task, like that of Peter was in a sense unique, for the risen Lord had given him a special commission to preach the gospel among the Gentiles "as Peter had been entrusted with the gospel to the circumcised" (Gal. 2:7). Paul's commission had a very special significance in the history of salvation. For according to Paul, after the Jews had rejected the Messiah, the Gentiles were to become the ones who would receive the gospel; and through their conversion the Jews, who are now hardened and refuse to accept Christ, would ultimately receive salvation (cf. Rom. 11:11, and J. Munck, *Christus und Israel*, 1956).

We must note that Paul does not conceive of his work as propaganda for certain ideas. This was not the conception of preaching in the ancient church. Paul regarded the various work of the apostles as the divine activity in the final and decisive time before the return of Christ. The apostles were to be the foundation of the church. Peter and Paul, who seem to have divided the Christian mission between themselves, stand one on each side of the portal leading into the coming kingdom of God (A. Fridrichsen, *The Apostle and His Message*). The one who had appointed them was the God of Israel. What Paul proclaimed was not human ideas, nor did he speak on his own authority. His message had become clear to him through a revelation of Christ. Paul was not, therefore, working for himself, nor for any human interests in general. He had the same office as the greatest servants of God in the Old Testament. God had consecrated him to his task even before he had been born, just as he had done with Jeremiah. But his commission was as much greater than that of any prophet as the fulfilment and realization of a decisive event are greater than its promise and preparation.

Paul's apostleship was therefore of divine character. Since it was a commission given him directly by God (or by God through Christ), it was unthinkable that other human authorities should come into conflict with him. His divine commission could not be recalled or changed by any human authorities.

On the basis of the institution of *shaliach* in late Judaism we must not draw the conclusion that Paul's apostleship meant that he was an authorized messenger in common with such others who, for example, had been given a limited authority by a congregation in order to perform a specific task. His apostleship meant something more and was of a special nature. Christ himself had given

Paul a special commission which was a part of God's activity in the last days. Paul understood his task as a link in the final and decisive events through which God would create a new order and change the life of the world. His apostleship belonged in the time between the resurrection and the return of Christ and had therefore an eschatological significance.

Paul emphasizes, therefore, that his call was from Jesus Christ and from God who had raised him from the dead. The resurrection of Christ was the starting point for the connection with the coming age. The resurrection was not an ordinary miracle. In order to understand its significance we must reject the modern conception according to which the marvelous, or unacceptable, element is the claim that a dead man became alive again. What was decisive for Paul was that the promised Messiah had come. The resurrection was the resurrection of the *Messiah,* and it was the dawn of the new age. What Paul had to proclaim was not that a man, or a prophet, had come back to life after death, but that Jesus was the Messiah of God, the Lord, who now—as God— exercised the authority of righteousness and judgment. That he was the Lord had been demonstrated when he, the Crucified, had risen again. This event could not be compared with the stories of other people who had been restored to life. The significance of his resurrection cannot be understood except in connection with the redemptive act of the Messiah and with the righteousness which he represents and bestows. The coming and the resurrection of the Messiah was a unique act of God. The resurrection fitted in as a link in the chain of God's redemptive acts.

It is not possible to decide definitely just what congregations Paul is addressing. In the Introduction we indicated that many leading exegetes now favor the so-called North-Galatian theory, according to which the letter was addressed to congregations in the ethnic province of Galatia. The inhabitants of Pisidia and Lycaonia may not properly have been called "Galatians."

In his introductory greeting Paul speaks also about the brethren who are with him. It is not definitely known from what place the letter was sent. In Acts there are two visits mentioned to "the region of Phrygia and Galatia" (16:6; 18:23). Gal. 4:13 indicates that Paul had visited them twice. It is possible that the letter was written during Paul's long ministry in Ephesus on his third missionary journey (Acts 19:1ff.). Since he sends no greeting from the congregation in Ephesus but only from the brethren who are with him, it is possible that he had left the city and was on a journey to some other place.

When Paul includes a greeting from all the brethren with him, it indicates that the gospel he proclaims has been received in true faith. The unity of faith among the brethren might show the Galatians that Paul does not stand alone with extreme and radical claims. His preaching has been successful in other places, and the brethren who are with him are a living testimony to his work.

The greeting is directed to the churches of Galatia. The letter seems to be a circular letter intended for all the congregations. The problems which Paul deals with affected them all through the propaganda of the Judaizers. What was a Christian's relationship to the Jewish law and circumcision? This question involved not only external ceremonies but also the very significance of Christian faith. Did Paul's preaching represent an extreme and one-sided emphasis? Was his message incomplete in that he had indeed preached Christ but had neglected the law, so that now the law and circumcision had to be added to faith in Christ as the Messiah?

This question of circumcision and obedience to the law was a great deal more serious than the Galatians had understood. The gospel he had proclaimed would be jeopardized if the Judaizers succeeded in winning the Galatians, because they represented a conception of the Old Testament and of the meaning of the salvation which came through Christ, that was contrary to the gospel.

When Paul in vs. 3 greets them with grace and peace, he uses an expression which reminds us of a solemn liturgical formula possibly belonging in the ancient Christian cultus. The formula may be a Jewish blessing that had been adapted to Christian usage. These words had a greater sense of reality to the readers of the letter than it may have to modern man. This greeting was not merely a pious phrase, it was an actual bestowal of grace and peace. We may compare it to the words in Matt. 10:12-13 (Luke 10:5): "As you enter the house, salute it. And if the house is worthy, let your peace come upon it; but if it is not worthy, let your peace return to you" (cf. John 14:27). Grace and peace are parallel concepts. The word "peace" represents the Hebrew *shalom,* a creative peace involving spiritual and physical growth, strength, and power in contrast to anxiety, conflict, and everything that retards, divides, and injures life. This includes both physical life and the life in Christ. Grace and peace come from God and through Christ. "Grace" is closely related to mercy and compassion, although it not only involves leniency but is an expression of God's gracious activity through which he makes man partaker of his abundant blessings.

Grace and peace had their foundation in the fact that Christ had come and had accomplished his work. For Paul this work was a part of the historical and eschatological context of salvation; its significance was that it delivered us "from the present evil age." "This age" is characterized by the lack of God's righteousness and also by positive and active evil. In this age man stands before God as a guilty sinner. The function of the law is precisely to accuse and to reveal the guilt of all (cf. Rom. 5:20; Gal. 3:19). The law thus affirms that even in this age God is man's true Lord. The separation from God is revealed through the fact that man is found as a guilty sinner without excuse (cf. Rom. 2:1ff.). Man is guilty before God (Rom. 3:19) and in need of righteousness. He lacks that which is most essential, the foundation of life here and hereafter. He is instead in bondage under the power of death in all its forms and with all its consequences.

Salvation from all that is involved in this state comes only when God fulfils his promise of righteousness and blessing. This fulfilment took place when he sent the Messiah-Christ. Through his death and resurrection Christ redeemed man from bondage to the powers of this age, and related him to the righteousness to be fully revealed at his return.

When Paul here in the greeting speaks of Christ who has given himself in order to deliver us from the present evil age, he indicates in a sense the theme of the whole letter. The content of the letter deals with this redemption and its consequences, especially in reference to the law.

That Christ "gave himself for our sins to deliver us from the present evil age" was also the foundation of Paul's apostleship, because this office was entirely in the service of the gospel. The gospel itself was a power, God's *dunamis* (Rom. 1:16), through which the spiritual content and might of the promised new age was transmitted to men here on earth. If it could be said that Paul thought a new aeon, a new age, began in Christ, this event was not something one could observe passively and contemplate objectively. This age, to be fully revealed at the return of Christ, manifests its reality through the power of the Spirit and the presence of Christ in his church. By faith the Christian lives in Christ, and Christ in the Christian. Fellowship with the risen Lord makes the life of the new age a reality in the present. The preaching of the gospel was the way in which this power of the new age was to reach the Galatians and become operative among them. Through the gospel men were incorporated into this sphere of power, and were thus liberated from bondage under the powers which rule in this present age. That these powers were evil is obvious because Paul calls this whole present age evil (vs. 4).

The law had been given by God, and was therefore in itself good. But its function was to condemn and to convict of sin. It had to show that man lives in bondage under the powers of sin and death. But because of man's indwelling sin the law itself had been misused and had become an instrument of sin. It had become a means of establishing a righteousness by the law. As such it belonged among the evil powers. Sinful man would not permit the law to convict him of sin, but instead used the commandments of the law to establish his own righteousness.

Now the time had come when freedom from these evil powers could begin to be realized. The struggle between the evil powers of this age and the *dunamis* of the gospel was going on now through the ministry of Paul in his service of Christ, who was active through the gospel himself.

The Galatians had accepted Paul's gospel but later on had deserted him. They had been enticed by a proclamation which purported to be more faithful than Paul's to the holy Scriptures of the old covenant, and which quoted its ancient precepts in regard to circumcision and the observance of the law. To Paul this legalism of the Judaizers was in the service of the powers of this present evil age. It was tempting and appealing, and appeared pious and faithful to the letter of the Scriptures of the old covenant, but it robbed the Galatians of their participation in the truth of the gospel. Paul had to show them how Scripture was to be understood in the light of the revelation in Christ. The whole letter is an attempt to open the way again for the power of the gospel to work among the Galatians. Through the letter he brings the light of the gospel to the Galatians who had been led astray by this enticing legalism. Even though the proclamation of the Judaizers appeared attractive and demanded a strict life, it involved a return to the bondage under the powers of this present age and a rejection of the redemption from this bondage which had come through Christ.

The statement in vs. 4 that Christ "gave himself for our sins to

24

deliver us from the present evil age" indicates therefore the theme and the purpose of the letter. What all the holy Scriptures had testified and pointed to, viz., the fulfilment of the promise and the appearance of righteousness in the world, had now come, and through it that which the law could not produce was now beginning to work. Now God had sent his Messiah, and through him had made atonement for sin and removed the curse. Those who did not submit to the powers of this age and did not observe the law in order to procure their own righteousness (observance was really a sign of bondage under the powers of this age) could now through faith receive righteousness and life. The gospel provided participation in the resurrection life of Christ and in the righteousness of God.

In other letters Paul closes the greeting with thanksgiving for what has taken place in the congregation. Here, however, he proceeds at once to express his astonishment that the Galatians have so quickly deserted him. Hence the thanksgiving becomes instead an ascription of praise to God. It was His will that through Christ freedom from the powers of this present age should be secured. It was not what had happened in the congregations that was a source of joy. Rather he looks away from the present sorrow to the real and great joy: that according to the will of God Christ had given himself for us to deliver us from the powers of the present evil age.

Attention is thus directed to God's "glory," an expression which corresponds to the *kebod Yahweh*—God's power and majesty— of the Old Testament. It was this power and majesty of God which was revealed in Christ. God rules over all the ages; he is the Lord in every age. It was not, as Marcion thought later, a new God who revealed himself in Christ and was now proclaimed by Paul; it was the same God who had been active in the Old Testament and who had created the world. This God had now appeared in Christ in the fulness of his divine glory. He had now fulfilled the promise of righteousness and life, so that the relationship to him could now take a new form.

After this ascription of praise Paul adds an affirmative *Amen.*

PART ONE

In the gospel, through which the Spirit is given, the law is fulfilled, but the righteousness by the law is excluded (1:6—5:12)

In the first part of the Letter to the Galatians Paul deals primarily with faith and *law* (*pistis* and *nomos*), and in the second part he discusses the relationship between faith and *love* (*agape*). Since the occasion for the letter was the Judaistic heresy, it is natural that Paul should deal most extensively with the relationship between faith and the law. The Judaizers had demanded circumcision and observance of the law as conditions for membership in the church, so that the law would complement the gospel. It was necessary, therefore, for Paul to explain the relationship of the gospel and faith to the law. For Paul the word of Scripture is the revelation of God. He proceeds on the basis of the self-evident authority of the Scripture (i.e., of the Old Testament) in a way which may easily be overlooked by those for whom the authority of Scripture has become a problem. His argument with the Judaizers has therefore at times been misinterpreted in terms of an emancipation from the Old Testament. In such a case Paul would have been directly contradicting himself. On the one hand, he would be trying to liberate himself from the Old Testament, and, on the other hand, he would be claiming the Old Testament as authority for his own arguments and reasoning.

One may easily get the impression that Paul contradicts himself frequently. In the first chapter, for instance, he starts with declaring his independence of the original apostles, but in the second chapter he relates how he visited them and was anxious to gain their approval. These contradictions, however, are more apparent than real, and arise because Paul's words are interpreted from a wrong point of view. In the first chapter he is not contending for his own personal authority, but for the gospel entrusted to him and for its divine character. He does not want to liberate men from law and Scripture, but from that righteousness by the law which is contrary to both the law and the gospel.

Paul claims that the gospel had been revealed to him on the Damascus road. There he had submitted in faith to God's action and judgment, and through this faith he had received the righteousness of Christ and had become a partaker in his fulfilment of the law through death on the cross. He had met the risen Lord and become *one* with him, so that he could confess that he himself lives no more, but Christ lives in him, and his life in the flesh is a life by faith in Christ who had given himself for him (Gal. 2:20).

This gospel meant for Paul that his prenatal election to become the slave and apostle of Christ had now been fulfilled. Christ (and God who raised Christ from the dead) brought him into the Christian church and gave him a special commission of preaching the gospel to the Gentiles, an appointment which seems to have been confirmed to him later (cf. Acts 22:21).

Paul was the one who saw most clearly the significance of the gospel and the consequences involved. His relationship to the original apostles, which some exegetes find contradictory, was a direct result of this fact. Paul was called as an apostle in a church in which there were apostles before him. If unity with them could not be established, the church, the body of Christ, would be divided. But this did not mean that the truth of the gospel, which Paul had received from Christ, had been mediated to him through those apostles. In that case, because of their human limitations, they might obscure that gospel whose deepest meaning and consequences Paul had been given to see and to proclaim. In the first chapter Paul shows that in principle they had no authority to act as lords over the gospel, as if it were a doctrine of men; but in the second chapter he indicates that they had not even attempted to do so. In obedience to the God who was active in the gospel proclaimed by Paul they had given to him the right hand of fellowship (2:7-10). Paul's attitude becomes contradictory and difficult to understand only when we ignore his fundamental point of view that the gospel was not a human teaching which men could develop and control, and fail to see that it was not his own peculiar conception for which he contended against his opponents.

I. The Gospel and the Tradition from the Older Apostles in the Church (1:6—2:21)

A. *Jesus Christ himself had revealed the gospel to Paul* (1:6-24)

1. The apostasy of the Galatians (1:6-9)

Immediately after the greeting Paul expresses his astonishment that the Galatians have so quickly deserted the God who had called them in the grace of Christ. The God who had created the world and made man subject to his will had given the law to Israel for a definite purpose. Now he had fulfilled the promise and sent Christ. All those who received the gospel became partakers of the grace of Christ. But the Galatians had fallen away and turned to a teaching which falsely claimed to be a real gospel. This other so-called gospel was not at all a different form of the gospel, as, for instance, a more original and genuine version dependent on the older apostles. It was not a more complete and comprehensive message in which the law was given its proper place. On the contrary, it was pure heresy and a perversion of the true gospel. The Judaizers did not represent the gospel because they had never understood its meaning. They had perverted its message.

According to Paul the gospel was a divine message, back of which stood God himself. It was not as if Paul had received a kind of divinely sanctioned or authorized doctrine; it was rather that Christ himself was living and active in the gospel. Christ had appeared to Paul as the living Lord, and now he used Paul as his servant. God himself had raised Christ, and Christ spoke now through the gospel. It was therefore not at all a question of a teaching which could be defined and examined in regard to its origin, authority, and purity. In the gospel it was God and Christ who were revealing themselves. The content in the gospel was therefore firmly fixed, not as in a human teaching, but as in God's own speech. It was perfectly meaningless to discuss the personality and authority of the one who proclaimed the gospel. The Galatians could claim that their new teachers had a gospel of

higher authority than that of Paul. But Paul could retort that the
content of the Judaizers' proclamation was false and contrary to
the divine gospel. If that was the case, no apparent or real agreement with the opinions of men would avail, no matter who these
men might be.

The words of Paul in vss. 6ff., "a different gospel—not that
there is another gospel," seem to be a characteristic manner of
expression. Paul was astonished and dismayed that the Galatians
had deserted the gospel for propaganda which could not possibly
be reconciled to his own proclamation of the gospel, but would
completely nullify it. But this propaganda through which the
Galatians had been seduced claimed to be a gospel; the correct
and complete gospel in accordance with Scripture, complemented
by the demand for obedience to the requirements of the scriptural
law. It was, to be sure, a different message from that of Paul.
But it was not a *gospel,* because in reality there can be only one
gospel. Paul was therefore anxious, as we can see from his statements in Galatians 2, that his agreement with the older apostles
should be made known. This one gospel was not at all a human
teaching, but a message not only *from* God but one *in which* God
and Christ themselves were present and active. The Galatians had
forsaken this message for a human teaching which claimed to be
a gospel.

The relation of this false "gospel" to the one true gospel was
the same as the relation of the Jewish conception of righteousness
to righteousness from God. This Jewish conception of righteousness, righteousness of one's own or of the law, which is secured
through observance of the law, and which enables a person to
glory, was a false righteousness, and, according to Paul, no
righteousness at all (cf. Phil. 3:7ff).

This false righteousness, therefore, was not that kind of righteousness which corresponds to God's demands, his perfect will, and
the deepest intention of the law. The Jewish claim that this
righteousness was the only real and true one was altogether false.
Righteousness by the law was not what it claimed to be; it was
simply vanity and illusion. But from another point of view it
could be regarded as something real, viz., an evil, lying power
which struggles against the truth of God's righteousness. Idols
represented both something that did not exist and evil powers
which contended against God and seduced men to enmity and to
putting their trust in actions designed to win the favor of these

powers by various works and observances. In the same way the false "gospel" of the Judaizers was not at all a gospel but a lie, and yet it represented a real spiritual power in conflict with the gospel.

According to Paul a false faith not only was a subjective mistake, but also involved slavery under an objective power opposed to God. In the same way the true faith was not merely subjective, but involved such a relation to God's objective activity that God or Christ could be said to be present and working in the believer. False faith did not really represent an objective power in the same sense as the true, but in practice the object of faith appeared as a power or powers which subjected men to bondage.

The propaganda of the Judaizers brought a curse upon every one who proclaimed it. Paul adds that if he or his associates were to bring a message or a form of the Christian faith contrary to what he had originally proclaimed, a curse would rest on them also. Even if an angel from heaven should do this, he would be accursed. The message was God's own message, and anyone who opposed or perverted it would come under a curse, since he would be in opposition to the true life. To change the gospel was to lead men astray, and that is strictly condemned (cf. Matt. 18:7; Luke 17:1-2). Paul's pronouncement of a curse, therefore, was not an expression of anger, or lust for power, or a fanatical, one-sided, and egocentric demand that only what he proposed should be accepted. The curse was a part of the whole situation. The curse was the opposite of God's blessing. The gospel of Christ contained that divine blessing which had been promised to Abraham and had now been fulfilled in Christ. This blessing was now really present and had come to the Galatians through Paul's preaching. To confuse the hearers so that they could not receive the blessing was to shut them out from life and keep them in the power of death. The curse would inevitably come upon those who thus confused the Galatians and prevented them from receiving the blessing of the gospel. It involved a denial of Christ who had come with redemption from the present evil age, and implied instead a confession of adherence to the powers of this age. In this situation there could be no partiality.

We must note carefully that a curse was pronounced also upon Paul himself if he should preach a gospel contrary to what he had preached. This indicates that it was a question of a sacred matter, not of personal prestige. Christ himself spoke in the gospel. The gospel was not dependent on Paul's *personal* authority. The decisive element was not the *person* proclaiming it, but the content. To oppose that content was to go contrary to God's own revelation, and to contend against that God who had spoken in all the Scriptures of the Old Testament, who had given the law, and who had now raised Christ from the dead.

The tremendous demand for obedience to his preaching which Paul had to make might seem to involve a claim of obedience to him as a person and an intolerance against all who would compete with him for converts. Intolerance means to put one's own self in the center, and to refuse to recognize or regard the interests and viewpoints of others. But Paul's zeal and exclusiveness is of a different nature. It has nothing to do with subjective one-sidedness, personal power, or desire for self-enhancement. He did not speak in his own behalf, but carried out a commission entrusted to him. His impetuous words testify to his zeal for the matter entrusted to him.

2.   Paul, the bond servant of Jesus Christ (1:10)

Paul's conception of his commission in the gospel helps to explain the relationship between the detailed description of his call in the first chapter and his exposition of the content of the gospel in the later chapters. To Paul's mind his apostolic commission and the content of his gospel are two sides of the same coin. Since Paul knew that he had met Christ on the Damascus road and had received from him the appointment as his servant and apostle to the Gentiles, his authority rested entirely on this commission.

As we have seen, it would have been easy to misinterpret Paul and claim that his zeal was motivated by a desire for personal prestige. Paul therefore asks whether his zeal for the gospel is now intended to please men? To those who did not understand the significance of the gospel Paul's proclamation could easily appear as lacking in moral earnestness. A strong moral program and a life regulated by definite commandments often appear as the highest and most unimpeachable standpoint. The Judaizers may have accused Paul of laxity and lawlessness. But Paul answers that to make the proclamation such that it pleases men is impossible for a servant of Christ. For Paul there are only two alternatives: either to stand in the service of Christ or to seek his own power and success by catering to the opinions and favor of men. To serve Christ as his bond servant totally excludes the second alternative. The Judaizers had evidently accused Paul of preaching freedom from the law in order to win those who found obedience to the law too difficult, of trimming off some of the demands of the gospel in order to please men. But by his anathema on the seducers Paul shows clearly that he does not seek the favor of men by yielding easily to different opinions. There is a certain sarcasm in his words: "Am I now seeking the favor of men?"

From the Jewish standpoint there were only two religious attitudes possible: either moral laxity or that strict observance of the law which was the glory and the joy of the Jews. But to Paul the alternative was entirely different. As he states elsewhere (5:13), freedom from law must not provide "an opportunity for the flesh." Both the moralism of the righteousness by the law and moral laxity were to Paul expressions of concern for the enhancement of self and belonged to "the flesh." To belong to Christ and to serve him was the opposite of both of these attitudes.

Paul cannot seek any personal honor by obtaining followers. He has no other honor than that which to the world is a dishonor, namely, the cross of Christ; just as he does not claim any other wisdom than that which to the world is foolishness (I Cor. 1:21ff.). When he glories, he must glory in his weakness (II Cor. 11:30; 12:9).

In I Thess. 2:4-5 Paul contrasts, just as he does here, a proclamation which seeks the favor of men and one which seeks to please God who tests our hearts: "we speak, not to please men, but to please God who tests our hearts. For we never used either words of flattery, as you know, or a cloak for greed, as God is witness." The solemn declaration in Gal. 1:10-11 has in a sense the character of an oath, as it is actually expressed in the Thessalonian passage. Later in the Letter to the Galatians Paul declares that the Judaizers themselves did not keep the law. They were the ones who were driven by selfish motives. They sought their own honor, glory, and power by their propaganda and their severity in regard to the observance of the law (6:13). A servant of Christ, however, could not seek his own power and glory, nor could he work in order to please other men. He was bound to his Lord and to his commission. He had to do what had been commanded him. As the servant and authorized messenger of Christ Paul had to be the representative of Christ in the proclamation of the gospel.

To pay heed to men would be impossible. That could be done by one who was not subject to a higher power, but served his own interests or his own objective by seeking the favor of others.

It may seem strange that precisely in this letter Paul points out that he is the bond servant of Christ. In the whole letter he contends for freedom, freedom from the slavery under the righteousness of the law. He urges the Galatians not to return to bondage after they have been set free by the gospel (4:9-10; 5:1). But freedom from the law does not mean a capricious freedom in which man does completely what he pleases (cf. 5:13). The basis of freedom is commitment to Christ and to everything he gives. This commitment is likened to a service which involves belonging completely to Christ. But in this case commitment and freedom are the same thing. Real freedom is not used in such a way as to give an opportunity for the flesh, but rather so that men serve one another in love (5:13). To be a servant of Christ and to serve in love is to be free, free from what really enslaves man: covert slavery to self, to the flesh, to a false use of the law, and to serve in love is to be free, free from what really enslaves man: righteousness, it becomes an expression of man's inner lack of freedom and gives concrete form to this bondage, while slavery in the service of Christ sets man free. We may say paradoxically that according to Paul slavery to Christ is not slavery but a total commitment to a power which gives man the greatest freedom he can attain; while freedom from Christ means slavery under all the powers that *de facto* enslave life. Slavery under Christ can therefore be likened to adoption as sons. Complete commitment to Christ can be likened to a son's entry into his inheritance after he has come of age, and it signifies therefore the most complete freedom (cf. 4:1ff.).

It may also be said that the law becomes one of "the powers of this world" as long as it is conceived of and used in the external, pharisaic sense. But in its deepest significance and fulfilment the law sets free; and this function has been realized in Christ, who could speak with the same authority as God who had given the law. Through his obedience unto death and through his resurrection Christ has proved himself a direct representative of God. The freedom from the law which Paul contends for in Galatians is not freedom from the God who had given the law and from his will enshrined in that law, because his will was God's own righteousness which included life and freedom. Freedom from the law was concerned with that situation in which the law was "weakened by the flesh" (Rom. 8:3) and stood in the service of sin. In that situation the law enslaved men.

It was on the basis of his experience on the Damascus road that Paul regarded himself as the bond servant of Christ. It is possible that the words in Acts 26:14 are to be understood as referring to the future: "It hurts you to kick against the goads," i.e., it will be difficult for you to live otherwise than as the servant of him who has now given you his commission (J. Munck so understood them in his *Paulus und die Heilsgeschichte*). The expression was a common Greek proverb, meaning that resistance to Christ was useless. It need not, therefore, refer to an inner struggle in the past. But the experience on the Damascus road, where Paul was overwhelmed and apprehended by One who was stronger than he (cf. Jer. 20:7ff.), was of such a nature that it bound Paul definitely and for life to the task given to him there, a task that had special reference to the Gentiles.

Another expression of Paul's commitment to Christ is found in I Cor. 9:16 where he says that "necessity is laid upon" him to preach the gospel. This preaching gives him no ground for boasting, nor can he demand a reward. It is a commission given to him which he is under obligation to fulfil (I Cor. 9:16-17). "Woe to me if I do not preach the gospel!"

3. The gospel is not man's gospel (1:11-12)

Paul declares solemnly that the gospel which he has proclaimed is not according to men. He has not received it from or been instructed in it by any man, for he has received it through a revelation of Jesus Christ. It is therefore of a nature entirely different from those of all human ideologies and teachings. It is not a propaganda for human ideas, nor an expression of his own theories and desires. When he declares that the gospel he had proclaimed is not a human doctrine, he indicates clearly that the Galatians ought to have understood this and not permitted themselves to be confused by the Judaizers. He addresses the Galatians here as "brethren," not as strangers but as bewildered and confused brethren in the faith. That the gospel he proclaimed was not a human doctrine is evidenced further by the fact that he had not received it from or been instructed in it by any man. Evidently the Judaizers had claimed that his preaching was dependent on someone else, possibly Barnabas with whom he had been in Antioch, and who had already befriended him in Jerusalem (cf., e.g., Acts 4:36; 9:27; 11:22; 13:1ff.).

The emphasis in vs. 12 is on the fact that Paul did not receive his message from any man. His commission was not to develop an already existing tradition. His opponents had evidently claimed that Paul, who had not been one of those who had associated with Jesus, must have received the tradition from one who was an apostle before him, or from the Jewish congregations. It was natural for them therefore to refer to what they claimed was the original tradition and to place this in opposition to Paul.

In this situation Paul had to make two things very clear. On the one hand, he was not the bearer of a tradition which had to be tested by reference to the older apostles. On the other hand, there was no essential contradiction between the gospel he proclaimed and that which the original apostles represented. Paul starts, therefore, by showing that he was not simply the bearer of a tradition from others, but a witness to the Christ he had met who had given him the apostolic commission with precisely the content he had delivered to them. He shows that his activity as an apostle has the full approval of the other apostles, and is not contrary to their preaching and principles. That the gospel is not a human doctrine was a negative statement of the fact that it was divine in content and origin. This is one of the chief theses of the letter. It had not been entrusted to Paul by men, nor had he received it through a human tradition. A corollary of that is that the gospel is on a plane wholly different from that of the law conceived of as a means for justification.

When a messenger from a recognized authority or a congregation travelled around, he may have carried letters of recommendation. On the basis of II Cor. 3:1 we understand that Paul's opponents claimed that he did not possess any such letters. If the Judaizers in Galatia had said something similar, it was natural that Paul should emphasize that his apostleship was not of such a nature that he needed recommendations or authorization from men. The gospel was not a human doctrine, or like a rabbinical tradition from learned men regarded as authorities and from whom one received instruction. Nor had he received the commission of preaching the gospel from men. Instead of instruction by men as the source of his insight and instead of a commission from men to preach, he had received a revelation from Jesus

Christ who is the foundation of the gospel. He did not need a
letter of recommendation. The truth of the gospel which his disciples and hearers received and which was confirmed by the Spirit
took the place of such a letter. In II Cor. 3:1-3 Paul addresses
the Corinthians, saying that they are "a letter from Christ delivered by us, written not with ink but with the Spirit of the
living God, not on tablets of stone but on tablets of human hearts."
In Galatians he refers to the Spirit which the Galatians had received when in faith they listened to the gospel (3:3ff; 4:6), and
shows that the law itself in Scripture bears witness to the gospel
(3:10ff.; 4:21ff.). The Spirit and the Scriptures testify to the
truth of the gospel. Consequently the gospel comes from God, not
from men.

That the gospel was not a human doctrine which could be
propagated by human authority and tradition, and that it was not
of the same nature as the law according to the Jewish conception,
were different aspects of the same matter. According to the
Jewish interpretation the law contained a moral code which instructed men in regard to God's will. This code was explained by
men, and the interpretation was transmitted by the tradition of
the scribes. As a Pharisee Paul had received from Gamaliel and
appropriated just such a tradition. The Jews indeed regarded the
law as of divine origin. But the use made of the requirements of
the law, which in principle could be fulfilled by men of their own
free will, and which were explained by scholars and understood
on the basis of the expositions and additions of the scribes, reduced the law to the level of a human teaching.

The gospel was of a different nature. Christ was not only the
object of the preaching; he himself acted and spoke in it. The
gospel was not a dead instrument and argument in the hands of
the apostles, it was an independent and living power which they
had to serve, but which they did not possess. They did not control the gospel; it controlled them. In the expression, "the gospel
of Christ," "Christ" is not simply objective genitive (the gospel
about Christ) but primarily subjective genetive (that gospel which
Christ proclaims and in which he is active).

There is indeed also an evangelical tradition. The words he
had spoken and the message he brought during his earthly ministry were proclaimed through the risen and exalted Christ. Only
now could that message be fully understood in the light of his
death and resurrection. The apostles and the disciples shared in

39

this preaching activity as agents and witnesses. But they themselves did not originate and formulate the tradition. Christ spoke and acted in it. This tradition was validated by the fact that the words of the Old Testament were illuminated by the gospel and their meaning was clarified. The true tradition, therefore, was not a human teaching which men could control. Peter and the Jerusalem apostles were not masters over it. The tradition had the character of a revelation from God, a work of the Holy Spirit. What was proclaimed according to this tradition could never be separated from what God had made known through the Spirit and his revelation. If the revelation took the form of visions and dreams, they received their significance, value, and truth because they became a part of this continuing revelation in which Christ himself was active. The words of Scripture, the words of Jesus, his whole ministry, his death and resurrection, the activity of the Spirit in the present, and the appearances of Christ after his resurrection—all this the early Christians regarded as a unit. Nothing could be removed. It could not be transformed into a tradition in which were decisive human decisions and regulations, authorized by those who like the apostles "were reputed to be pillars." Consequently the gospel could not be complemented by requirements of the law, or be made dependent upon anything extraneous to itself. To incorporate circumcision as a condition of salvation would be contrary to the revelation in which Christ was active. Legal requirements as conditions for membership in the church would bring together two contradictory traditions: the one in which Christ was active (the gospel), and the one in which human interpretation of the law prevailed. If anyone attempted to declare these legal requirements necessary for salvation by referring to the authority of the apostles or the Jewish Christians in Jerusalem, the whole gospel would be transformed into the commandments of men. In that case the messianic tradition and interpretation of Scripture would be replaced by one based on rabbinical principles. But just as Jesus in the Sermon on the Mount placed his "I say to you" (speaking with the authority of the God who had given the law) in contrast to the rabbinical interpretation, so also in the ancient church the gospel was placed in opposition to a Jewish tradition resting on human authorities and representing an interpretation of Scripture which led to righteousness by the law.

Paul emphasizes, therefore, that the gospel cannot in principle be dependent on men, not even on the leaders in Jerusalem. The gospel would then become a doctrine of men, just as the Old Testament Scriptures had become in Judaism. This attitude did not imply any suspicion of the apostles; it was simply a rejection of a false conception of their function and authority.

It is obvious, therefore, that Paul's account of certain experiences and events in his life in the first two chapters and his theological exposition of the significance of the gospel and its independence of law and circumcision (yes, its incompatability with them if they are understood as conditions for or additions to the gospel) are very closely related. The subject under discussion is the same throughout. Paul does not first provide an autobiographical account of his life and then proceed to his discussion of the gospel free from the law. In the first two chapters he deals with the same subject as he does in the latter chapters, but from a different point of view and about other aspects of it.

If the law were to become a human norm which could be observed by human effort in the sense that man could achieve righteousness through circumcision and observance of its precepts, it would serve as an instrument for man's self-righteousness (Phil. 3:9; Rom. 10:3). This righteousness, produced by man's own efforts and works, could also be regarded as a power to which man submits. But this would not be God's power and will which are found in Scripture and the law, but a power separated from God and comparable to those powers under which the Gentiles live. These powers, under which even the Jews stood because of their false conception of righteousness (cf. Rom. 10:3), had exercised control over men (Gal. 4:3, 8ff., Col. 2:20), but Christ had come to set them free. To be in slavery to "the elemental spirits of the universe" (*ta stoicheia tou kosmou*) and to seek righteousness through one's own works are really two aspects of the same thing. The observance of human teachings and commands in order to gain security becomes servitude under powers which are enemies to the will and power of God.

Precisely because he proclaims a gospel which is not a human teaching and has not come from or through men, Paul really maintains the true divine character of Scripture and the law. He wants to bring the Jews back to a right reception of the revelation of God in the law and to liberate them as well as the Gentiles from servitude to foreign gods and powers. He instructs the Gentiles in the Scriptures and finds in them the testimony to that righteousness which has been fulfilled in Christ. If law and gospel are contrasted, it is necessary, as far as Paul is concerned, to distinguish between Scripture and the law on the one hand, as their essential meaning was revealed when the veil was removed (II Cor. 3:14ff. and 4:2ff.), and the righteousness by the law on the other hand, which was a perversion of the true meaning of both Scripture and the law. It was against the law in this sense (righteousness by the law) that Paul warned the Galatians. This was the new, false gospel to which they had been enticed. Righteousness by the law was a false, human teaching in contrast to the gospel. But the whole divine meaning of Scripture and the law was made known through the gospel revealed by God. When the Galatians fell away, they were forsaking the God revealed in the Old Testament. Subjectively they had become attached to the false and erroneous conception of the law; and objectively they had become subject to the false gods and powers connected with righteousness by the law. As far as Paul was concerned both of these aspects were one.

4. Jesus Christ himself chose Paul (1:13-24)

a) Paul the persecutor chosen as the Apostle to the Gentiles (1:13-17)

(1) Paul's earlier zeal for the tradition of the fathers (1:13-14)

Paul refers to the circumstances of his conversion to show the significance of the fact that he received the gospel from Christ himself. He had been a very active Pharisee and had surpassed many of his own age in his zeal for the tradition of the fathers (vs. 14). This tradition interpreted the written law and supplied detailed instructions as an ethical foundation for living. The Pharisees had been deeply concerned about the tradition and had incorporated it as a part of the *Torah*. According to them a life in righteousness consisted in a faithful observance of the tradition. Paul had manifested a fanatical zeal for the tradition and could say that in regard to it he was found blameless (cf. Phil. 3:6).

To the Gentile Christians to whom he writes he can claim that in this respect he had been a more faithful Jew than the others. He had advanced in Judaism beyond many of his own age. When the Judaizers criticized his preaching because the observance of the law had no place in it, he could point to his life before conversion and show that he knew the law better than they, and that he had shown greater zeal for it than anyone else. That he did not urge the law's observance now was not because he was ignorant of the severity of the law. Nor had he for the present left out the demand for observance of the law in order to please men, so that later on he would have to supplement his proclamation by the message of the Judaizers. The way of salvation by works of the law did not belong with the gospel, and could not be reconciled with it. What Paul had once gained along this line he now calls loss (Phil. 3:7ff.).

The result of Paul's zeal for the law according to the Jewish interpretation had been that he persecuted the Christian congregations (cf. Acts 8:3; 9:1ff.; 22:4ff.; 26:9) and sought to destroy God's church. His emphasis on obedience to the law had brought him to this point. He had become an enemy of the Holy One of God and of God's people who were the true Israel, the church. He had come into conflict with God and his plan of redemption. Thus it was evident that the Pharisaic conception of the law was against God. According to Paul's earlier, Pharisaic understanding the church and the gospel appeared as an antithesis and total perversion of the law. From the very beginning he had perceived that the Pharisaic and Christian conceptions of the law could never be reconciled. But through the revelation of Christ God himself had explained the meaning of everything in the Old Testament, and Paul had acknowledged God's righteousness and submitted to his will. He had been brought to this understanding of Scripture not through other men but by God himself through Christ. He had become more clearly aware of this new insight than anyone else. Since Paul tells the Galatians that he had been zealous for the law and had been a bitter enemy of the Christians, it is clear that he had not received any instruction in Christianity before his conversion. His enmity against the Christians had been so violent that he had sought to find and arrest them even outside of Jerusalem. If the Judaizers accused Paul of laxity in regard to the law, his earlier life proved abundantly that he had been much stricter in his observance of the law than anyone else. Paul points out, however, that his zeal for the works of the law led him to persecute that remnant which God had chosen (Rom. 9:27; 11:5; Isa. 10:22ff.). This little flock was the bearer of God's will. That

Paul had persecuted this remnant meant that he had become an enemy of that God whose action and election were recorded in the Old Testament. His Pharisaic interpretation of and zeal for the law had made him an enemy of the law and completely perverted its meaning.

(2) Paul receives the call (1:15-17)

We may emphasize again that Paul's account is not autobiographical in the modern sense, but rather a reference to the activity and revelation of God. This is shown clearly in vs. 15: "But when he who had set me apart before I was born, and had called me through his grace, was pleased to reveal his Son to me, in order that I might preach him among the Gentiles. . . ." The account deals with *God's* election, call, and revelation. The connection with the Old Testament appears even in these words. His election was a continuation of those acts of election and salvation which are recorded in the Scriptures and the law. Since Paul had become a participant in this revelation, he needed not seek information about the significance of the message of salvation from men but simply accept obediently the commission given to him. Paul knows that he was called by God's *grace,* and this realization determines the conception of his task. He called himself the slave (*doulos*) of Christ. He was constrained by the love of God in his work. Even here there is a connection with the Old Testament, for Jeremiah too was compelled to serve God (cf. Jer. 20:7ff.).

There is a contrast between one who voluntarily accepts a task which will bring him some personal profit and one who is called as Paul was. His service in the gospel was not of his own free will in the sense that he could leave it. Although he was not worthy of his service, he was called by grace alone to the task of preaching the gospel among the Gentiles. He had, therefore, no claim to any wages (cf. I Cor. 9:17). In Paul's time a steward was often a slave. Paul's stewardship was of such a nature that he could not seek other employment, nor could he claim any rewards (cf. Rom. 4:4). In spite of his persecution of Christ he had received a commission similar to but greater than that of Israel's greatest prophets.

Although Paul in this chapter asserts his independence of the older apostles, he nevertheless emphasizes that he was called by *grace* and to a status of **bond** servant. This fact also indicates the kind of authority he claims. His is not the personal authority of one who voluntarily accepts a task, for the authority is contained exclusively in the gospel itself which has been entrusted to him in such a way that he is its bond servant.

The expression *en emoi* (in me) in his statement, "was pleased to reveal his Son in me," may linguistically also be rendered "for me." But possibly it indicates the intensity of the revelation as it illumined his whole being and filled him with spiritual power, and is therefore best rendered "in me." The revelation constituted an event that so changed his whole life that Paul could say (2:20) that he no longer lived but Christ lived in him.

The word "pleased" indicates that this was an act of God's free choice. The same word occurs in I Cor. 1:21: "It pleased God through the folly of what we preach to save those who believe"; and in Col. 1:19: "For in him all the fulness of God was pleased to dwell." Through the revelation on the Damascus road Paul was caught up in this act of God's election which primarily referred to Christ. Election and revelation are related concepts. Revelation is God's intervention in human history. Through this action Paul understood the significance of the death of Christ, and God's actions in Christ were shown to be exactly what the Scriptures had said should happen in the last days. When Paul saw the Crucified as the living and divine Lord, surrounded by the glory of God, his prenatal call and election were realized. The God who had appeared and made himself known by mighty works throughout the whole of Israel's history had now appeared to Paul. At Damascus, Paul as it were recognized in Christ the God whose works were recorded in the Scriptures. He accepted immediately in faith this act of God in the death of Christ through which God had brought his revelation in Scripture and the law to its climax. The death of Christ on the cross, who was designated Son of God in power by his resurrection from the dead (cf. Rom. 1:4) and appointed Lord over both Jews and Gentiles, was not the curse of the law upon a blasphemer and deceiver, because Christ took the curse of the law upon himself in order to redeem those who were under the law. The righteous One submitted to the judgment of the law and removed the curse from all who are united with him. Thus the promises of Scripture were fulfilled through the cross.

According to Paul a revelation may be described either as a vision, as on the road to Damascus, or as a personal insight

given by God (I Cor. 2:10; Gal. 3:23; Phil. 3:15; Eph. 3:5).
The Damascus revelation had an eschatological significance.
According to the Old Testament God appeared in his glory to
Moses at Sinai. Christ reveals the glory of God, and it is probable
that Paul claims to have seen on the Damascus road the divine
majesty of Christ as he will appear at his return. It is clear therefore that the Crucified represented God himself and that now he
shares in the glory of God. Thus there can be no doubt but that
God himself appeared in Christ. Since the God who had spoken
to the fathers and to Moses had revealed himself in Christ, the
Scriptures must be interpreted in line with this fact. Since God
was in Christ, the gospel had divine authority. The preaching of
the gospel was the manifestation of a mystery (cf. Col. 1:26) in
which Christ himself was active.

According to vs. 16 God's intention was that Paul should
become a servant of the gospel especially to the Gentiles. His
preaching of the gospel did not involve only obedience to the
revelation but also a participation in the activity of which the
revelation was an expression. His preaching of the gospel continued in a sense the activity of the revelation.

Just as his reference in vs. 13 to his persecution of Christians
shows that he had not been prepared for conversion by their
influence, so he emphasizes in vs. 16 that after his conversion
he did not confer with anyone, not with "flesh and blood." The
contrast between human doctrines and the gospel appears in this
expression, "flesh and blood," which designates the area to which
all human teaching belongs. But the gospel does not belong to the
realm of "flesh and blood." Consequently Paul had not even gone
up to Jerusalem but had withdrawn into Arabia.

In order to understand the ideas connected with Paul's
words about his election and call to the apostleship and his clear
understanding of the gospel we must note how Paul in other
passages speaks about the revelation of the glory of Christ, and
how God the Creator had in Christ manifested his glory.

When Paul interpreted Scripture on the basis of his Damascus
experience, he knew that there had been taken away the veil that
obscured "the light of the gospel of the glory of Christ, who is
the likeness of God" (II Cor. 4:4). To receive the gospel was
to see something of the glory of God. It was the God who had
created the world and had spoken in the law whose glory had

surrounded Paul at his meeting with Christ. The God who in creation had let light shine out of darkness (II Cor. 4:6, quoting freely from Gen. 1:3) had caused his glory to appear in Christ. The same God who had created the world now revealed his glory through the gospel and gave Paul his commission to preach the gospel among the Gentiles. It is therefore natural for Paul to assume that his whole life was comprehended within God's decree and election, and that even before birth he had been selected for the commission given him in Damascus. The veil had been lifted from Scripture so that he saw the testimony of God's own glory in Christ (cf. II Cor. 3:14ff). If the ministration of the law had had a share in God's glory, the revelation of glory to which Paul was a witness was much greater and clearer so that as it were the ministration of the law lost its splendor. The ministration of the law was a dispensation of death and condemnation. It was the negative aspect of God's power. But the revelation in Christ stood in the service of life and righteousness. Those who had received the ministry of the gospel were to behold the glory of the Lord "with unveiled face," and be changed into his likeness from one degree of glory to another (II Cor. 3:7-18).

We need to keep in mind this view of the significance of the gospel in order to understand Paul's claim that the gospel is not a doctrine of men. It is of the nature of a light shining and revealing its power. The Christians are lights in the Lord (Eph. 5:8). "For once you were darkness, but now you are light in the Lord; walk as children of light." In I Pet. 2:9 we read: "That you may declare the wonderful deeds of him who called you out of darkness into his marvelous light." That the gospel can be said to be God's *dunamis* and a light in which God's own glory is revealed shows that Paul did not think of it as a human teaching, not even as a divine doctrine. It shows its power by its ability to transform those whom it reaches so that they advance "from one degree of glory to another." And to misunderstand this gospel as if Paul had preached himself (cf. II Cor. 4:5) or had made his own desires and ideas prevail would be to pervert it and totally extinguish its light. The preacher of the gospel was nothing in himself, simply a servant (cf. I Cor. 3:5). He simply transmitted a truth which had been entrusted to him.

Paul declares that Christ is the image of God. "In [him] we have redemption, the forgiveness of sins. He is the image of the

invisible God, the first-born of all creation" (Col. 1:14-15). Paul
had met this Christ who reflected the glory of God and through
whom the world was created. He, the risen Lord, had appeared
to Paul. The Letter to the Hebrews expresses the same thought:
"God . . . in these last days . . . has spoken to us by a Son, whom
he appointed the heir of all things, through whom also he created
the world. He reflects the glory of God and bears the very stamp
of his nature, upholding the universe by his word of power. When
he had made purification for sins, he sat down at the right hand
of the Majesty on high" (Heb. 1:1ff). When Jesus says, "He who
has seen me has seen the Father" (John 14:9), the idea of Christ
as the image of God appears. For the interpretation of Galatians
it is especially important to make clear that Paul claims to have
met the very God who spoke in and through the Law and the
Prophets in the Old Testament, since otherwise his words may be
understood as an attempt to emancipate himself from the Old
Testament. This God has revealed his divine glory in Christ.

God himself, the God of Israel who had spoken and acted in
Scripture and had given the law, had now appeared in Christ,
not in a veiled manner as in the law but in his full glory. At
Damascus Paul had seen the glory of God's power, and he knew
now beyond doubt that Jesus was the Messiah. The Gentiles in
their worship had "exchanged the glory of the immortal God for
images resembling mortal man" (Rom. 1:23). The Jews by their
false understanding of the law as a means of righteousness had
become like the Gentiles. But in Christ God's own glory really
appeared. In the resurrection God had bestowed on him his own
glory so that it shone forth "in his face." Therefore it was clear
that Christ also fulfilled the law. The reflection of God's glory
in the law was transformed into a full manifestation of his glory
(cf. II Cor. 3:12—4:6). What had been hidden was revealed.
The written code kills, but that code had been permeated by
the Spirit of God in Christ. Christ fulfilled the law, and in a sense
he was God's perfect law. The gospel is the fulfilment of the
law. We may also say that, according to Paul, Christ is the fulfilment; thus may be interpreted the words in Rom. 10:4.

The law, which earlier had been the highest expression of God's
will, had now become overshadowed because God's perfect light
had come. The rabbis called the law a light. But Paul wants to
show that the light which was only a reflection of God's light

has now been replaced by the true Light—Christ. He was therefore the perfect law through which God's light appeared directly. According to the Jews and to Paul the law, *Torah,* was not merely a juridical code. The law expressed the meaning of creation and of God's purpose for man. Christ was the incarnation of God's law. He was the image of God and the expression of his will. The life which man could not produce for himself came into victorious being through his resurrection. This life was the goal of God's law and of his whole creation. In Christ Paul had met and received the perfect law, and it was He who was active in the gospel.

When Paul speaks of his call to become Christ's apostle, he takes his stand on that decree of God which had determined the events in his life. In these events of his life he recognizes the God who had also dealt with the greatest prophets. As God had chosen Jeremiah even before birth, so Paul's call rested ultimately on God's decree. Paul understood that he had been chosen before his birth to receive the revelation and to become the apostle to the Gentiles. God said to Jeremiah: "Before I formed you in the womb I knew you, and before you were born I consecrated you; I appointed you a prophet to the nations" (Jer. 1:5). A similar statement is found in Isa. 49:1: "The Lord called me from the womb, from the body of my mother he named my name." Paul's words here remind us of these texts.

In these words about his election and call Paul has connected his gospel with the revelation in Scripture. When the Galatians read these words, they may have been reminded of the passages in Isaiah and Jeremiah. Indirectly Paul not only asserted his independence of the other apostles but also began his interpretation of the significance of his gospel by his reference to Scripture. His words must have reminded the Galatians of the passage just quoted: "And now the Lord says, who formed me from the womb to be his servant . . ." (Isa. 49:5).

According to Paul's point of view there is therefore a connection between his life before and after his conversion. But this connection is not to be sought in psychological preparation for conversion but in God's election. Even before his conversion Paul had been chosen as a witness of the gospel. God had chosen him for his service and in Christ had revealed to him his glory. Now Paul saw that the whole Scripture had been fulfilled. He regarded his earlier life as a struggle against the gospel in which the God of Scripture was now active. This struggle had made him unworthy of being an apostle (I Cor. 15:9), and yet he understood now that even from his mother's womb he had been chosen and set apart for this service.

We should note particularly that in the passages alluded to in connection with his election before his birth, his commission is like that of the prophet to go to *"the nations,"* to the *Gentiles*. "It is too light a thing that you should be my servant to raise up the tribes of Jacob and to restore the preserved of Israel; I will give you as a light to the nations, that my salvation may reach to the ends of the earth" (Isa. 49:6).

It is suggested here in Second Isaiah that the salvation which was to come through the Suffering Servant of the Lord should include the Gentiles. On the basis of such texts Paul declares that he has been selected to bring the gospel to them. He had been entrusted with the gospel in its most complete form, for God's plan was to be realized by including the Gentiles in salvation. Paul was carrying out the commission of which the prophets had spoken. This meant that the Messianic salvation of which he was the means and the apostle was already active. To oppose *this* gospel was to resist the salvation God had prepared, and opposition would invite a curse (vs. 8). To make Paul's apostolate dependent on the Jerusalem apostles or on anyone else was to reject God's charge and Christ's command.

It had been tentatively suggested in the Old Testament that the sufferings of Israel would prove to be a blessing to the Gentiles. It was clear to Paul that the inclusion of the Gentiles in the kingdom of God was a preparation for the final salvation. Israel too would fully share in it, and thus everything would be ready for the new age. The Messiah was sent also to the Gentiles. Paul had been chosen and called from his mother's womb for this very purpose of proclaiming and realizing that truth.

To understand the uniqueness of Paul's conception that he was entrusted with the gospel *in order that* he might preach it to the Gentiles we must keep in mind the Jewish attitude toward the Gentiles. The Gentiles had always opposed God's work, and in Israel's history they represented the powers hostile to God. Paul's Jewish contemporaries drew the conclusion that the Gentiles were not worthy of the divine blessings Israel had received through the law, which contained the way to righteousness. According to the Jewish conception the law had been given them by God as a means to attaining righteousness (cf. Rom. 2:17ff). The law thus separated the Jews and the Gentiles. The Gentiles were sinners and enemies of God, who did not share in the light and joy of the law. Some of the rabbis suggested that the Gentiles had been offered the law and rejected it. This idea agreed with the rationalization of the law and the conception that the basis of sin was man's free will.

This rationalization was a perversion of the law. The Jews thought that the law could be fulfilled by the observance of commandments which people could keep. In this way they made themselves masters of the law instead of letting the law rule them and waiting for its fulfilment through the Messiah. That the circumcised received the fulfilment of the law through Christ and in faith became partakers of God's righteousness was a testimony to God's truthfulness in fulfilling his promises (Rom. 15:8). The Jewish conception resulted in turning the Gentiles away from God's righteousness, but Scripture included them in his plan of salvation and the Messiah was sent to them also. They could therefore praise God for his mercy (Rom. 15:9).

According to Paul's understanding of Scripture the preaching of the gospel to the Gentiles was the fulfilment of the law. This fact could neither be validated, explained, or corrected through ideas of other people. He had not consulted with "flesh and blood," nor had he thought that human reason could either add to it or detract anything from it.

It would have seemed proper for Paul after he had received his new insight, to have gone back to Jerusalem to be instructed by the leading apostles and then consecrated as a preacher of the gospel. In that way the Christian tradition might have been transmitted. But Paul emphasizes that it was not a question of a succession in teaching or authority from the foremost apostles. Instead he went away into Arabia, possibly to the kingdom of the Nabataeans southeast of Damascus (cf. II Cor. 11:32). The reason for his withdrawal cannot be deduced with any certainty. Probably he withdrew to attain greater clarity in regard to his new insights. From Arabia he returned to Damascus. The chief point is that he did *not* go to Jerusalem to seek instruction and authorization through the earlier apostles. That he did not seek the counsel of men marks the difference between a tradition mediated by men and a teaching which has its basis in a direct divine revelation.

b) Christ, not the Christians, had instructed Paul (1:18-24)

(1) Paul's visit to Peter (1:18-20)

Paul did not go to Jerusalem until three years after the experience at Damascus. He would naturally be interested in learning to know Peter, whom he regularly calls Cephas (2:9, 11, 14; I Cor. 1:12; 3:22; 9:5; 15:5) although in 2:7 he calls him Peter. Paul had remained with Peter only two weeks. In that short a time one can learn to know a person, but not really receive fundamental instruction in a theology covering the whole proclamation and the Christian life. Since the visit took place three years after his conversion, it could not have been decisive for Paul's theological knowledge and thought. He emphasizes that he had not received the gospel from Peter. According to Paul an apostle was one who had received the gospel directly from Christ. This is what Paul had done, and consequently he did not need to go to Jerusalem at once in order to receive instruction from the older apostles.

It would be natural, however, during this visit for Paul to become acquainted with the tradition represented by Peter. He may have received some of that tradition already in Damascus. Through his conversion Paul had attained to clarity in the essential content and meaning of the gospel and of his own commission. But the common faith could be strengthened and enriched through mutual association. Unity among the apostles appeared in the fact that the same Spirit was active in them all. The Lord Christ himself was active in the gospel which both Paul and the older apostles served. The risen Christ had given Paul the office of servant of the gospel, and he himself was active as the life-giving Spirit (I Cor. 15:45). Peter was an apostle not merely because he was the bearer of a tradition, which of course he was, but because he had received his commission from the risen Lord.

If what Paul had received from Peter and James had been the basis of his gospel, and if the gospel had been of the same nature as the tradition the scribes transmitted and annotated in their interpretation of the law, his relationship to the apostles would have been the same as that of a disciple to his rabbi. This is what Paul denies. He had not received *the gospel* and his commission from them. God had chosen him before he was born, and he had received his commission from Christ. When it pleased God to reveal his Son to him, Paul had received in that experience his understanding of the significance of the gospel and his commission to preach it among the Gentiles. The preaching of the gospel also involved a tradition which could be enriched by information from the older apostles, but the gospel was the basis for the tradition, rather than the tradition serving as a basis for the gospel. The gospel was a proclamation of Christ in which he himself was active. The tradition recounted and transmitted the story of the events which had taken place. The stream of tradition continued from those who had been present to later generations. There was therefore a *formal* resemblance to the Jewish tradition. But while the rabbinical tradition was an ethical teaching declaring what God wanted man to do in order to become righteous and good, the Christian gospel was a message about the person and work of Christ and the salvation available in him.

In vs. 12 Paul maintains that he had not received the gospel from man. The question has been asked how he can say this and at the same time declare (I Cor. 15:3) that he had received it, and that the risen Christ had been seen by others before him. But this question arises because of a misunderstanding. It assumes that the gospel is similar to a rabbinical tradition, and the difficulty lies in the fact that we find two statements as to its origin. But although the content of the gospel tradition could be transmitted from person to person, it was not of the same type as the rabbinical. That tradition lacked the living Spirit. It broke off and replaced the works of the prophets who had interpreted the Scriptures through the Spirit. The gospel renewed the prophetic interpretation of Scripture and tradition. The content of the message of salvation was essentially the same whether Paul or the other apostles proclaimed it. Consequently Paul could tell the Galatians *both* that he had received the gospel by a revelation, that he was not related to the older apostles as a disciple to his master, *and* that his message was the same as theirs. This is the claim he makes in I Cor. 15:3.

We must remember that knowledge of Jesus was not knowledge "according to the flesh." When Paul says in II Cor. 5:16, "Even though we once regarded Christ from a human point of view, we regard him thus no longer," he does not mean that knowledge of the concrete events, words, and deeds of Jesus' life would as such be knowledge "from a human point of view." But the *nature* of knowledge of Christ could be both spiritual and "according to the flesh." Paul maintains that his knowledge of both the

historical Jesus and the risen Christ was spiritual (cf. W. D.
Davies, *Paul and Rabbinical Judaism*, p. 195). The concrete, historical events in Jesus' life were understood as a part of redemptive history. They remained historical, but their significance was seen in a new light.

Even the disciples who had walked with Jesus learned to regard him no longer "from a human point of view." Their faith in him as the one who had died and risen again meant that they knew him in the Spirit as the living Christ. Through the Spirit he was continually at work among them. The living and indwelling Christ himself revealed to them the meaning of his life and work. No one can understand the teaching of Jesus unless he has received the new life and the living Spirit of Christ. For one who does not live in Christ his teaching is just as impossible to understand as are the Old Testament Scriptures—in which he also speaks —for one who does not belong to Christ.

It might easily be assumed that a spiritual understanding of God's acts would mean making historical events symbolize inner experiences. For Paul, however, who had been nurtured in the realism of the Old Testament, the act of God's election was his essential point of reference. The significance of this activity of God had become clear to him in his Damascus experience. He saw that everything in the event of Christ was a part of God's election and salvation. He received a new insight into the meaning of the Old Testament. He understood it "according to the Spirit," not "according to the flesh." But this spiritual understanding did not eliminate the concrete and historical events but meant finding God's purpose in them. Paul's "spiritual" conception continues the Old Testament interpretation of God's activity. It is not a question of the spiritual development of a few important men, but of God's dealing with ordinary people. Paul is not concerned with "the inner life" or the personality of Jesus, but with what God has done with and through him in whom God's redemptive purpose has reached its climax. On the basis of this general conception it is easy to understand that the center of Paul's interest is in the redemptive significance of the work of Christ and specifically in the decisive events of the cross and the resurrection. The institution of the Lord's Supper was therefore of great importance to him. It had great significance for that gospel in which Christ continued to live and work.

The message of salvation revealed to Paul illumined and helped him to understand the deepest significance of everything he had learned of the tradition about Jesus' life and death. The older apostles had met the risen Christ before him, and he characterized his own meeting with Christ as the last manifestation of the risen Lord to his disciples (I Cor. 15:8). Paul's knowledge of Christ was a part of the gospel in which Christ was present and active. This knowledge gave content and meaning to everything the tradition could tell Paul about the life and work of Jesus.

Paul emphasizes that he had not seen any of the other apostles except James the Lord's brother. Probably the Judaizers had declared that immediately after his conversion he had gone to Jerusalem and received his instruction there. Afterwards he had been sent by the congregations in Jerusalem and Judea to preach the gospel. He was entirely dependent on them. He was, they claimed, a *shaliach* who simply had to deliver the message entrusted to him. But in order to please men Paul had delivered only a part of the message, leaving out the law which might have been difficult for the Gentiles to accept. Against all such accusations Paul declares with an oath that the situation had been rather as he stated now in vss. 18-19. His words in vs. 20, "In what I am writing to you, before God, I do not lie!" have the nature of an oath. The expression may be compared with I Thess. 2:5, "as God is witness," which is of similar significance.

In saying that he did not learn to know Peter until three years after his conversion Paul meant to indicate his independence of him and his equality with the Jerusalem apostles. But although he maintains that he had received his apostleship from the risen Lord, we must also note that he is the servant of the *same Lord* and the *same* gospel as the other apostles. He does not preach himself, nor does he seek to please men. He *assumes* the unity of the church. By claiming his place as apostle in the church where Peter was an apostle before him, he emphasizes the unity of the church. In the second chapter he shows how this unity was affirmed by their recognition of him and his apostleship. Here in the first chapter he shows how through his call he received a commission from Christ in this one church.

Paul never denied that the Jerusalem apostles were servants of Christ. The church was one because it belonged to Christ. The gospel in which Christ himself was at work gave to the church its meaning, significance, existence, and unity. His insistence on the fact that he had been called by the risen Lord meant *not only*

55

that he had the same authority as the older apostles but also that he had been called to serve the *same* gospel. Christ had called both him and them. The call gave him power not to preach himself but to serve this Lord who already had other apostles.

If Paul had received his commission from others, and if it were essentially a doctrine of men, it might be limited and subject to misunderstanding. If such a commission were enlarged beyond the original scope, and set forth as embracing a larger truth than it actually did, the result might have been the emergence of a sectarian emphasis and the division of the church. But this could not be because the gospel he proclaimed came from Christ himself and represented the whole evangelical truth which was constitutive for the church and made it what it was. Paul's assumption is that he and the other apostles represented the one church. In insisting that the gospel was not from men and that he had been called as an apostle by Christ and God who had raised Jesus from the dead, he is not trying to enhance himself and demand recognition for a sectarian emphasis. He emphasizes rather the unity of the church. He is the servant of the same Lord who has called the others and who is active in the gospel himself.

> (2) Paul's independence of the congregations in Judea (1:21-24)

After his short visit to Jerusalem Paul went into the regions of Syria and Cilicia. He left Judea and remained personally unknown to the inhabitants there. It was evidently important for Paul to insist that he was not sent out by any Jewish congregations, and that he had not received his apostleship from them. Nor had he been influenced by any special emphasis in Judea, or sent by the Christians there.

What Paul emphasizes in this chapter is that the gospel he proclaims is not a human tradition taken over by him. It could not be handled as a human teaching. The whole church was united in the gospel, including the Jewish-Christian congregations. He had not been sent by the congregations in Judea nor was he their agent, for he was the apostle of Christ and was responsible for his task to God only. His preaching had not caused division in the church; on the contrary, the report of his activity had been received with joy. The accusation that he had caused a schism, or that he had exceeded the commission given to him, and caused dissatisfaction among the Christians in Jerusalem or Judea, was altogether false. He who had been a zealous Pharisee and had held more strictly to the law than many of his countrymen (vs. 13; cf. Phil. 3:5-6), had become an apostle of the faith he had persecuted. His attitude at that time ought to convince the Galatians under the influence of the Judaizers that he would not curtail his message for fear of the severity of the law. His message was not a gospel that needed to be complemented by the proclamation of the law. He himself had been much stricter in his observance of the law than the Judaizers. But he had found the fulfilment of the law in Christ, and Christ himself was the fulfiller of the law.

The relationship between Paul's account and the narrative in Acts (9:26ff.) is a very difficult problem which we cannot discuss fully here. This is a part of the whole question of the relationship between the narratives in Acts and in Galatians. The discussion of this problem belongs properly to the interpretation of Acts and can only be alluded to here. We must remember, however, that Galatians is an older document than Acts, and that we have not a transmission of traditional material here but the authentic account of Paul himself. But his words must not be understood as an autobiography. Everything he says is intended to clarify the nature of the gospel as a divine revelation. He omits whatever does not directly concern this question. Acts mentions that the Hellenists sought to kill him in Jerusalem, but Paul says nothing about this. It is very probable that through the preaching of Paul the Jews recognized more clearly the difference between the gospel and the Jewish conception of the law, and therefore regarded him as a dangerous leader. Paul evidently had no occasion to mention this attempt on his life nor his preaching in Jerusalem. The author of Acts seems to have believed that Paul's visit to Jerusalem was of longer duration than Galatians indicates. He also seems to imply that Paul went directly to Jerusalem from Damascus. The tradition on which Acts is based seems not to have known of any sojourn in Arabia. It is impossible to reconcile these differences. Attempts to harmonize them result in mere speculations. But some of the differences that have been found are due to the fact that interpreters have regarded the first two chapters of Galatians as an autobiography and have assumed a sharp antithesis between Paul and the original apostles.

B. The gospel is the sufficient, necessary, and exclusive foundation of the unity of the church (2:1-21)

1. Paul's second visit to Jerusalem; the gospel is sufficient to preserve the unity of the church (2:1-10)

a) The reason for the visit (2:1-2)

In the beginning of Galatians 2 Paul tells us of his second visit to Jerusalem fourteen years after his first visit. The narrative is a part of his explanation of his relationship to the Jerusalem apostles. It is not an autobiography in the usual sense. The purpose was to explain to the Galatians how his position and message were related to the leaders in Jerusalem, and to refute the accusations of the Judaizers.

Paul did not deny that the administrative leadership of the church was located in Jerusalem. But his position nevertheless involved a problem. Through revelation he had received the commission as an apostle of Christ, but this commission was held in the church already established by Christ whose leaders were in Jerusalem. His apostleship was not in rebellion against these leaders. He had not been sent out from Jerusalem and did not carry letters of recommendation from them. He had received the gospel from Christ himself. But this did not mean that he was to establish his own church, or that he repudiated the administration of the older apostles. Paul did *not* "preach himself" (II Cor. 4:5); he preached Christ, and he was united with the Jerusalem apostles in the same faith. It is easy to understand how contentions and uncertainties might arise in the early church because it was difficult to explain the theoretical and practical attitude to the law contained in Scripture. No one doubted the divine authority of Scripture, and Paul did not question it at all. The difficulty was in the understanding of the profound meaning of the law and its application in the new situation created by the fact that God had declared Jesus to be the promised Messiah by the resurrection from the dead. He had made the One rejected by the Jews both "Lord and Christ" (Acts 2:36). The leaders in Jerusalem understood that this event introduced something new in their relationship to the law. But it was natural that many who had come to believe in Jesus as the Messiah found it difficult to comprehend the full consequences of their faith (Acts 15:1-5; Gal. 2:4). The center of the difficulty concerned circumcision and the question whether Gentile Christians had to observe the Jewish law. The rules of clean and unclean food would be important at the common meals, especially in the celebration of the Lord's Supper.

The second chapter tells us how in spite of all difficulties agreement was reached in regard to the law, and how Paul's clear and certain recognition of the implications of the gospel won recognition from the leaders in Jerusalem. Here Paul discusses in detail his relationship to the older apostles, mentions certain difficult situations, and proceeds to the theological discussion of the significance of the gospel.

By the time Paul after fourteen years returned to Jerusalem, he had lived in Syria and Cilicia, his home province, and in Antioch which had become a center of missionary expansion. It has been assumed that his first missionary journey took place during this period, and the narrative order in Acts supports this assumption. But it has also been suggested that the visit mentioned here took place shortly before the first journey.

Paul's account of this visit to Jerusalem has caused a great deal of discussion. How does this narrative agree with the sequence of events in Acts? Most commentators hold that the meeting described in Gal. 2:1-10 is identical with the one related in Acts 15. There are, however, some differences in the two accounts, and therefore some scholars would identify this visit with the one mentioned in Acts 11:30. Even if some historical problems will always remain unsolved, there is no reason to doubt the accuracy of Paul's account. If we keep in mind the character and purpose of the discussion and do not read it as a purely historical narrative, his presentation appears logical and clear. The Letter to the Galatians is older than Acts. Here we have Paul's direct words, not traditions and narratives compiled by others. The evidence seems to be in favor of identifying the visit with the Jerusalem council in Acts 15.

Paul states that his reason for going to Jerusalem was a revelation. In saying this he apparently refutes a claim by the Juadizers that he had been requested to give an account of his activity by the leaders in Jerusalem and had been reprimanded by them. Paul's account shows clearly that he had not gone there to receive instructions, or to be sent out by the Jerusalem congregation as its representative. According to Acts 15 it had been decided that Paul and Barnabas and some others were to go up to Jerusalem because of uncertainty in regard to the law and circumcision.

When Paul makes the claim that he went up because of a revelation, we must remember that, as he said, his whole commission originated in and rested on a revelation. His trip to Jerusalem did not invalidate this fact. He who had called him as a servant of the gospel had now made clear to him that he ought to go to Jerusalem and confer with the other apostles about the work of the gospel. It was not because of doubts about his apostolic call or the truth of the gospel that he went to Jerusalem, as if he had to ask advice of the older apostles about the relationship between the gospel and circumcision.

There are several visions or revelations recorded in Paul's life. After his meeting with Christ on the Damascus road he is reported to have seen Ananias in a vision (Acts 9:12). He had received revelations through visions and dreams (Acts 16:9; 18:9; 23:11; 27:23); he had ecstatic experiences and visions (Acts 22:17ff.; II Cor. 12:1ff.); and he was guided in his work by the Spirit (Acts 16:16; 19:21; 20:22). Even though these later experiences were not as decisive as the one on the Damascus road, they were of the same nature and guided him in his obedience to the commission given to him. What the nature of this particular revelation was we do not know. He must have been convinced, however, that what may well have been suggested by the congregation in Antioch or some other Christians was not contrary to the commission given him in Damascus.

Barnabas accompanied Paul on this journey. They were to confer with the Jerusalem apostles. Paul took Titus along also. Titus was not circumcised and did not have the same status as Paul and Barnabas. Barnabas was Joseph from Cyprus (Acts 4:36) who had befriended Paul during his first visit to Jerusalem after his conversion (Acts 9:27). Later he had been sent to Antioch, where he acted as a representative of the Jerusalem church and as teacher (Acts 11:22; 13:1; 15:35). He accompanied Paul on the first missionary journey but separated from him before the beginning of the second (Acts 15:36ff.). It was natural that Barnabas should go to Jerusalem since he was very close to Paul and enjoyed the confidence of the Jerusalem congregation.

The question has been raised how this journey could be reconciled with Paul's claim of being an apostle whose commission had not been given him by the older apostles. In a sense he seems to accord a special authority to the Jerusalem apostles. But, as we have stated above, there was no real contradiction between the Jerusalem apostles' and Paul's conception of righteousness through Christ, nor had Paul ever intended to establish a church or a sect separated from the administration in Jerusalem. It could be said that it was precisely Paul's concern for *the unity of the church in the truth of the gospel* that caused his anxiety. He was disturbed because "false brethren" had appeared who had never understood the deep significance of the gospel, but had combined faith in Christ as the Messiah with a Jewish interpretation of the law. They represented the same standpoint as the Judaizers in Galatia. Paul could not recognize them as Christians. But they could influence the leadership in Jerusalem in regard to rules and regulations for missionary work. Even if the leaders held firmly to justification through Christ, as Jewish Christians they might not be able to judge clearly in matters which from a Jewish-Christian point of view appeared to be inherited legal requirements that ought to be observed to avoid offending the Jews. Paul himself could be as a Jew to the circumcised when there was no danger of encouraging righteousness by the law. But he saw clearly the implications of the gospel with respect to the Gentiles, who did not need to submit to circumcision when they received the gospel.

If the leaders were to yield to the demands of the false brethren without seeing clearly that this must lead to righteousness by the law and destroy the gospel from within, all the work Paul had done might be in vain. Under the guise of directions designed to make the Gentile Christians conform to the Jewish Christians, the bondage of righteousness by works would exclude righteousness by faith and the freedom given by the Spirit.

Neither Paul nor the Jerusalem apostles regarded the extension of the Christian faith as propaganda for certain human ideas and ideologies in a modern sense. For all of them it was a question of a new and clearer view of God's purpose and acts of salvation. They regarded themselves as his instruments, servants, and messengers. This fact should make us hesitate to present their relationship as a struggle for power. The difference in their theological views arose because the Jerusalem apostles seem not to have perceived as clearly as Paul the full implications of the gospel with respect to the Gentiles. In general the first Christians in Jerusalem conceived of Jesus as the Messiah of the Jews who had appeared as the Suffering Servant of the Lord. Since salvation had come through him, they expected the Gentiles to join the Jewish-Christian church. The gospel must be preached first of all to the Jews. Since the Spirit had also been given to the Gentiles, the apostles perceived that observance of the law should not be required of them. This decision was of a practical nature. Because of the unity of the Spirit and their faith in Christ the Gentiles nevertheless became accepted as members of the Jewish-Christian church in spite of their deficiencies from the strict Jewish point of view. Paul, however, saw more clearly than anyone else the implications of the common faith in justification through Christ, and he had analyzed the significance of the law more sharply than others.

This difference between them could lead to a dangerous division. The Jerusalem apostles held that the conversion of Israel must come first, and they were concerned therefore with the mission to the Jews. They might have experienced or been told about the tremendous offense caused by the gospel when freedom from circumcision and the law was emphasized in principle. At times the early church had been regarded favorably by Jewish people (Acts 2:47) and could be tolerated, even though the leading Jews disapproved (Acts 5:13, 38-39). Persecution arose from time to time, but the conflict with Judaism did not become irrevocable and violent as long as the equality of the Gentiles with the Jews and their participation in the church without circumcision were not emphasized too strongly (cf. Acts 21:21; 22:21-22). As long as this aspect did not occupy the center in preaching, the Christians might be regarded as a Jewish sect or a special tendency, which was of course heretical, but with which it was possible nevertheless to carry on discussion.

No doubt there were many who had never considered or understood what consequences the righteousness revealed in Christ really had in reference to the law and its application. This problem became acute as soon as Gentiles were admitted into the church. If the Jerusalem apostles retreated and sought to make the gospel less offensive to the Jews (cf. I Cor. 1:23), the truth of the gospel would be corrupted. This attitude might be justified on practical grounds, but it would affect the very content of the gospel proclamation. A division along these lines would have serious consequences for Paul's work. The harvest he expected might be destroyed. The mission was not a part of Paul's own ambition and desire for power. He had not originated the gospel (II Cor. 3:5).

But on the day of judgment he must give an account of his work before God. In vs. 2 he voices his concern lest he be working or had worked in vain. That the gospel had borne fruit would be Paul's boast at the return of Christ (I Thess. 2:19ff.; II Cor. 1:14; cf. I Cor. 3:10-15). Similarly he encourages the Philippians to hold fast to the word of life "so that in the day of Christ I may be proud that I did not run in vain or labor in vain" (Phil. 2:16).

If a schism should occur, there was danger that the fruit of Paul's work might be destroyed, and the truth of the gospel would be obscured among the Gentile Christians (cf. vs. 5). It was necessary therefore for Paul to lay before the brethren and especially "before those who were of repute" the content of the gospel he preached.

What happened was that the leaders gave him "the right hand of fellowship" (vs. 9). They rejected the claims of the false brethren. It is not certain that the false brethren were present. Their claims could have been brought to Jerusalem in many ways. Paul did not come to Jerusalem as one accused; he went up "by revelation," possibly in order to secure the help of the older apostles against the false brethren, which they gladly gave him. They agreed that the gospel Paul preached among the Gentiles was equivalent to the gospel Peter preached among the circumcised. This did not mean that Peter had preached a gospel different from that of Paul. But Peter became responsible for the Jews, and among them circumcision was not such an acute problem as it was among the Gentiles. That the gospel was one and the same Paul shows in vss. 15ff.

b) The circumcision of Titus (2:3-5)

The Judaizers had evidently claimed that there was a difference in principle between Paul and the leaders in the preaching of the gospel. It is clear, however, that the leaders did *not* share the conception of the Judaizers. The episode of Titus may have been cited by Paul to establish this fact.

Paul had taken the uncircumcised Titus along to Jerusalem. The best attested text states that not even Titus was "compelled to be circumcised, though he was a Greek." If the Jerusalem apostles had insisted in principle that Gentile Christians must be circumcised, certainly a companion and fellow worker of Paul would have had to be circumcised.

The text, however, is a little uncertain, and in the so-called

"Western" text the words "not" and "even" are omitted from verse 5⁰. The meaning would then be that Titus was indeed circumcised as a concession to those who insisted on circumcision, but Paul had not been *compelled* to do so. He had simply consented to have it done in the interest of peace.

This text variant must, however, be regarded as wrong both on philological and logical grounds. The rule of textual criticism is that the more difficult reading must be accepted as authentic, since it is obvious that a difficult text may easily be simplified by a scribe. The text used in the Revised Standard Version is the best attested and also most difficult in the passage as a whole. The Greek sentence presents an anacoluthon, which the scribes would be tempted to remove.

In principle it would seem impossible for Paul to have yielded in this matter since the question at issue was the significance of the law for salvation. Some have pointed out that according to Acts 16:3 Paul circumcised Timothy. It is certainly possible that Acts may have reported an erroneous tradition, that this story may be due to reports which the Judaizers had circulated about Paul and which he denies in Gal. 5:11 (E. Haenchen, *Apostelgeschichte* [1956], p. 427). But there is really no reason to doubt the report in Acts that Paul circumcised Timothy. The question about the necessity of circumcision for salvation was not involved in this instance. Timothy was the son of a Jewish mother and might be regarded as an apostate unless he was circumcised. In this case Paul could obey the law in deference to the Jews and regard it as an ordinary custom without significance for justification. In such a situation Paul could "become as a Jew to the Jews" (I Cor. 9:20).

Since Paul had taken Titus along on his own initiative, the situation in this case was different. Possibly the intention had been for Titus to serve as a means to force the issue and compel the leaders to decide whether they would side with "the false brethren" or with Paul. When the issue was joined, they had placed themselves unreservedly on the side of Paul.

The actual cause of the difficulty, according to vs. 4, was that "false brethren . . . slipped in to spy out our freedom."

As indicated above, it is not necessary to assume that this happened in Jerusalem, although in that church there were "believers who belonged to the party of the Pharisees" and insisted that circumcision and observance of the law were necessary for salvation (Acts 15:5). Much theological reflection and a deep experience of the power of the Spirit were required before the early Jewish Christians could fully understand that the fellowship of the church was built on the foundation of the gospel without the observance of the law which distinguished the Jews from the Gentiles (cf. Acts 11:2ff.). Naturally this difficulty may have been particularly acute among the Jewish Christians in Judea (Gal. 2:12; Acts 15:24). But as we have emphasized, this situation must not be interpreted to mean that the leaders in Jerusalem supported the Judaizers. Rather, these leaders had probably had some difficulties with those people who were not yet able to see in the church a wholly independent entity based on the gospel, in which the prophecies of the Messiah's sufferings had been fulfilled. Paul was possibly the first one who consistently realized that the gospel involved as well the fulfilment of *the law,* and that therefore the gospel needed no complementation by the observance of legalistic requirements as a condition for salvation. It seems to be true, however, that the other apostles also submitted to this truth given in the fact that the Gentiles too became partakers of the Spirit, the sign of the people belonging to the new age.

In Antioch a Christian congregation with both Jewish and Gentile members appears to have been organized. It is possible that Paul's words about "false brethren . . . who slipped in to spy out our freedom" may refer to something which had taken place in Antioch. There may not even have been any one particular occasion. Paul's account in Galatians 2 does not have the character of a historical narrative, but is intended to show that the relationship of Paul to the Jerusalem apostles was not what the Judaizers claimed. Paul wants to refute the claims of the Judaizers, and "the false brethren" were evidently of that stripe. "False brethren" may have appeared in Antioch, in congregations founded by Paul, and in Jerusalem. According to Paul they did not belong to the true church. Their participation in the life of the congregation was for the purpose of spying out how the Christians observed the law. When they discovered that the Christians did not observe it in accordance with the Judaizers' conception of its significance and practice, they began propaganda against those Christians who had not submitted to the law according to the Jewish fashion.

The question of where these false brethren had appeared is not essential for our understanding of Paul's words. In order to clarify this point it would be necessary to discuss the report in Acts about the Jerusalem council and its decree more thoroughly than is possible in this connection.

Paul says that the false brethren "spied out" the freedom which the Christian possessed. Consequently their freedom could be observed; it was not simply a matter of inner freedom. It was evidently visible because of the fact that the Christians were not circumcised and did not observe the food laws. It is obvious that table fellowship at the Christian love feasts and in general the unrestricted social intercourse between Jews and Gentiles were matters which from a Jewish point of view could easily be attacked.

For those who had accepted the Jewish way of understanding Scripture it was easy to believe in Jesus as the Messiah and at the same time retain circumcision and the Jewish conception of the law. It was therefore quite natural that these people should seek to hinder Paul in his proclamation of freedom from the Jewish law as a condition for participation in the salvation of Christ. But to that demand Paul could not yield for a moment. Yielding would result in obscuring the truth of the gospel revealed to him. It was that gospel which he had proclaimed to the Galatians. He tells them that his appearance in Jerusalem had been in the interest of preserving the truth of the gospel for such people as the Galatians. If they had yielded to the views of the false brethren, the gospel could no longer have been proclaimed as Paul had in Galatia. Insistence on circumcision as a principle would lead to righteousness by the law, because it would imply that righteousness depended on the observance of the ordinances of the law in the Jewish sense. The position of the law as a testimony to a coming righteousness would then become obscured.

c) The older apostles agreed with Paul (2:6-10)

    (1) Those who were of repute made no demand that Paul add anything to his proclamation (2:6)

The sentences in vss. 6-8 are broken up by inserted phrases. Paul expresses himself in anacoluthons. A translation would run somewhat like this: From those who were reputed to be something (what they were makes no difference to me; God shows no partiality)—those who were of repute imposed nothing extra on me; but on the contrary, when they saw that I had been entrusted with the gospel to the Gentiles, just as Peter had been entrusted with the gospel to the Jews (for he who worked through Peter for the mission to the Jews worked through me also for the Gentiles), and when they perceived the grace that was given to me, James and Cephas and John, these who were reputed to be pillars, gave to me and Barnabas the right hand of fellowship, that we should go to the Gentiles and they to the Jews; only they would have us remember the poor, which very thing I have been eager to do.

To break up a sentence and leave it incomplete is possible in Greek in a way that it is not in English. Whether he dictated or wrote this, Paul has used an unusual number of anacoluthons in this passage. Possibly he was especially anxious to guard against misinterpretations.

Paul points out especially that "those of repute" did not impose any new requirements on him. They gave their complete recognition to the gospel Paul had preached. It was not necessary to add anything to it such as circumcision or observance of the law. The only thing they wanted to emphasize in the interest of unity and co-operation was that Paul should "remember" the ingathering for the congregation in Jerusalem (vs. 10). This had of course nothing to do with the content of the gospel.

That the older apostles did not impose anything extra on Paul implied that they did not demand, as the Judaizers wanted, that the Gentile Christians should be circumcised and required to observe the law of Moses. The Judaizers had evidently maintained that Paul's proclamation was incomplete. To please men (1:10) and not scare anyone away from the gospel he had proclaimed *only* the gospel and had left out the requirements of the law. His preaching ought to be corrected by including these requirements. Very likely the Judaizers had intimated that the older apostles always preached *both* the grace through Jesus the Messiah *and* the requirements of the law. Paul understood at once that this law was not the law fulfilled in Christ, nor was it the demands legitimately imposed on a Christian. Observance of the law could not be added to the gospel. The gospel which the Judaizers wanted to complement with the righteousness of the law was not the real and true gospel. Their whole proclamation was not a different gospel (1:6-7) but a perversion. It was a different proclamation, not at all identical with the one true gospel.

Paul emphasizes that those of repute in Jerusalem did *not* place any such demands upon him. They had preserved the truth of the gospel, and the unity of the church was manifested through their brotherly attitude toward Paul and Barnabas. "Those of repute" had no such control over Christian preaching that they could tell Paul how and what he should preach. He notes that the One who worked through Peter worked through him also, and thus their attitude becomes a confession of the unity which the church possessed through the living and active Lord. The story of Paul's meeting with them became therefore a refutation of the false "gospel" of the Judaizers. It was an attempt to present the Christian message as faith in Jesus the Messiah and in addition the demand for the observance of the law (or at least a part of the law) according to the Jewish interpretation. Righteousness would then be dependent on the observance of the requirements of the law in their external and literal form. The essential tendency of the gospel to obliterate the boundary between Jew and Gentile would then have been denied, and Christianity would have become a Jewish sect.

But the Jerusalem apostles had not taken this attitude. Even though the Jews in Judea lived according to the law, its observance was not a means of righteousness. They also held that righteousness was the result of the action of Christ, "by the grace of our Lord Jesus Christ" (Acts 15:11). The words of Paul in 2:16 express the faith of the older apostles also.

In exegetical literature there has been much discussion about Paul omitting all reference here to the decree mentioned in Acts 15:19-29, and the rules which according to that decree were to be observed by the Gentile Christians. Although the presentations cannot be harmonized, in Galatians it is not a question of what the Gentile Christians were to observe; it is a question of circumcision and the observance of the law as requirements for salvation. If Paul knew of the decree, he may have felt that its requirements did not touch the gospel itself, since it was not a question of circumcision or of conditions required for participation in salvation.

It has also been suggested that the broken sentences in vss. 6ff. indicate that Paul had known about the decree, but that he wanted to emphasize that the intention of the apostles was not to add anything to the gospel. He insists that there were no requirements which would constitute a condition for righteousness. Many exegetes, however, among them Oscar Cullmann in his book, *Peter:*

Disciple—Apostle—Martyr (Philadelphia: 1953), believe that Paul could not have known about the decree. Cullmann holds that Gal. 2:1-10 describes the same meeting with the apostles as Acts 15, but that the decree itself belongs to a later date. At Paul's last visit in Jerusalem (Acts 21:25) it is intimated that the decree was relatively recent. The speech by James may of course be Luke's literary production, but there are indications that the decree was not authorized at the meeting Paul attended.

In any case there are no reasons to hold that circumcision was required by the leaders in Jerusalem. These leaders did *not* adhere to the Judaistic position. If the decree was authorized at the Jerusalem meeting, it apparently emphasizes that circumcision was not required, but that certain precepts should be observed in deference to the customs and traditions of the Jews. It may be noted that the rules mentioned in Acts 15:29 are such ritual precepts which according to the law of Moses (Lev. 17:8ff.; 18:6ff.) applied also to *strangers* who dwelt among the people. These were rules relating to clean and unclean matters; they had nothing to do with observances whereby a man might attain righteousness.

In general it is clear that the Christian doctrine of justification by the grace of Christ indirectly gave a different significance to the law as far as the Jewish Christians were concerned. It may be true that circumcision and the observance of the law had a religious significance for the Jews of Paul's day. But if Christ was the ground of salvation, and the Gentiles were able to receive baptism and salvation, the Jewish-Christian conception of the law must move more and more in the direction that it was significant only as custom and tradition. Paul declares that circumcision was *a seal* to Abraham of the righteousness by faith, not a condition or a means of righteousness (Rom. 4:10ff.).

It may be possible, as we have said, that Paul did not know anything about the apostolic decree. It may have been authorized at a later time, possibly after the episode in Antioch. Since the rules mentioned in the decree applied to strangers living among the Israelites (Lev. 17-18), it may be that they were intended to apply in the congregations where the majority of the members were Jews and where a few Gentiles were to be admitted. They would serve, therefore, to make table fellowship possible, to remove Jewish scruples about the observance of the law, and to reduce Jewish antagonism against the Gentile Christians.

The side remark in vs. 6 about those who were reputed to be pillars has been interpreted in various ways. It has been generally understood that here Paul expresses his real conviction that the apostles, to whom he appealed in the interest of unity, did not have any absolute authority just because they were the older apostles and had been associated with Jesus during his earthly life. God shows no partiality. Paul's apostleship was just as good as theirs. The implication of his words would be that the Galatians overestimated the importance of the original apostles.

Another interpretation (suggested by J. Munck) holds that here Paul points to the contrast between what the apostles are now and what they had been earlier. They had been ignorant, they had forsaken Christ, and Peter had denied him. But God paid no attention to these things; he used them nevertheless in his service. In the same way He used Paul, even though he had earlier persecuted the Christians. God was not concerned with what either they or Paul had been in the past.

It seems more natural, however, to assume that the expression, "God shows no partiality," means that God judges all alike, the Gentiles as well as the Jews. The statement that God shows no partiality occurs in Deut. 10:17: "For the Lord your God is God of gods and Lord of lords, the great, the mighty, and the terrible God, who is not partial and takes no bribe. He executes justice for the fatherless and the widow, and loves the sojourner." Here the stranger and the Israelite, the Gentile and the Jew, are placed side by side. Acts 10:34 tells us that after Peter had seen his vision and had been called to Cornelius, he exclaims: "Truly I perceive that God shows no partiality" (cf. Deut. 10:17, and II Chron. 19:7). Paul uses this well-known expression to indicate that God judges righteously and gives no preference to the Jew. When Paul uses the same expression in Rom. 2:11, he affirms that God judges justly without reference to whether a person has had the law or not. It seems, therefore, that the expression refers to God's righteous judgment according to works (cf. also Eph. 6:9; Col. 3:25; I Pet. 1:17).

Just as the Galatians tended to have faith in circumcision and the law, they also regarded the Jerusalem apostles as the real authorities. These apostles were Jews, they observed the law, they had been closely associated with Jesus during his earthly life, and according to the Judaizers they represented the true Messianic faith. Paul shows that the apostles sided with him and did not agree with the Judaizers. He may have purposely inserted these broken sentences, however, in view of the tendency of the Galatians to think of a person's high office and reputation as a basis of the gospel. The truth of the gospel had no such foundation. It was a revelation of God. Just as in his judgment God shows no partiality between Jew and Gentile, so does he take no account of the reputation certain people enjoy. The interpretation of the gospel does not depend on men, and the truth is not subject to them. The fact that the older apostles had a favorable reputation and were regarded as of highest rank did not mean that they could establish norms and definitions of the gospel. In reality their comprehension could be quite circumscribed. Paul indicates this here in his report on Peter's action in Antioch. *The fact that Paul received the support of the older apostles in an important question did not mean that he regarded them as infallible authorities in their interpretation of the significance of the gospel.* They were servants of the gospel and could be mistaken in regard to its implications. But in this case they had understood its implications correctly. However, the gospel came from God, and he judges without partiality.

In agreement with this general principle Paul can say that he himself counts everything "as refuse" that caused him to "have confidence in the flesh." Whatever gain he had had he now counts as loss (Phil. 3:7ff.). Such personal advantages as for instance circumcision were not significant in the sight of God, nor could external authority and prestige become normative for the truth of the gospel. This fact must be clearly stated even in the midst of joy over the preservation of the unity of the church by the leaders' obedience to the truth of the gospel. The foundation of the truth does not depend on persons but on God, who reveals it and judges both Jews and Gentiles in righteousness. He inserts this idea even in the statement where he records the agreement between himself and the other apostles. Now the truth of the gospel is given; God affirms its truth and bestows righteousness. The gospel signifies a divine reality in the present, and it must not be made to depend on authority and tradition "of the flesh." Christ is active in the gospel, and the Spirit reveals the truth proclaimed in it.

The inserted statement, "who were reputed to be something," does not imply, therefore, that Paul is opposed to the apostles in Jerusalem or that he is irritated at a theology not quite like his own. In spite of the actual unity in faith Paul warns in principle against basing this unity on anything "physical," on the reputation of certain people, or on rumors about their opinions. The gospel, through which the Spirit is given, validates itself (cf. 3:2).

The decision taken in Jerusalem meant that the leaders understood and agreed in principle that the gospel should not be proclaimed as if it were a tendency within Judaism. They acknowledged God's work through Paul and accepted in faith the implications of the gospel which Paul had drawn and the fact that Christ worked through Paul for the Gentiles. For Paul the sign of the new Israel was not "a circumcision that is outward in the flesh" (Rom. 2:28ff.; Phil. 3:3). Those uncircumcised who were received into the church through baptism were not to be compelled to receive circumcision and become like Jews. The question whether and to what extent Paul's points of view prevailed will be discussed later in the exegesis of 2:11-14.

(2) The apostolic authority of Peter among the Jews and that of Paul among the Gentiles was on a par (2:7-9)

Among the leaders Paul mentions James, Cephas, and John in vs. 9. The name of James is placed before Peter (Cephas) in the best manuscripts. Evidently James was at this time the leader of the congregation. Peter had assumed the direction of the mission to the Jews and possibly no longer resided in Jerusalem but had come there to attend the meeting. From the point of view of the ancient church Peter and Paul were the foremost apostles and had been entrusted with the missionary task of the gospel. Their appointments had been given by revelation of the risen Christ. Peter had been entrusted with the gospel to the Jews and Paul with the gospel to the Gentiles. This seems to have involved a recognition of the grace given to each of them. He who had worked through Peter for the mission to the Jews worked through Paul for the mission to the Gentiles. The unity between them is emphasized by the insistence that the same God assisted both. The Jerusalem apostles recognized this unity in the work of the gospel, and Paul underscores the fact.

Did this division mean that Paul had to go exclusively to the Gentiles and Peter exclusively to the Jews? Possibly it meant that different territories were assigned to them where either the Jews or the Gentiles were in the majority. We know that Paul on his missionary journeys turned first to the Jews and preached in their synagogues (Acts 9:20; 13:14-15, 46; 14:1; 17.1ff.; 18:4-6, 19ff.;

19:8ff.; I Cor. 9:20). The reference seems to be to geographical regions, so that Peter was assigned to those areas where the Jews were in the majority, or where there were great concentrations of Jewish people, especially in Palestine and possibly in Syria.

It is possible, however, that geographical regions were not involved. In Jerusalem it was not a question of deciding between different spheres of influence or power. Once we free ourselves from the notion that the conference involved a struggle for power by different parties, the significance of the decision might be understood thus: Paul assumed the *chief responsibility* for the mission to the Gentiles, and Peter likewise for the mission to the Jews. Paul could therefore in general follow the principle he states in Rom. 15:20ff. and II Cor. 10:14, but it would also be possible for him to preach the gospel in the synagogues. It is, of course, also possible that no division of the missionary task was involved in either a geographical or a religious sense, but that the apostles recognized Paul to be free to preach the gospel according to the grace given to him without any instructions or corrections by the church in Jerusalem.

Whatever the details might have been, it is clear that Paul's work was recognized as the work of the church to the same extent as the work among the Jews. The Gentile mission was placed on a par with the Jewish mission. Since both were "by grace," the living Lord himself determined how the gospel was to be proclaimed. At the meeting there was no presentation of a theological conception differing from that of Paul, as the Judaizers claimed. Paul's preaching was accepted as being essentially equivalent to that of the older apostles. We must, however, define the shade of the differences between them more clearly.

Many scholars have been inclined to posit a theological conflict between Paul and Peter. The hypothesis of the Tübingen school was that the author of Acts wanted to minimize the conflict between Paul and the Jerusalem apostles who were supposed to have sided with the Judaizers. After this theory had to be abandoned, the relative agreement between Paul and the Jerusalem apostles has been emphasized. But this agreement in essentials does not exclude differences in detail. We will consider here only the shade of difference between Peter and Paul. Even if James was not quite the Judaizer he is sometimes made out to be, the difference between him and Paul would have been considerably greater than that between Paul and Peter.

It cannot be denied that Paul meant something specific when he spoke of "my gospel." We must note especially two aspects. 1) Paul's gospel was the divine truth concerning salvation and righteousness which had been clearly revealed to him. That truth was essentially the same as the gospel the other apostles preached. 2) Through the revelation he had been especially enlightened about one aspect of the common gospel, viz., the significance of the conversion of the Gentiles and the understanding of the law. Even though we cannot with certainty speak of a theology of Peter, we can distinguish certain aspects of his thinking as it is presented in Acts. Even though Peter's sermons in Acts 2-4 were edited by Luke, they may reflect Peter's ideas. He thus proclaimed this Jesus who suffered and died on behalf of Israel, who rose again from the dead, and whom God has made both Lord and Christ (Messiah). He was the Suffering Servant of the Lord. His death on the cross involved a vicarious suffering, a sacrifice. He was the Messiah promised in Scripture. Peter labored to prevail upon the Jews to believe in Jesus as the Suffering Servant of the Lord whom God had made Messiah and Lord. But it was an old expectation in Israel that in the last days the Gentiles were to come to Zion in order to worship the God of Israel, bring their gifts and sacrifices, and become incorporated in or subject to the people of Israel. It was natural for the early Christians to believe that these prophecies were now beginning to be fulfilled, even if it did not happen the way the Jews had expected. Through the resurrection Jesus had been declared to be the Messiah, the Son of God, the Suffering Servant of the Lord. That Israel should accept this Messiah who had suffered and died for the people, and that the Gentiles should join Christian Israel were a part of the events of these last days.

It is evident that the revelation on which Paul based his proclamation dealt with his commission as the apostle to the *Gentiles.* What made Paul the apostle to the Gentiles was not merely the formal commission to preach the gospel to them, but also a certain quality in his proclamation through which some aspects of the gospel were emphasized and assumed a significance differing in some respects from Peter's preaching. Paul, of course, regularly began his preaching in the synagogues, and Peter also preached to the Gentiles.

These ideas of Paul seem to have been connected with his conception of the events of the last days (cf. Rom. 11:1ff.). In accordance with God's plan the apostasy of Israel and their rejection of the Messiah served to provide an opportunity for the salvation of the Gentiles (cf. Rom. 10:14-21). When Israel refused to believe in Christ, it rejected the Scriptures and the real meaning of the law. Through the death and resurrection of Christ the transgression of Israel became a means through which the gospel was brought to the Gentiles, who thus became partakers of the promises given to Israel. The church in Jerusalem thought primarily of the conversion of *Israel,* and assumed that even now the Gentiles might join them without first having to become Jews. Paul seems to have understood God's plan of salvation to mean that the Gentiles were first to receive the gospel, and afterwards all Israel would participate in salvation. Then the new age would appear in its full glory (cf. Rom. 11:7-18). Through the death of Christ on the cross the circumcised were redeemed from the curse of the law so that they would receive salvation together with the Gentiles. In this way the blessing of Abraham would come upon the Gentiles (Gal. 3:14). A small remnant of apostate Israel had come to faith through election, not through the law (Rom. 11:1-6). Paul's theology was unique not only in the order in which the gospel was to be preached, but the meaning of the gospel itself in its relationship to the law was developed with great power and clarity.

Since the observance of the law did not prevent the hardening of Israel, it is evident that the law had been misinterpreted and misapplied. But God permitted the hardening of Israel to promote the salvation of the Gentiles. The Israel which rejected Christ misused and perverted the law. A new way for the salvation of the chosen people, through the conversion of the Gentiles, corresponds to a new way of understanding and applying the law as fulfilled in Christ. If the Gentiles were to practice circumcision and observe the law, they would adopt apostate Israel's conception of the law. Using the law and circumcision as means of attaining righteousness was tantamount to rejection of Christ. The Gentiles' acceptance of Christ, of the new understanding of the law, and of righteousness by faith would have the paradoxical result that all Israel would turn to their true Messiah. This was not simply the conversion of a people to a new religion; it was a part of the history of redemption. The conversion of Israel had a special place in God's plan of salvation. Since Israel was the chosen people, and God remains faithful (Rom. 3:3ff; 11:29), the conversion of Israel would mean the full inauguration of the new age, "life from the dead," the coming of the kingdom of God (Rom. 11:15).

This theology of Paul had its basis in that gospel concerning the suffering Son of God, who had died and risen again, which was preached also in the congregation in Jerusalem, but it places the Gentiles and freedom from the law in the center of the message in a way quite different from that of Peter in the sermons in Acts. In his theology the conception of justification by faith was developed with special care and its ramifications thought through with great intensity. Paul's preaching agrees with the common Christian faith in Jesus Christ as the Suffering Servant of the Lord, in his atoning death and in salvation through him, rather than faith in salvation by works of the law. But he seems to have changed the accent in the early Christian proclamation so that the Gentiles' acceptance as heirs of the promises (Gal. 3:26—4:7) became the first event and the condition for the ultimate coming of the Messianic age. Paul's ability to comprehend the implications of the faith in Christ in reference to the law may have been due to his rabbinical training. He *knew* the Scripture and the tradition as he had learned it in their school. After he had received new light, he could see more clearly the significance of the history of salvation.

(3) Unity was sealed through the ingathering for the Jerusalem church (2:10)

The unity of the church was especially accentuated through the common responsibility for the ingathering in behalf of the Christians in Jerusalem. This ingathering indicates how closely Paul felt himself related to the Jerusalem congregation. Paul indicates that he was eager to do his part in this matter. This practical task had a unifying result. "The poor" means the poor in the church in Jerusalem. The only request the Jerusalem apostles made of Paul was that he should "remember the poor." Paul's participation in this collection indicates clearly that he did not intend to found a separate church. He belonged to the same church as the Christians in Jerusalem. He mentions this collection in Rom. 15:25, 31; I Cor. 16:1; II Cor. 8:4; 9:1, 12. They felt a special concern for the home base of the church. There is no doubt but that the Christians in Jerusalem, who were frequently subject to persecution, really needed this help.

The collection for the saints emphasizes therefore the unity of the whole church. But there was also another element in the situation. We have seen that Paul regarded his work as a part of the events of the last days. The work of the gospel was understood from an eschatological point of view. It was not propaganda for human ideologies. The apostles were not great religious personalities; they were servants in the work through which the word of Scripture was now fulfilled in Christ. But Scripture said that in the last days the Gentiles were to come with gifts to Jerusalem (cf. Hag. 2:8; Zech. 14:14; Isa. 60:5, 11). Through the servants of the gospel the events of the last days were now coming to pass. The poor saints in Jerusalem could apply to themselves the word of Scripture that Israel was to be humbled by poverty and suffering. But they were to be restored when God himself bestowed his blessing on them in the world and gave them the life of the age of salvation. The collection fulfilled a condition for the coming of the kingdom of God. The congregation in Jerusalem which suffered persecution and poverty stands as a representative of the pious and humble, the *ebionim,* who were to experience the fulfilment of the promises, and to whom all peoples would come and join themselves. The Gentiles had shared in their spiritual blessings, and they ought therefore to serve them in material blessings (Rom. 15:27).

It is to be noted, however, that Paul's readiness to participate in the collection was connected with the full recognition by the apostles that the gospel was to be brought to the Gentiles without any demand for circumcision and the observance of the law. According to the Jewish understanding of the Old Testament the Gentiles were to come to Jerusalem as subjects, and according to custom as a subject people who submitted to a powerful nation, they were to bring gifts. Jerusalem remained the holy place to which all must turn, and the Jews became the ruling people to whom their subjects paid homage. The gospel destroyed this nationalistic idea. It knew nothing of a ruling people, nor of a holy place which would serve as a perpetual center and capital. The gospel was to go into all the world independently of specific places and of Israel's religious laws and traditions in the external sense. But when the apostles had agreed that the gospel was to be brought to the Gentiles without the demand of circumcision and observance of the law, the prophecies could receive a new interpretation. The Gentiles' gifts to the congregation in Jerusalem could be seen as a fulfilment of the prophecies and a sign that the new age of salvation had come (II Cor. 6:2; Luke 4:21; II Cor. 8:3ff.; 9:1ff.). The basis on which the gifts were to be sent was not the victory of Israel over external enemies but the victory of Christ's death on the cross, when he took upon himself the curse of the law so that the Gentiles could participate in the blessing given to Abraham (cf. the exposition of 3:13ff.).

2. The gospel is a necessary guide for the unity of the church—Peter and Paul in Antioch (2:11-14)

In order to understand the significance of Paul's narrative of his conflict with Peter in Antioch we must consider the place it has in his whole argument. Paul explained first of all that he had received his apostleship by a revelation of Christ, and that it was not dependent on the older apostles or on the churches in Judea (Galatians 1). He went on to show that there was complete agreement in principle between him and the leaders in Jerusalem in regard to the content and proclamation of the gospel (2:1-10), and he closes his account by saying that the only request made of him was that he should remember the poor. The story of his two visits to Jerusalem is an integral part of his concern to instruct the Galatians in the basis of the gospel and the unity of the church.

He then proceeds in 2:11 to relate an episode which illustrates how the gospel must be applied consistently. (The Judaizers may have used the same story for their own purpose.) The truth of the gospel must be maintained at all times. Peter agreed with Paul, but on one occasion he had departed from the narrow path of the gospel, and Paul had had to correct him.

The account of this episode is a part of Paul's argument. He speaks of justification by faith as the basis of the Christian church. But for Paul who was well versed in the Old Testament "faith" is connected with trust, consecration, and faithfulness in response to God's acts of redemption. After the Christian has been brought to faith through revelation and his own experience, he must walk consistently in the truth which he has seen and accepted. Paul uses the figure of running in a race (I Cor. 9:24ff.; Phil. 3:11ff.). If one does not hold consistently to righteousness by faith, and does not walk in the truth, he will go astray. Peter fell into hypocrisy and endangered the unity of the church by his vacillation.

If the Galatians had heard that Peter in Antioch had insisted on the law as a basis for table fellowship, they were now told that this was a temporary deviation and that Paul had officially reprimanded him. At the same time Paul illustrated his contention that the truth of the gospel did not depend on the actions of those who were of repute, and that he himself was a servant of that gospel whose truth God had revealed to him. This truth could not be understood and secured if it was regarded as instruction in which one had to ask how the leaders acted, as when a great rabbi could be cited as irrefutable authority.

What Paul wants to do in this chapter, where the incident in Antioch is incorporated, is not simply to relate in succession a series of events. We might say that the real purpose of the whole chapter is to illustrate how justification by faith, as Paul proclaimed it, was recognized by the older apostles and how it was consistently maintained in the incident in Antioch.

It is perfectly natural, therefore, for Paul to proceed at once to an exposition of righteousness by faith in vs. 15. There has been some question as to whether vss. 15-21 constitute Paul's words to Peter or are addressed to the Galatians. If the report of the incident in Antioch is understood as a historical narrative of a conflict with Peter, it is strange that the following section is attached to it without any clear indication that it belongs in this context. But if we understand that Paul's purpose was to illustrate the truth of justification by faith, it is quite natural for him to begin clarifying this doctrine for the Galatians. He can do this in behalf of both himself and Peter, because on this point they were in complete agreement.

It is quite natural that after pointing out the equality between the mission to the Jews and the mission to the Gentiles, Paul insists also that the gospel is the same for both. The same gospel of righteousness through Christ must be proclaimed to both groups. There was a danger that the observance of the law by Jewish Christians might be regarded as a condition for participation in salvation, even if it was not openly proclaimed. If in a congregation of both Jews and Gentiles the Gentiles were excluded according to the Jewish tradition, the observance of the law might be regarded as an extra condition for participation in salvation. Jewish custom thus became a qualification for righteousness and the gospel was perverted.

The account of this incident in Antioch may have been included here by Paul to show that he had made clear even to Peter that one must never act in such a way as to raise an ambiguity in the relationship between Jewish and Gentile Christians. The Judaizers had told the Galatians that circumcision and observance of the law were conditions for table fellowship. Paul proves that this was a mistaken idea.

It is generally assumed that the incident occurred after the second visit to Jerusalem, or in the order in which Paul tells it here in the second chapter. We have emphasized, however, that Paul's presentation in these two chapters is not primarily historical. What he has written is intended to refute the Judaizers and to instruct the Galatians in the truth of the gospel. In this argument the two visits of Paul to Jerusalem have their proper place. But the incident in Antioch is not related as something that happened *after* these events. There is no *epeita,* "thereafter," in the text as in 1:18; 1:21; and 2:1. Some exegetes maintain that the incident took place before the second visit to Jerusalem. Others feel that it is more natural to assume that it happened in the order it is narrated. Even if it did take place after the council in Jerusalem, there is no attempt to minimize the unity of the apostles. It is rather a presentation of the basis and condition of unity, and indicates that the basis of unity must be defined more carefully.

Some scholars suggest that the apostolic decree (Acts 15:23ff.) was a result of this incident in Antioch. It was a kind of compromise intended to remove any further uncertainty about table fellowship.

If we assume that the decree of the council of Jerusalem originated as Acts tells us, the episode in Antioch may be regarded as a commentary on it. The purpose of the decree seems to have been to avoid causing unnecessary offense to the Jews, "for from early generations Moses has had in every city those who preach him, for he is read every sabbath in the synagogues." Though such consideration was shown to the Jews that indirectly the Gentile Christians came to be regarded as strangers living within Israel, and though these Gentile Christians nevertheless were accepted into full membership in the church, it was also clearly demonstrated that Gentile Christians need not *become* Jews. The important fact about the situation in Galatia was that the demand of the Judaizers for circumcision and observance of the law (which applied to the *Jews*) was not imposed on the *Gentile* Christians. This was a real victory for Paul.

If the decree was accepted in Jerusalem before the episode in Antioch, Paul may have related the incident in order to show that what the gospel had built up must not be torn down by subterfuge and evasion. This would happen if a conception of the law prevailed that the *law* instead of the righteousness of Christ became the foundation of fellowship (cf. 2:18). If Paul's account of the episode was intended to establish the basis of Christian fellowship, it is natural for him to pass on to the theological exposition without supplying a historical conclusion. The exposition takes the place of the conclusion we might have expected in a historical narrative. Indirectly he shows that no rules observed in deference to others can be interpreted to mean a restriction of righteousness by faith. If we believe that he participated in the decision and even in the decree, he has shown by his mention of this incident how the existing unity is to be understood and applied.

We may say that Paul presented in his account of the incident in Antioch what from his point of view was lacking in the decision in Jerusalem, and what the Galatians needed to be informed about. The fact that the work of Peter and Paul was placed on a par did not mean that the only difference was that Peter turned to the Jews and Paul to the Gentiles. When the whole gospel is proclaimed, the wall of partition between Jew and Gentile must be broken down. This development is a sign of the last days, the days of the promised salvation. The gospel among the Jews was also according to Paul a gospel, and Paul generally began his preaching in the synagogues. But the gospel must always break down the separation between Jews and Gentiles wherever that was found. Even if the Jewish Christians were allowed to practice their customary observances, this practice must not separate them from the Gentiles. If *this* situation arose, observances must cease because then they would become a hindrance to the gospel.

While the Jerusalem apostles proclaimed salvation by the grace of Christ to the Jews and expected the Gentile Christians to join the Jewish Christian church, Paul had come to the conclusion that when they became Christians, Jews must become like Gentiles in the sense that circumcision gave them no preference. The nature of the gospel is such that it is addressed to Gentiles. Even if the Jewish Christians continued to observe the ordinances, the Jewish interpretation of the law and its position as a condition of salvation were eliminated. The story of the episode in Antioch shows that Peter's commission to preach the gospel to the Jews did not imply that Jewish Christians had a greater share in salvation because they possessed the law. Such an assumption would involve a perversion and a loss of the gospel.

In modern theology the incident has often been used as a proof of the tension between the Jerusalem apostles and Paul. In reality, however, its function in Galatians is to refute the propaganda of the Judaizers who maintained that the tension existed. It indicates how necessary it is to realize all the implications of the gospel.

Paul assumes as a fact that he and Peter agree in principle. Peter is not presented as a Judaizer, or as a leader having a different conception of the faith. What was involved was a failure to apply the gospel consistently, and this failure led to his sin. Paul thus compelled Peter to see the implications of the gospel more clearly. The real authority was the truth and consistency of the gospel. Peter evidently acknowledged this authority, because the text implies that he accepted Paul's rebuke. Paul therefore continues in vss. 15ff. with an exposition of that gospel which both he and Peter had in common.

It has been assumed that the men who came from James (some manuscripts mention only one) had been sent by him. Since it was held that there was a sharp antithesis between James, Peter, and the Jewish Christians on the one hand and Paul on the other, it was thought that James sent a messenger to inspect the congregation in Antioch and to make sure that they observed the Jewish law. But the men need not have been special messengers. In any case James did not hold the same opinion as the Judaizers in Galatia. If he did send any messengers to Antioch, he wanted merely to warn against such things that would cause excitement and aversion among the Jews. The Judaizers had no doubt claimed that Peter demanded circumcision and observance of the law of the Christians in Antioch. But he had not done so. On the contrary, he had at first participated in the table fellowship with the Gentile Christians. But the Judaizers denied that justification was by faith without the works of the law. In this respect they differed decisively from Peter.

The Jewish Christians who came from Jerusalem where James was the leader were evidently hesitant to join in table fellowship with the Gentiles who did not observe the Jewish law. Peter himself had realized that the Christians were free from the law. But when these people came, he withdrew from the table fellowship, and Barnabas and the other Jewish Christians joined him. The expression, "fearing the circumcision party," is generally taken to refer to Jewish Christians. If it does, it must not be made to refer to Jewish Christians in general and especially not to the Jerusalem apostles, but to such as had not yet realized the freedom from the law. The expression may however refer to non-Christian Jews. But it is more likely that it refers to all who *think* according to Jewish patterns. However it is translated, the object of the fear may have been the reaction of the Jews if the report should come to them that the Christians consistently ignored the Jewish ordinances of clean and unclean food. The men from James may have pointed this out and referred to the fact that the Christians in Jerusalem, who at the beginning had "favor with all the people" (Acts 2:47), would run into difficulties if it became known they ate regularly with the Gentiles and did not observe the laws of purity.

We might ask whether the table fellowship refers to the Lord's Supper or to common meals in the homes of Christians. It is doubtful that the distinction between the Eucharist and the ordinary common meals had been made at this early stage. Peter had regularly participated in these meals without observing the laws of purity until the men from James came. Paul regarded his withdrawal as a transgression and hypocrisy, because he acted contrary to his real conviction. Peter did not really hold that the laws of purity and the prohibition against eating with Gentiles applied to Christians (cf. Acts 10 and 11:1-17), but he withdrew from fear of the Jews or of those who held that position. The result would have been that the Gentile Christians would have to begin living as Jews in order to share in salvation and the fellowship of the whole church. Peter vacillated between two points of view. The first implied that the Christian table fellowship broke through the Jewish conception and was based entirely on participation in the gospel. According to the second point of view Jewish Christians should continue to observe the Jewish ordinances for table fellowship, especially if doing otherwise would cause difficulties. But this second standpoint might then nullify the first.

It was therefore necessary for Paul to oppose Peter. By reporting the incident in the letter Paul also corrected a false report of the incident. The account of the episode serves also to show that the gospel itself is the norm of faith and life, and not individuals however great they may be. The fact that Paul had rebuked Peter

"before them all" (vs. 14) indicates that the authority of Peter
was not such that his opinions and actions were in themselves
normative for the church.

The account shows how difficult it was to define the relation
to the Jewish law. The pressing problem of the relation of Jewish
Christians to Gentile Christians had become acute in the question
of table fellowship (cf. Acts 10:13). The pious Jew of that time
was careful lest he should become unclean by eating with a Gentile.
The scrupulous observance of the food laws in order to avoid
eating meat sacrificed to idols, blood, etc., was general among
the Jews, possibly as a result of the cruel attempt of the Syrians
to hellenize them in the time of the Maccabees. (Cf. T. W. Manson,
St. Paul in Ephesus, John Ryland's Library, Bulletin 24, p. 72.)
Table fellowship with Gentiles had become a serious transgression
of the law. It must have been very difficult for the Jewish Christians who lived in this tradition to consent to table fellowship
with uncircumcised people. Furthermore such an action would
separate them from the Jews and make them the object of their
hatred and persecution.

It is customary to interpret Peter's action here as indicating
a certain changeableness and instability of character. The context
of the story however indicates rather a theological uncertainty.
The fact that Barnabas supported Peter shows that the situation
was complicated. Paul does not seem to have attacked Peter personally but to have criticized his inconsistency, his theological
thinking and his practical judgment. It was this which led him to
hypocrisy and transgression. Even though Peter did not wish to
impose the observance of the law on Gentile Christians but
preached justification by faith, he acted as if the observance of
the law was a prerequisite for justification. His conduct in regard
to table fellowship did not agree with the theology he had manifested earlier.

It has been said that in this situation Peter was in a more difficult position than Paul since he was dependent upon the Christians in Jerusalem and not as free in his work as Paul. But the
real difference was rather that his theology was concerned mostly
with the Jews. From that point of view it was natural to hold that
fellowship with the Gentiles was indeed permissible, but in deference to others it might at certain times be avoided. Although
justification is not by the law, the law should in general be ob-

served. That the whole law had received a new significance had not become clear prior to Paul, even though they had understood the Scriptures in the light of faith. Paul's call to the office of apostle to the Gentiles by a special revelation gave him a clearer insight into the proclamation of righteousness through Christ and its consequences for the Christian life. If according to Peter God's plan of salvation implied that Israel was now to be converted to faith in Christ, and the Gentiles were to join the Jewish church, it would have been easy for him to think in traditional Jewish forms. But if Paul's view of the conversion of the Gentiles prevailed, the Christian fellowship, exemplified in the common meals, would be firmly established on that righteousness by faith which united Jews and Gentiles into one body. It is clear that Paul pointed out an inconsistency in Peter's action. It was Paul's unique insight into the significance of the gospel which gave him a greater stability.

In the history of theology the incident in Antioch has served to point out that in apostolic times the gospel itself was the highest authority, and not persons who might have a great reputation and high office in the church. The actual implications of the gospel were superior to the leadership of the organization. These implications could be proclaimed openly even though a man of great reputation had ignored them and yielded to another opinion. Luther regarded this incident as of great significance, and it strengthened his certainty that he had the right and the duty to proclaim the truth of the gospel in opposition to the contemporary leadership in the church.

3. Justification by faith, which is the content of the gospel, excludes righteousness by the law (2:15-21)

a) Righteousness by the law cannot be made to agree with the gospel (2:15-18)

As we have indicated above these verses (2:15-18) need not be regarded as a direct quotation of Paul's words to Peter. The rebuke in vs. 14 was brief and clear, and revealed the inconsistency in Peter's action. But this was a temporary deviation resulting from a certain theological unsteadiness and confusion. In principle Peter and Paul agreed in regard to the righteousness through Christ, "We" in vs. 15 seems to include Paul, Peter, and all Jewish Christians.

It seems most natural therefore to understand vss. 15-21 as a brief theological summary of the thoughts which constitute the basis of Paul's presentation of his relation to the Jerusalem apostles. His account of this relationship, of his meeting with the leaders in Jerusalem and of the incident in Antioch serves to explain his conception of the gospel. This gospel was not a doctrine of men. It was founded on a revelation, on the unity in faith, and on the necessity to walk firmly and faithfully in the truth. It must not be obscured or perverted by being made dependent on the observance of the law, as if this were necessary to receive the righteousness contained in the gospel. He now summarizes and declares solemnly the content of what the previous narratives were intended to set forth. Here he deals directly with the significance of the gospel in theological terms rather than in narrative form.

It seems most probable, therefore, that on the basis of the whole previous presentation Paul now turns to the Galatians and addresses them directly. In this passage he reveals the consequences not only of his own theology but also of the theology which Peter truly held, as Paul sees it. In vss. 15-16 he presents the principle of justification by faith without the works of the law which later on he expounds more fully, and on the basis of the incident in Antioch he presents it as essentially the theology of *the church*. It is probable that the Judaizers had presented the Jewish Christians as the norm and had told the Galatians that these Christians not only believed in Jesus as the Messiah but also held to the Jewish faith in justification by obedience to the law. Against all this Paul maintains that Jewish Christians after coming to faith in Christ rejected the righteousness by the law, and that they ought not to return to this false righteousness.

The Judaizers wanted to place the Galatians in the antithesis between the Jews and "Gentile sinners." They had accepted the Jewish conception of the uncircumcised as Gentile sinners, and they urged the practice of circumcision so the Galatians would be counted among those who were not sinners. "Gentile sinners" did not have the law. According to the Jews they were opposed to God. They were not worthy to receive the law. From the Jewish viewpoint the law was directed against the unrighteousness of the Gentiles. That Israel had received the law was a sign of God's special love for them and of his desire to make them righteous. Through the law their righteousness was augmented. Paul assumes that he as well as Peter were Jews and belonged to the people of the law. They were not "Gentile sinners." They did not need to be circumcised as the Judaizers urged. They had been "circumcised on the eighth day" (Phil. 3:5).

But instead of remaining in this state and trying to make others partakers of such "privileges" Paul had, as he says in Philippians, counted all his gain as loss for the sake of the knowledge of Christ (Phil. 3:7ff.). The righteousness which he earlier had trusted in was not a real righteousness. In the light of the righteousness obtained through faith in Christ he regarded it now as "loss" and "refuse."

This new attitude did not mean that Paul now repudiated the law in the Old Testament. On the contrary the law now became fully established. In the light of the righteousness of Christ righteousness by the law was found to deny the law. It could not really function properly by legal observances. Zeal for the law had led to the rejection of God's Messiah. The observance of the law did not lead to righteousness but to unrighteousness, to disobedience of God's will and work in the law. Christ was the fulfilment of the law. He was the real law, for in his life, death, and resurrection he represented the righteousness of God. Whoever did not realize that Christ was the fulfilment of the law, that his words were spoken in the name of the law, and that he made the law what God had really intended it to be, destroyed the law. The works of the law by which the Jew considered himself to be righteous as distinguished from the Gentile made the law something over which man himself ruled. The Jew did not realize that the fulfilment of the law was given in Christ. In Christ righteousness came into the world and broke down the power of unrighteousness. Whoever rejected Christ made the law of no effect and denied its inmost intention of serving righteousness. The works of the law, therefore, which severed the connection with the promised blessing in Christ, became a denial of the law.

It is precisely *the law* that speaks *against* righteousness by the law. It speaks of a curse and a blessing: a curse on those who do not keep all the commandments, and blessing and life to those who keep them. Paul does not interpret *the law* as containing the principle of righteousness by the law. He means rather that the law itself points to Christ (cf. 3:10ff.). The law speaks of God's

righteousness and man's unrighteousness. But the intention of
righteousness by the law is to make man righteous by his own
effort and therefore free from guilt before God.

What he said here on this subject is not fully developed but
implicit in his whole presentation. We will consider this again in
the exposition of Galatians 3 and 4. Paul writes to Galatians
who had already heard his preaching, and this letter is not their
first instruction in the gospel. It is rather a clarification of that
which Paul had previously proclaimed, but now presented in
opposition to those who had perverted and rejected his teaching.

On the basis of what we have just said it is clear that Paul can
reject the works of the law. No one becomes righteous "by the
works of the law." This is repeated three times in this verse. If
the repetition is due to Paul himself and not to a subsequent
scribe, he must have wanted to impress this fact on the Judaizers.
Scripture declares, he says, that no one is righteous in the sight
of God. Paul alludes to Ps. 143:2; *to be made righteous* (*dikaio-
thenai*) is a Septuagint expression. The verb means to be declared
righteous, to be granted righteousness, and to be incorporated into
the sphere where righteousness is a transforming power. Man
who had been made a sinner through the transgression of Adam
was made righteous through Christ and incorporated into the realm
of the age to come. God is active in conferring righteousness and
in the life of the man who is reckoned righteous. His power to
make righteous applies to all men, Jews and Gentiles alike. Christ
was sent not only to the Jews but also to the Gentiles to bring
them righteousness and thereby salvation from evil. Scripture
bore witness to this righteousness; the law had it in view and prepared for it through its demand for righteousness and its judgment
on sin. But in that sense the law did not lead to "works of the
law." According to the Jewish view these works represented the
advantage of the Jews over the Gentiles. Those who had the law
were regarded as righteous, or in a position to attain to righteousness; while the Gentiles who did not have the law were regarded
as sinners who were not worthy to receive it, or who had rejected it.

Although the law bore witness to that righteousness which
had come into the world through Christ and which operated in
the Christian church, it could not produce it. Paul speaks of this
in Rom. 3:21ff.: "But now the righteousness of God has been
manifested apart from law, although the law and the prophets

bear witness to it, the righteousness of God through faith in Jesus Christ for all who believe." Men did not participate in justification because they had the law, or because they labored in observing it. Righteousness was to be given both to the Jews and to the Gentiles. It was not dependent on works of the law, and it was not "of the law" (cf. Rom. 3:22ff.). It was given to those who in faith received Christ's fulfilment of the law (cf. Rom. 9:30—10:4). But in this faith God and Christ were active. Faith is a sign that the power of righteousness is active in man. It was set over against the works of the law, i.e., the attainment of righteousness by the law, which involved an attempt to enter into the sphere of the law through one's own righteousness. The Jews held that anyone who thus belonged to the law and lived in and by the law would be declared righteous in the judgment and would receive eternal life. But according to Paul the righteousness that avails before God is righteousness by faith, God's own righteousness. In it God's own righteousness is acknowledged and received. To seek righteousness through the law thus was the opposite of receiving it through faith. Paul understands faith as a life in which God is active in the present. In the same way he regards the works of the law as a life in which a power other than God is active. This power stands in conflict with God, just as did the powers which ruled in the religions of the Gentiles, and also falsely promised righteousness to men.

In the light of the revelation given to him Paul understood that during his pre-Christian life he had pursued a false righteousness. The content of his idea of righteousness was changed through his Damascus experience. Since righteousness is given only through faith, we, says Paul, have entered on the way of faith. Circumcision as a means of righteousness became a sign of false righteousness as over against baptism which represented and provided participation in the righteousness of faith in which Christ is active. In some other passages (cf. I Cor. 6:11; Rom. 6:3) Paul showed that being united with Christ in baptism means a participation in his righteousness and a union with him in his death and resurrection (cf. vs. 19 below). Faith in Christ means to have forsaken the way of righteousness by the law. The gospel would be destroyed if additions were made to it in the form of demands for circumcision and observance of the law.

The works of the law were those which the law of Moses demanded and which the rabbis claimed would lead to righteousness.

The rabbis, too, could speak about faith, but to them faith was a work. They explained the law and developed it further with comments and additions. These works of the law were to them the opposite of those selected by man himself which would be of lesser value. Paul had learned, however, that even those works which the rabbis regarded as works of righteousness did not lead to righteousness. According to him they belonged in the sphere of one's own works. That righteousness is "by faith" is the opposite of "by works of the law" (*ek ergon nomou*) or, what is the same thing, "by law" (*ek nomou*).

But faith must not be conceived of as a work or an accomplishment which would take the place of *the works of the law.* That would be a perversion of Paul's meaning. Faith means participation in the life where Christ is active. To live in faith is for Paul equivalent to being in Christ (*einai en Christo*). In Paul's usage "being righteous in Christ" is equivalent to "being righteous by faith or through faith." To be justified *in* Christ is grammatically the same as *through* Christ. In justification Christ is understood as the one who is active in man. The faith-relationship to Christ in or through which the Christian is justified is not correctly understood if faith is interpreted as a means of attaining a goal. Justification occurs *in* Christ in such a manner that the Christian can be said to be *in* Christ, and also that Christ is *in* the believer as the power active in his faith (cf. vs. 20). The one active in faith is the living Christ.

When justification in and through Christ is set over against justification in and through the law, the law in this case is understood as a power opposed to Christ, not as the revelation of God's will in the law. It is separated from God's will in the law and becomes associated with "the weak and beggarly elemental spirits" which the Galatians had previously served (cf. 4:9). Here the power of the law appears in direct conflict with Scripture. Consequently righteousness of the law is the opposite of the most profound meaning and purpose of the law as it has been revealed and fulfilled in Christ.

Real righteousness can be found only in Christ through whom God sent the promised redemption. But, Paul asks in vs. 17, if we in our endeavor to be justified in Christ have also been found to be sinners, is Christ then an agent of sin? Paul's answer is, certainly not!

Paul answers his question in the negative. The expression,

"certainly not," "may it not be," "God forbid," (*me genoito*) occurs in many passages (Rom. 3:4, 6, 31; 6:2, 15; 7:7, 13; 9:14; 11:1, 11; I Cor. 6:15; Gal. 3:21). What is it that Paul so vehemently denies? Is it, some have asked, the idea found also in Rom. 6:1, 15, that those who have been justified by grace must not remain in sin? The context does not seem to favor this interpretation. In vs. 15 Paul emphasized that "we" are Jews by birth and not sinners of the Gentiles; i.e., from the *Jewish* point of view "we" were not sinners as the uncircumcised Gentiles. Here Paul alluded to the Jewish conception of righteousness. i.e., to win and increase one's righteousness by means of the observance of the law. But in vs. 16 he placed the righteousness he met and found in Christ in opposition to this Jewish conception.

To understand the argument we must make clear that Paul is concerned with what a surrender to the demands of the Judaizers for circumcision and observance of the law would mean for the *Jewish Christians.*

The Judaizers wanted to add something of the old to the new, which they had not fully understood, i.e., they wanted to add the righteousness of the law to faith in Christ. They believed that this was done in Jerusalem. But what would the result be? Both the old and the new would be destroyed. The Jewish Christians had broken down the righteousness by the law through their faith in Christ. In principle the old was removed. If (vs. 18) they wanted to build up the righteousness by the law again through the demand for circumcision and observance of the law, they would thereby acknowledge that the tearing down involved in the Jews' acceptance of faith in Christ was sin. The tearing down took place because of their faith in Christ. By their demand for the observance of the law therefore the Judaizers made Christ a servant of that which the Jews regarded as sin. In their insistence on circumcision they accepted the Jewish criterion of what constitutes sin. In doing so they proved that anyone who sought righteousness in Christ became a transgressor of the law and a sinner. It would be better not to be Christian at all but completely Jewish. If à Jewish Christian did not hold fast to the righteousness by faith in Christ, but sought to add the observance of the law as a basis for his righteousness, his righteousness had to be defined from the Jewish point of view. According to this standard he was by his faith in Christ a transgressor. Insistence on circumcision and observance of the law made faith in Christ impossible. It is clear that what Paul decisively rejects is the attempt to add the righteousness by the law to the righteousness by faith. These two nullified one another. If the attempt were made to add observance of the law to faith in Christ, both would be destroyed. Both from Jewish and Christian points of view such a man was without righteousness, a transgressor and a sinner. Paul shows the absurdity of the righteousness by the law by pointing out that by accepting it Christ would appear as a servant of sin. This idea he dismisses by the exclamation, "certainly not."

The difficulty of interpreting Gal. 2:15-18 arises, therefore, because Paul uses the ideas of *sin, sinner,* and *transgressor* sometimes in the Jewish and sometimes in the Christian sense. In dealing with the Judaizers he had to have regard for the Jewish criterion of sin and righteousness, and also consider what sin and righteousness involved from the Christian point of view. The Galatians, led astray by the Judaizers, wanted to be Christians, but they were unable to follow this out consistently. The Jewish Christians, who sought righteousness through Christ, had given up the claim of a righteousness of their own and of being better than "the sinners of the Gentiles." They were on a par with the Gentiles and sinners like them, but they were justified through Christ. "Since all have sinned and fall short of the glory of God, they are justified by his grace as a gift, through the redemption which is in Christ Jesus" (Rom. 3:23ff.). In Gal. 2:16 and Rom. 3:20 Paul quotes Ps. 143:2 and points out that no living being is righteous. Faith in Christ and the surrender of the claim to righteousness by the law make the Jewish Christian a sinner from the *Jewish* point of view. But from the *Christian* point of view he has obtained the true righteousness. Anyone who makes circumcision and the law a condition of membership in the church and participation in righteousness returns to the Jewish conception of righteousness which holds all neglect of the Jewish law as sin. In that case Christ becomes a servant of sin, and justification by faith becomes a sin because it regards Christ as the basis of justification.

What Paul says here is in a certain sense the same as what he said to Peter in Antioch. A person who has accepted the righteousness of Christ, but who lives according to the Jewish pattern and makes this a condition of fellowship in the church and of participation in the righteousness of Christ, lands in hypocrisy and sin. Peter's defection was due to a temporary confusion. In vss.

15-18 Paul indicates what is involved both for Peter and Paul, as well as for all Jewish Christians. He makes clear that a person must act consistently in respect to his conception of sin and of righteousness. Otherwise Christ is made a servant of sin. In Rom. 15:7ff. Paul tells us that Christ "became a servant to the circumcised to show God's truthfulness, in order to confirm the promises given to the patriarchs, and in order that the Gentiles might glorify God for his mercy." The basis on which Israel obtained righteousness was the election of God. When the children of Israel received Christ in faith, the promises to the fathers were fulfilled, and they could praise God for the fulfilment of the promises in Christ. But in his mercy God gave his righteousness also to the Gentiles. The basis of righteousness is not glorying in the works of the law but the grace and election of God.

According to Paul Christ is the exact opposite of a servant of sin. The righteousness which he and faith in him destroy is a real power active in the world, but it is a false righteousness which is contrary to the truth of Scripture. Christ brings in the true righteousness. Scripture and the law bear witness to Christ and to his righteousness. The circumcised who have been converted to Christ do not break Scripture and the law when they do not observe the legal precepts; instead they now participate in the fulfilment of the law. Christ is a servant of the truth, not of sin. The truth of Scripture becomes powerful and clear through him (cf. Rom. 15:8). The promise is fulfilled in Christ, and Israel's faithlessness and rejection do not nullify God's truth. When the Gentiles have been converted, God will also fulfil his election in the case of Israel. Christ is not a servant of sin, but of the truth of Scripture and of the faithfulness of God. But in order rightly to receive Christ one must consistently hold fast to the truth and not try to combine righteousness by faith with the righteousness by the law.

b) To live by faith in the Son of God means to have died to the law (2:19-21)

In vs. 18 Paul had already changed from "we" to "I." This transition is emphasized in vs. 19 by placing "I" in an emphatic position, "I for my part." Against all the attempts by the Judaizers to confuse righteousness by faith and righteousness by works he opposes his own gospel which he states here in almost majestic terms. He speaks with power and authority as one of Israel's great prophets, and presents a severely concentrated statement of the meaning of his gospel. The subjective form does not imply that his words concern only himself. He speaks in the name of the gospel as its servant and presents its meaning in a few brief phrases.

In the statement in vs. 19, "I through the law died to the law," the words "through the law" have caused difficulties and have been variously interpreted. We might first compare the expression "through the law" in vss. 19 and 21. In vs. 21 he states that righteousness cannot be gained "through the law." If that had been possible, Christ need not have suffered death. The death of Christ secured righteousness, but the law could not produce it. Why then the law? Later in the letter (3:19) Paul says that it was added because of transgressions. According to Rom. 5:20 the law came in "to increase the trespass." The commandment revived sin, and consequently did not give life but rather produced death. "The very commandment which promised life proved to be death to me" (Rom. 7:9-10).

What happened through the law was therefore that "I" *died*. The law brought death because of sin (Rom. 7:13). Through the law "I" was constituted a sinner, so it was obvious that I could not secure life and righteousness for myself. "I" died through the law, and I was declared dead in reference to the real life, life with God, the life in righteousness.

The rabbinically-educated Paul had delighted in the attempt to fulfil the precepts and commandments of the law. The law had brought him to this point, but after his Damascus experience he had found that this striving was the false way of righteousness by works. Through the encounter with Christ he had gained a new insight. He had discovered that in general the function of the law was not to give life but to judge and to bring him to that death which he had tried to avoid by obedience to the law. Now through Christ he had been brought under the real judgment and death of the law, and had come to understand that the demands of the law meant that man must submit to its accusations and judgment. "Through the law" he knew himself sentenced to death. But this correct conception of the function of the law had come to him through Christ. We might have expected him to say, *"through Christ* I died to the law," but instead he says, "I died *through the law."* In itself the law was not contrary to Christ, so as to lose its significance as soon as Christ had come and revealed the truth. On the contrary, through Christ the real function of the law was revealed: not to procure righteousness, but to make man's sin evident and put him to death. Thus it performed its service to God in the death of Christ. He who by faith has been united with Christ in death and thus has been made dead through the law, has also become a partaker of that life which came in Christ.

To understand Paul's meaning, we must distinguish between the different ways in which the law kills man (cf. Rom. 7:11). We may say that the law destroys man in two different ways. The misused law destroys. Righteousness by the law (the misused law) always destroys man, and death in that case does not produce life. The law used to obtain a false righteousness (law used as a means by which man creates his own righteousness) does not lead to eternal life. When the law is used in a false way, it kills but not according to God's will.

The true purpose of the law however is indeed to kill man, but in another sense. If the law really is to fulfil its God-given task it has to destroy man in order to reveal his sin and worthiness of condemnation. No ordinary man would be able to endure this death. Only Christ could bear the condemnation of the law. He died, killed by the law. But he died in faith and in the righteousness from God, not in the manner of a sinful man who is destroyed by the falsely used law in a false righteousness of his own. And to be *one* with Christ, to be baptized into him, is to die and to be buried with him. This is the true way by which the law kills man. This way Paul himself had died through the law.

Death through the law is connected with the fact that Christ took upon himself the judgment and curse of the law, and therefore died. The function of the law in reference to fallen man was revealed and the knowledge of the real significance of the law was given in the cross of Christ. He died through that law whose function was to judge and put to death. Since through Christ Paul had been enabled to accept the judgment of the *law* and had died through the law, the law could no longer hold him in servitude. In union with Christ by faith he shared in the death of Christ which was transformed into life, because Christ's death, which assumed the whole condemnation of the law, resulted in the resurrection life. Consequently Paul was dead to the law both in the sense that it could no longer impose a final sentence of death, and in the sense that the law as a false way to righteousness was set aside.

The significance of the phrase "died *through* the law" is not what a later theology has suggested in assuming that the demands of the law were so many and difficult that it was impossible to keep them. The realization of the impossibility of keeping the commandments in a strict sense was supposed to have driven Paul to a different road in search of righteousness. Paul does not reason this way. His life under the law was not, as far as we know, a life in despair and anguish, which would have prepared him for the gospel. In general the law was a pride and joy to the Jew, and not something under which he suffered and from which he desired to be free.

The expression, "through the law," does not refer primarily to eagerness for righteousness by the law—this would not in itself lead to despair—but to the judgment and death imposed by the law. This work of the law had appeared to Paul in all its clarity through his encounter with Christ. The law expresses God's just judgment on sin, and both the Jew and the Gentile were subject to the judgment. Through Christ it is possible to face this death and judgment. But this death freed man from all further judgment, because the law had now fulfilled its righteous condemnation. This condemnation, the seriousness of which was revealed when Christ endured it, led through Christ to life. Consequently it would be absurd to seek later for life through the observance of the law.

Through this new Christian insight which Paul had obtained, and the light it shed on the significance of Scripture, the law had been able to show him that apart from Christ he stood completely under the dominion of death. Thus the Christian insight validated the Old Testament witness that through the law God's righteous judgment had been revealed.

The correct thing to do, therefore, would be to acknowledge God's judgment through the law and to expect righteousness through God's promised act. In the light of the righteousness in Christ it became clear that, after sin had achieved its dominion, the function of the law was to impose judgment and death; a death which expressed God's righteousness, and which could therefore not be avoided by means of man's own work. Rightly interpreted the law itself led to death, and this death could not be avoided by any observance of the law. Nor could it be maintained that because the law did not bring life it could be ignored. God's judgments cannot be ignored. It was not a question of an emancipation from the law. The death which set man free from the observance of the law came only *through the law.*

It could be said, however, that this law itself, which kills and which man by himself cannot escape, died in and through Christ. Christ had entered under its judgment and in his death had assumed its curse. When he fulfilled the law, he abolished the curse. He became a curse for us (3:13), and was made to be sin for us (II Cor. 5:21). When the law had once accomplished its destructive work, first in respect to Christ, and then in everyone who on that basis acknowledged its right to kill and who was united with Christ in faith and was buried with him into death, it had no longer any right to condemn (Rom. 8:1). Then the law itself was dead, i.e., for him who is in Christ.

The expression in vs. 19, *nomo apethanon,* means really "died to the law." "I through the law died to the law." The meaning is not primarily that I ceased to live by the righteousness of the law, which may be included; but that through faith in Christ I have died *in relation to the law,* so that the law has no longer any authority over me and cannot judge me or put me to death. Through faith in Christ "I live to God;" I died in order to live to God. But the death that the law brought about because I was a sinner became also a death to the law. The law could no longer reach "me" with its condemnation because my death through faith in Christ was united with his death. This death led to life in God. Paul continues therefore: "I am crucified with Christ." When the law's sentence of death came to the Christian, it encountered one who was dead to the law and whom it could no longer hurt. We may remind ourselves here that the trial of an accused man must cease if the accused dies. A dead person cannot be tried and convicted. He who is dead to the law cannot be judged by it. Through faith in Christ "I" died in relation to the law, and then there is no one to judge; there is no condemnation for one who is in Christ Jesus (Rom. 8:1). "I" am dead to the law. The condemning law became for me a dead letter, because in my death with Christ the judgment has been fulfilled and sin has been put to death. He who has died is freed from sin (Rom. 6:7). Because the Christian died with Christ (as the following verse states: "I have been crucified with Christ; it is no longer I who live"), the judgment of the law on sin became a judgment which could not affect him in the same way as before.

To die to the law therefore means to die with Christ so that the law can no longer condemn and put to death.

The law rightly condemns sinful man to death. In doing so it performs the function God gave to it. The man condemned to death by the law, who has no life and nothing of his own, receives life in and through Christ. The law cannot deprive him of the new life. About this man Paul can say both that he is dead to the law and that the law is dead to him. That he is dead implies primarily that the law cannot extend its judgment to him since he is dead. That the law is dead to him means that the law lost its authority to condemn, since the Christian lives in Christ.

The righteousness which the law could not produce was secured through the death of Christ (Rom. 8:3). Then life was given through death. "For the law of the Spirit of life in Christ Jesus has set me free from the law of sin and death" (Rom. 8:2). When I died with Christ, I was made free from that law which on account of sin had brought death.

Paul means, therefore, that the law puts man to death, but when his death is incorporated into the death of Christ, it becomes transformed into a life which cannot be affected any further by the judgment and condemnation of the law. Man is therefore free from the law.

Paul developed this line of thought further in Romans 6 and 7. In Rom. 7:4 he states that we have died to the law through the body of Christ in order that we might belong to another, to him who has been raised from the dead. The only one who can release us from the authority of the law is death. As we have already said, just to decide to set the law aside would be an absurdity to Paul, because the law expressed God's will and his judgment on sin. But the death which the law imposes on account of sin becomes transformed into life, because it is incorporated and absorbed into the death of Christ. "I have been crucified with Christ."

Because man dies to the *law,* the law has lost its authority to condemn. There is another side to this statement, viz., that death to the law is also a death to *sin.* The objective power of sin over man, which the law revealed and thus gave sin full sway, lost its dominion through the death of Christ. Through him the way was prepared for a life over which sin had no power: the life of the righteousness of God. Faith in Christ involved a participation in this life. Here righteousness was reckoned to man, and the gift of the Spirit bestowed. The Spirit released man from law-righteousness and destroyed the things of the flesh. In the Spirit the enmity of the flesh against God (Rom. 8:7) was taken away, both the desire to establish man's own righteousness and the kind of fleshly lusts which Paul describes in Gal. 5:19ff.

The result of dying is therefore also that through the law I died to the law. To die to the law is to die to the judgment of the law, but also to die to that righteousness which is by the law. The Judaizers wanted to add circumcision and the observance of the law as a complement to faith in Christ, but this would nullify righteousness by faith. Paul, who could boast of his observance of the law (Phil. 3:4ff.), explained (Gal. 2:18) that he would have made faith in Christ appear to be transgression if he were to accept again the Jewish conception of righteousness and base his righteousness on observance of the law. No, righteousness by the law was now impossible to Paul. After he had found righteousness in Christ, the law could no longer drive him to seek his own righteousness.

The law that led to law-righteousness was the law in the service of sin. The real meaning of the law was then obscured and perverted by sin, so that the demands of the law were understood to mean that observing them resulted in righteousness. It was a false insight, a false understanding of the law that led to this result. But by virtue of this false attitude the law operated as an objective power, a false god, similar to the powers and gods which the Gentiles served.

Christ represented and bestowed the righteousness which God demanded through the law. When Christ died and took upon himself the curse of the law by being hanged on the tree (3:13), the law itself died as a power that condemns and incites to self-righteousness. It lost its power over him who is united with Christ in his death. Consequently Paul can say in Col. 2:14 that Christ has cancelled the bond which stood against us with its legal demands by nailing it to the cross.

Participation in the death of Christ is suggested here simply with the words: "I have been crucified with Christ." In Romans 6, which contains and discusses further many ideas similar to the theme under discussion, he says: "Our old self was crucified with him so that the sinful body might be destroyed, and we might no longer be enslaved to sin" (Rom. 6:6). And in Gal. 6:14 he says that through the cross of Christ "the world has been crucified to me, and I to the world."

That which came with Christ—righteousness and life—incorporates every believer in an entirely new situation. Everything which belongs to this world and its allure, the flesh and the selfish desire to obtain one's own righteousness, has lost its power. As far as the believer is concerned baptism incorporates him into everything Christ has come to bestow. This involved baptism into his death (Rom. 6:3). The believer's relationship to the death of Christ on the cross, which also involved the beginning of a new life, was established in baptism. The idea of baptism as a symbol and realization of the union with Christ appears in Gal. 3:27. Baptism is not directly mentioned here, but in Romans 6, to which we have repeatedly referred, he develops this idea more fully.

Paul's statement that he has been crucified with Christ is often interpreted as indicating a mystical conception peculiar to him. But even if these words are given a meaning peculiar to Paul, we must recognize that they represent a conception common to primitive Christianity.

The death of Christ was a death leading to life. The significance of freedom from the law was not a human freedom to do whatever anyone desired, but a freedom to live for God. God's righteousness and life were bestowed through Jesus Christ, and this freedom implied freedom from the condemnation of the law and from slavery under righteousness by the law. Living for God means being dead to the law. This thought is expressed in Rom. 7:4: "Likewise, my brethren, you have died to the law through the body of Christ, so that you may belong to another, to him who has been raised from the dead in order that we may bear fruit for God." A similar thought meets us also in II Cor. 5:15: "And he died for all; that those who live might live no longer for themselves but for him who for their sake died and was raised." "To put off the old man" and "to put on the new man," and similar statements (Eph. 4:22ff.; 2:1ff.; Col. 3:9ff.; Rom. 6:6; 12:2; II Cor. 5:17) touch on the same reality discussed in this verse.

To die to the law resulted in a life for God, just as the words that Paul has been crucified with Christ correspond to the fact that Christ lives in him. To be "buried with Christ" by baptism and being "united with him in a death like his" involves also being "united with him in a resurrection like his" (Rom. 6:4ff.; cf. Gal. 3:27).

The significance of living for God and being crucified with Christ is developed in vs. 20 in a statement that belongs among the great sayings of Paul and one which is frequently quoted. The statement is, however, rather brief.

As we have noted above, the words, "it is no longer I who live, but Christ who lives in me," have been regarded as a typical expression of Paul's mysticism. It is a question whether it is proper to use this term. It is so ambiguous that it hardly contributes to a clear understanding. It is thus taken to refer to a peculiar, individual piety which can be expressed only as a man's private confession about his life. But Paul wants to bring out the meaning of the gospel as a message. He wants to clarify this meaning for the Galatians as something belonging to their Christian life.

We may start our elucidation of these words with a reference to Paul's eschatological conception. Life in this age is in bondage under sin and death. Even the law which was given by God was taken into the service of sin. With Christ came something new, something which did not belong to this age. Christ came to set us free from the present evil age (1:4). To be united with Christ and to participate in his righteousness meant that the center of life is transferred from this age to that age which God promised when he gave Abraham the promise of a coming blessing. Salvation is bestowed in that realm, that new kingdom, which God promised and which began in Christ. Through him the powers of the age to come became operative already in this realm of death and sin (cf. John 5:24). The Christian does not live according to the flesh, but according to the Spirit (Rom. 8:4). By his resurrection Christ has become life-giving Spirit (I Cor. 15:45). To be in Christ and to be in the Spirit mean the same thing, because the Spirit is the Spirit of Christ (II Cor. 3:17-18).

As we have indicated in the exegesis of vs. 19, the Christian has died with Christ, and he has been buried with Christ in order to live to God (Cf. Gal. 3:27). This life may be described both as a life in Christ (cf. Rom. 6:11; 12:5; 8:10; I Cor. 1:30; II Cor. 5:17; Eph. 2:13) and as the life of Christ in the believer. In a corresponding statement it may be said that Paul knew himself to be dead to the law and to the world, and that the law and the world were dead to him. The life of the believer is no longer only the natural life "in the flesh;" his life is hidden in God. "For you have died, and your life is hid with Christ in God" (Col. 3:3). This new, hidden life is really the life of Christ in the believer (Col. 3:4; cf. Phil. 1:21, "For to me to live is Christ"). Christ dwells in the believer through his Spirit (cf. Rom. 8:10). To receive the gospel was to be born to a life in which Christ is the effective power. The apostle was his servant, and to those among whom he worked he had to impart the life and power of Christ. The statement that Christ dwells in the believer may be compared to his words in Gal. 4:19: "My little children, with whom I am again in travail until Christ be formed in you!" (cf. II Cor. 13:5). In Col. 1:27 he uses a similar expression: "God chose to make known how great among the Gentiles are the riches of the glory of this mystery, which is Christ in you, the hope of glory" (cf. John 14:10).

Life here on earth "in the flesh" is lived now "in faith." The expressions "faith," "in Christ," and "Christ in the believer" are so closely related that they may be said to represent the same reality. Life in faith and life in Christ or in the Spirit are equivalent, and designate life here on earth defined and determined by the powers and righteousness of the new age. Faith is faith in Christ who manifested his love to men. Christ "gave himself for me," says Paul. The source and object of faith is the sacrificial love of Christ. All of life on earth is life "by faith in the Son of God, who loved me and gave himself for me." This life is the opposite of seeking one's own righteousness by works of the law, or of living to oneself (Rom. 14:7) and not for the neighbor. Works of the law and living for self are expressions of man's natural concern for self. But that kind of life lacks the real righteousness. To live in righteousness by the law is to "nullify the grace of God" (vs. 21) which alone gives righteousness.

The grace of God included the redemptive activity in which God sent the Messiah-Christ and through him fulfilled all the promises of Scripture. He came with righteousness and life, which the law could not give. By his work he accomplished all that the Scriptures had promised and prepared. The rejection of this grace of God in Christ by the Jews became a denial and a destruction of that purpose which their law (*Torah*) in its deepest meaning served. But Paul did not reject God's grace. He received it in faith and acknowledged God's word and will revealed in the *Torah*. To act as if righteousness and life came through circumcision and observance of the law would be to despise the act of God in Christ and likewise the whole law which was fulfilled in him. It was Christ who set men free from the observance of the law and from the power of sin and death which ruled in this present age.

The phrase with which Paul closes this section is therefore quite natural. "If justification were through the law, then Christ died to no purpose." In that case the law as a way of salvation (as a rule of life, and as a means of righteousness) would have been sufficient and the death of Christ unnecessary. But Christ did not merely proclaim what righteousness really was, he himself had to bring the righteousness of God to men. But this could be done only by overcoming everything that compelled men to seek righteousness by works of the law. Christ had to fulfill and complete the law by taking its curse upon himself (cf. the exegesis of 3:13). Righteousness could become available only when God himself fulfilled the promise of redemption. This fulfilment had taken place in Christ's death on the cross. Here the distinction between Jew and Gentile was obliterated. Christ gave himself for all. When Christ gave men a new life and liberated them from the law that separated Jews and Gentiles, he brought to all a new righteousness. He liberated all men from any law that would lead to law-righteousness, and turned the judgment of the law into a blessing. He set men free from "the powers of this world" (cf. 4:3).

In the following section Paul expounds the significance of the gospel with a reference to what Scripture says about the commandments. Scripture does not urge men to seek righteousness by their efforts to keep the law. Such efforts do not bring anyone out from under the curse, but the new life of faith gives to men a share in the promised blessing. Faith is not an accomplishment. It is not like the obedience to the law which men labored to produce. Faith is a state (cf. 3:23, "before faith came . . .") which rests on the presupposition of the redemptive act of God in Christ. It signified a reality which separated men from "the present evil age" (1:4) to which they otherwise inevitably belonged. Faith is a life where the Spirit rules and where love to the neighbor is a natural expression (cf. 5:14-23).

II. The Witness of Scripture to the Gospel; the Place and Purpose of the Law in God's Redemptive Action (3:1—4:7)

A. The blessing through faith and the curse through the law (3:1-14)

1. The Spirit came through faith (3:1-6)

It is obvious that at the beginning of the third chapter Paul makes a new start in his letter. He turns again directly to the Galatians and expresses in sharp words his amazement at their vacillation and defection. Such expressions of astonishment as we found before in 1:6 occur later on in the letter (cf. 4:11, 19ff.; 5:7-12). But here as in other passages these personal references serve only as a transition to a renewed discussion and exposition of the principal argument.

The discussion concerns the relationship between faith and the law. The Galatians had not become fully grounded in their faith, and after listening to the propaganda of the Judaizers they had been prepared to accept their interpretation of the meaning of faith and the law. They had also realized the practical consequences of their view, in that they were now willing to be circumcised and to observe the requirements of the law. Even if they were not able to keep the law strictly, they accepted in principle the observance of the law as a condition for salvation.

The theme under discussion is the same as has been dealt with previously. From new points of view Paul wants to show that Scripture and the law bear witness to righteousness by faith and reject righteousness by the law. The Judaizers no doubt pictured Paul as not quite faithful to the Scriptures. They wanted to appear more faithful than he was. They claimed that he ignored certain aspects of Scripture, as, for instance, the demand for observance of the law.

In order to understand Paul's position and argument we must recall the circumstances of his missionary work. He had turned to the Gentiles, but many of them had probably been closely related to the synagogue. He had spoken of the God who had revealed himself in the Old Testament, the God of Abraham. Those who had been converted to Christianity had come under the influence of the holy Scriptures. It would be quite natural for them to understand these Scriptures in the same way as the Jews, or rather as the Judaizers understood them, who added the demand for circumcision and observance of the law to faith in Christ as the Messiah.

Paul's preaching was opposed to this development. As a human being Christ was descended from David, and through the resurrection he had been designated Son of God in power (cf. Rom. 1:4). According to Paul Jesus was not only the Messiah of the Jews, but God had made him also the Lord and Savior of the world.

The blessing and salvation which God had promised to Abraham had now come. A new covenant had thereby been established, and its consummation belonged to the coming age. In this covenant the righteousness which had been sought in vain by observance of the law was now available to those who in faith accepted the message of Christ. Thus man could share in the powers of the new age. But to go back and seek righteousness through the law would mean a rejection of that message which not only mediated a new insight but also provided participation in the fulfilment of the promise and in the power of the Spirit. Through Christ something new had come which in one sense did not belong to this present age. The work of Christ, his crucifixion, death, and resurrection signified that the righteousness of God had come into the world. This righteousness was active in the midst of this age which was in bondage under sin and death, and under that law which during this age could represent God's will and condemn sin, but which was unable to create righteousness and life.

What the law had pointed to in its judgment of sin but had been unable to produce had now become a reality. The law could not provide righteousness because it was "weakened by the flesh" (Rom. 8:3). But everything the law had pointed to in its witness to the righteousness demanded by God had now been given in and through Christ. He himself was the perfected law. Thus the law was fulfilled and at the same time it was freed from the state of weakness caused by the flesh and from the obscurity which hid its essential meaning.

We might say that the crucifixion of Christ marks the transition between the righteousness of the law and the new state ushered in by Christ. The necessity of the crucifixion may be said to reveal the spuriousness of the righteousness of the law, for in that way the true righteousness could not be found, but only unrighteousness (cf. 2:21). When the righteousness of God came, its bearer had to go the way of the cross. Here the absolute contrast between the righteousness of the law and the righteousness of God appears. But the righteousness from God which appeared in Christ was the true continuation and fulfilment of the revelation in the Scriptures of the old covenant. It meant also a release from that bondage in which the message of righteousness had been imprisoned in the law. Through the resurrection Christ appeared as the Lord of all the world, and what had separated Jew and Gentile had no longer any validity. Instead the word of Scripture was fulfilled that the blessing of Abraham was to come to all peoples, and that the salvation of God was to reach the Gentiles.

Just as the crucifixion shows the spuriousness of the righteousness of the law, so Paul can say in other passages that the wisdom of this world constitutes a false way to God. The divine truth cannot be secured either through the wisdom of the Greeks or through the righteousness of the law. There is a contrast between that which by its nature belongs to the wisdom of the age to come and that wisdom which belongs to this age and is highly regarded by the powers of this world. The contrast appears in that both the wisdom of this world and the righteousness of the law interpret the crucifixion of Christ as something foolish or offensive and contrary to their own conceptions (cf. I Cor. 1:21ff.; 2:1, 6ff.). In the Letter to the Galatians, however, the emphasis is on the contrast between righteousness by faith and righteousness of the law.

The Old Testament, however, bears witness to the righteousness of God. Paul can therefore refer those who were zealous for the law to the Scriptures of the old covenant. These Scriptures bear witness to Christ. He is the fulfilment of all that the law and the prophets have proclaimed and the goal of all that *Torah* represents. If only they could understand Scripture correctly, they would be guided in the right way. What the law promised to the one who kept it is now available through Christ and by faith in him. And the curse of the law is applicable to that world and that life which lacks the righteousness from God. Thus the law itself bore witness against the way of righteousness by the law.

Paul finds it incomprehensible that the Galatians could forsake the gospel for the Judaistic proclamation, or that they could be-

lieve this Judaistic proclamation was a more correct exposition of
the truth they had received. He thinks that they have been
so bewitched that they can no longer recognize reality as it is. Yet
Christ had been publicly portrayed to them as crucified.

When the Jews had not understood and submitted to God's
act in Christ, they showed that their righteousness of the law
did not correctly interpret Scripture. In the Gospel of John the
man born blind could point to the fact that he was healed and
could draw the conclusion that the Jewish interpretation of the
law, which rejected Jesus, was wrong (John 9:30ff.). Now Paul
refers to the whole ministry of Jesus and specifically to his *cross*.
That the Messiah had been rejected and crucified ought to convince the Galatians that the Jewish conception of the law as a
way of salvation was false. This point of view was connected with
their false conception of the Messiah as the one who would vindi-
cate them and as Abraham's children give them victory over the
Gentiles who had not been worthy to receive the law. Paul had
declared the glory of the gospel. We are reminded of his words
in II Cor. 4:4: "In their case the god of this world has blinded
the minds of the unbelievers, to keep them from seeing the light
of the gospel of the glory of Christ, who is the likeness of God."
Paul had publicly proclaimed to the Galatians the message of the
crucifixion of Christ. He can think of no other explanation of
their defection than that they had been led astray, blinded and
bewitched.

Paul further reminds the Galatians that they had come in
contact with something entirely new. This was the world of the
Spirit and of the righteousness of God which does not belong to
this age. They had become partakers of the powers of the age
to come and of the Spirit. But they had received this by faith,
not by submitting to circumcision and to a life regulated by the
Jewish law. We may compare this to Paul's question in 4:15:
"What has become of the satisfaction you felt?" The joy which
belonged to the reception of the gospel and the Spirit had disappeared. This fact alone should convince the Galatians that
they had been robbed of their great possession. Joy and blessedness did not come through observance of the law but through
the Spirit (cf. Phil. 4:4; 2:18; II Cor. 13:11; I Thess. 5:16;
Rom. 12:12).

To return now to the righteousness of the law would be the
greatest foolishness. It would mean forsaking the participation in

the fulfilment of the promise and in the righteousness now given, and returning to the dominion of the present, evil age. This is what Paul calls ending with the flesh after having begun in the Spirit. The Galatians had wanted to add the observance of the law to the proclamation of Paul. Did they want to complete faith by letting it turn into its opposite, the life of "the flesh," rather than continue the life in the Spirit in which they had begun when they received the faith? The law in which God spoke and carried out his judgment had been truly fulfilled in Christ. If one really lived in the law, one should always submit in faith to God's will and action. Because God had now fulfilled the law in Christ, and caused the revelation given in the law to be eclipsed by the revelation of himself in Christ—and had thus prepared a way for that righteousness which the law demanded but was unable to produce—man should receive all this in obedience and with thanksgiving. The Galatians, who had received the Spirit, seemed to make themselves "perfect" by ending in the flesh and returning to the old state. The Galatians were so foolish that they wanted to end "with the flesh" and "complete" the work of the Spirit by a denial of his power. It would be like "completing" freedom by returning to bondage as the final goal. Paul speaks ironically about completing, "ending with the flesh." The mistake of the Jewish interpreters of the law was that they conceived the law to be something finished and completed which could be used as a means of attaining righteousness. This character of the law as complete was enhanced by the comments and additions made by the rabbis. They strengthened the character of the law as a means available to man in his pursuit of righteousness. The Galatians, who wanted to complete what they had received in the Spirit, turned away from the real fulfilment of the law and sought to "fulfil" the gospel by returning to the false interpretation of the law which stood opposed to the gospel.

"Spirit" and "flesh" are opposites in Paul's theology (cf. 5: 16ff.). The Spirit is that Spirit of God who was given after the resurrection of Christ and signified that the power of the new age had begun to work. The Spirit therefore joined the Christians to the age to come. The flesh, on the contrary, belonged to this life and this age. It was corruptible and enslaved under the powers of sin and death, which were the opposite of God's Spirit and life. The law had no power to set one free from the flesh, even though it represented the will of God and his judgment on sin.

Ending in the flesh means therefore going back to that state from which faith had liberated them and thereafter helplessly remaining in its strong and final bondage. The powers of the Spirit belong to the new age, and the connection with that new age is established by faith. To forsake the new which they had experienced would be foolishness. It could not be done unless a person were so completely bewitched that he no longer understood the meaning of the experience he had had. That experience had come through faith, not through works of the law. But if they now attempted to complete the new through works of the law, they would establish the power of the flesh as final, deny the Spirit and exclude themselves from his fellowship and gifts.

"Did you suffer so many things in vain?—if it really is in vain." Paul had preached Christ to the Galatians and through his preaching had brought them under the influence of the Spirit, the power of the age to come. If the Galatians interpreted their experience as a conversion to obedience to the Jewish law, or if they wanted to be justified both through the law and through Christ, all his work had been in vain. Paul hopes, however, that it has not been in vain, and that they have become afflicted with only a temporary confusion and blindness. He admonishes them to recall how it had been when he visited them. Through his preaching he had made them participants in the Spirit and had done miracles among them. What power had done this? Did these signs come through works of the law? Or were they the powers of the coming age, which a person could receive by accepting in obedience and faith what God had wrought in Christ?

Paul repeats and thus emphasizes in vs. 5 the question he had asked in vs. 2: did the Spirit and the miracles come through works of the law or through faith? Since these had come through faith the Galatians ought to understand that the works of the law were not the means which had provided the salvation in which they now participated. The Spirit and the power had been given apart from the works of the law. These gifts indicated that the Messianic age had come because in that age the Spirit would be given. But since he had been given to them while they were uncircumcised, why were they now so anxious to add the demand for circumcision with all its consequences to the salvation they had already received?

The miracles which Paul had performed in Galatia had been done in the power which belonged to the age begun in the coming of the Messiah. As the disciples had been able in the name of Jesus to heal the sick and to do such deeds as belonged to the Messianic time (cf. Acts 3:2ff.; 9:32-41; 14:8ff.), so Paul also had done mighty works among the Galatians (cf. also Mark 6:7; Luke 10:17; Matt. 10:1, 8). The Galatians had accepted him and his proclamation, and they had not rejected him or by their unbelief prevented him from doing these works among them (cf. Matt. 13:58; Mark 6:5ff.).

Here Paul compares the faith of the Galatians at the time of his visit with the faith of Abraham. The Galatians had witnessed and participated in the works which could be done in the power of the Spirit of the Messianic age. Therefore, he equates the righteousness given to Abraham with the fruits of the Spirit which belong to the Messianic age. Righteousness meant for Paul a participation in the power of God. Abraham shared in that mighty work of God which meant the fulfilment of the promise in which he had believed even though the fulfilment appeared impossible. The first stage was the birth of Isaac. The promise implied first of all a multitude of descendants and possession of the land. But according to Paul Abraham also shared in the blessing which was the greater content of the promise. In faith he received the certainty concerning the coming Messiah who was to descend from him and through whom all the nations were to be blessed. This blessing, in which Abraham participated beforehand through faith, had now, according to Paul, come in Jesus. Paul interpreted the word of Scripture, that in Abraham all the nations should be blessed, to mean that the Gentiles were to share in that blessing the Messiah was to bring (vs. 8). This blessing had now come, and through the gospel it was brought to them also. By faith Abraham had been incorporated and given a share in that redemptive act of God which began with the promise of blessing to all nations through his offspring, and which had now been fulfilled in and through Christ.

2. The promise to Abraham is fulfilled in the gospel (3:7-9)

The reference to Abraham furnishes an example of how Paul understands Scripture. He regards Scripture as an expression of God's Word. God had reckoned Abraham's faith as righteousness. Even though the blessing promised to Abraham was concerned primarily with descendants and heirs, the story has for Paul a deeper meaning. The inheritance is concerned with righteousness. Abraham believed God's promise of descendants, life, and blessings. According to Paul he understood that the blessing would come from God; he could not earn it by his own efforts. Consequently the righteousness he received was a righteousness reckoned to him, not one he himself had acquired through his own works. As Paul later explains in the Letter to the Romans (Rom. 1:4ff.), it was the Abraham justified by faith who received circumcision as a seal of the righteousness given to him by God. Abraham was a type of *faith,* not of righteousness by the law. Not the Judaizers but those who lived by the righteousness of faith could appeal to Abraham.

The Jews prided themselves on being children of Abraham. Those who were not his descendants, but wanted to share in his blessing, had to be incorporated into the chosen people, the children of Abraham. It was circumcision through which the Gentiles were admitted into that fellowship which claimed a share in Abraham's blessing. According to Matt. 3:9 John the Baptist denounced the propensity of the Jews to regard themselves as secure, righteous, and superior to others because they could say: "We have Abraham as our father." We may compare Paul's words here with the statement in the Gospel of John about descent from Abraham, where the emphasis is not on the physical descent but on spiritual unity with Abraham. "If you were Abraham's children, you would do what Abraham did" (John 8:39). It was a common assumption in the ancient church that *the Christians* were the true children of Abraham. Paul especially emphasized this fact. The Old Testament bears witness to the righteousness by faith and to Abraham as the real spiritual father and example of the life in faith. The real descendants of Abraham, therefore, are those who follow the example of his faith. His faith did not rest on observance of the law but on regarding God's Word and promise as true. If the Galatians were to submit to circumcision, the result would not be a participation in the blessing of Abraham. The scriptural word to Abraham, "In thee shall all the nations be blessed," referred, according to Paul, to that blessing which through faith in Christ was to come to *all* peoples and therefore also to the Gentiles. We may also remind ourselves of the words of Isaiah and Jeremiah quoted in our interpretation of 1:15ff. Paul evidently saw in the mission to the Gentiles a fulfilment of prophecy as well as of the promise to Abraham.

It would be plausible to argue that the Old Testament contains the law and that the law is the principle of the righteousness by the law. But this was not Paul's thought. Abraham, the chief patriarch of the Old Testament, whom the Jews regarded as the father of circumcision, was in reality the forerunner of the coming, promised age and the father of its children. Thus Abraham was tied in with Christ who came as the promised One. God's promise, which was fulfilled in Christ, was primary and made Abraham what he was. We may remind ourselves of the words in the gospel of John that Christ was before Abraham (John 8:56ff.). Luther comes very close to Paul's thought when he says that Abraham's faith was faith in Christ.

According to Rom. 4:2 Paul held that the idea of righteousness by the law involved having something to boast about. Righteousness by the law leads to self-righteousness. In this age the law may very well speak of righteousness, and it can also forbid and condemn sin and injustice. But it can never really bestow righteousness. It rather enslaves man in self-righteousness. It does not mediate the power and life which belong to the age of the promise, the new covenant. Paul thus emphasizes that only through faith in Christ can we come into a right relation to the Scriptures and the law of the old covenant. Faith in Christ does not sever the connection with them, but makes it more secure.

In general Paul's reasoning, here as in Romans 4, is based on a view of Scripture entirely different from that of the Judaizing enthusiasts. The real people of God and the children of Abraham are those who participate in the promised blessing, but that blessing came through Christ. The Scriptures of the old covenant did not belong only to the circumcised. They speak also of a faith offered to the Gentiles. After the promise of righteousness was fulfilled in Christ, faith unites all people. Paul expresses similar views about circumcision in Col. 2:11 and Phil. 3:3. The true circumcision not made with hands was the circumcision in Christ. Through it, says Paul, you have put off "the body of flesh" (Col. 2:11). "We," the Christians, "are the true circumcision, who worship God in spirit, and glory in Christ Jesus, and put no confidence in the flesh" (Phil. 3:3). Through baptism the Christian became properly circumcised. But this implied really that he died to "the flesh." He died to his subjection under the powers of this age. The law also belonged among those powers insofar as it was understood as something which could furnish man with some basis of security and give him a preferred standing. Even some rabbis had spoken of a spiritual state corresponding to circumcision. Paul, too, interprets circumcision in a spiritual sense, but he rejects the idea that anything in man can serve as a basis for his righteousness. Nor can man be accounted righteous before God because of some self-acquired disposition or spiritual status. Paul points to the new objective divine act of God in Christ. This new act is the foundation of baptism through which man becomes incorporated into fellowship with Christ, dies and is buried with him, and participates in his resurrection life.

The thesis which Paul establishes here against the Judaizers may be said to be that the blessing Abraham received belonged to those who are righteous by faith. These were the true children of Abraham. This idea was naturally very offensive to the Pharisaic Jews. Abraham was for them a father and an example. He who had Abraham on his side also had the law on his side. Abraham was the great patriarch of Scripture and the prototype of the man who is righteous. Being a child of Abraham involved membership in that covenant of which all Scripture spoke and for which the law provided the norms. To keep the law was to walk in the footsteps of Abraham. When Paul says that Christians, who according to the Jews transgressed the law, are the children of Abraham and children of the promise given to Abraham, he completely reverses the Jewish conception.

In order to understand what Paul proclaims here we must understand clearly how *faith and election* belong together. *To believe* meant for Paul essentially that God is justified both in his judgments and in his promises, and that he is acknowledged as true, righteous, and faithful (cf. further the interpretation of 3:11). To be justified by faith is intimately connected with the conception of God as the one who elects, as this conception was expressed in Israel in the story of God's call and election of Abraham. Even in other parts of the Old Testament the name of Abraham is connected with the election. Thus we read in Isa. 51:1: "Harken to me, you who pursue deliverance, you who seek the Lord; look to the rock from which you were hewn, and to the quarry from which you were digged. Look to Abraham your father and to Sarah who bore you; for when he was but one I called him, and I blessed him and made him many."

But when the idea of God's election was interpreted to mean that certain people, the circumcision, had through this election received a special quality of which they could boast and despise others, and when the choice was understood to mean that through the law the Jews had obtained a means of making themselves righteous, then the conception of the election had become perverted. In that case what they rejoiced and trusted in was not really God's act of election, but something certain people possessed or could acquire. As Paul understood the narratives about Abraham, God's election excluded any quality in man which might serve as a basis for the blessing. The idea of election turned attention away from man's nature and actions, and focussed it on the sovereign act of God (cf. Rom. 9:9-11). The election of Abraham, therefore, pointed forward to the coming acts of God through which he would fulfil his promises. These fulfilments were to take place in new acts of election through which all peoples would be blessed. And now, according to Paul, the fulfilment of the promise has come through Christ, and the work of fulfilment continues as the gospel is brought to the Gentiles and they share in the promised blessing. It would be quite unreasonable, therefore, to seek for a basis of salvation in circumcision and works of the law. If anyone insisted on circumcision, he would turn away from God's election and join the Jews in their perverted trust in Abraham, as they made circumcision and their descent from him a privilege which distinguished them from other people. Because of their perverted view of the meaning of God's election of Israel the Jews rejected God's act in the present when he sent his Son, the promised Messiah, and through him fulfilled the promise to Abraham of a blessing for all peoples. For the Gentiles to accept circumcision, or to demand that they be circumcised that they might participate fully in salvation, did not mean at all that they became Abraham's children; it meant rather a denial of the promise to Abraham and a refusal to accept its fulfilment. Abraham himself had not received the promise on the basis of circumcision or of any works of the law, but in obedience he had justified God and trusted in the word of promise. Therefore he had become the example of all who in the same manner *believed* in God. To trust in circumcision and works of the law, which, as practiced by or demanded of the Gentiles, meant that they were a means of securing righteousness, was the opposite of the faith of Abraham. For God's elect there could be no boundaries between peoples; but when circumcision and works of the law become conditions for participation in salvation, they separate people from one another (the circumcised from the uncircumcised, those zealous for the law from those less zealous). But this is contrary to God's sovereign election. The only correct following of Abraham's example is by *faith*. In faith man receives God's call and election just as Abraham did, and in faith he accepts God's promise as true just as Abraham did.

Paul seems to spiritualize the conception of circumcision when he calls those who believe in Christ the true circumcision, but in reality he follows consistently the Old Testament idea of election. But if this idea is changed so as to provide for a quality of the elect which sets them apart above the rest, or if it is assumed that the elect can walk in the way of righteousness with the help of the law given to the chosen people and thus separate themselves from "the sinners of the Gentiles" (cf. 2:15), then in reality God's sovereign act of election is nullified. The very rejection of the fact that the Gentiles can participate in the gospel without circumcision and works of the law must nullify the gospel. But the meaning of the gospel is precisely the fulfilment of God's election in the old covenant and of the promise. In the Old Testament the prophets, too, opposed the idea that the election was to be understood as a privilege for the people (cf., for example, Amos 3:2).

3. Scripture combines righteousness by the law with a curse and righteousness by faith with life (3:10-12)

a) The law itself curses righteousness by the law (3:10)

This section, vss. 10-12, is a pregnant passage but difficult to interpret. It has been explained in many different ways. Even translation of the Greek text has in some respects been influenced by its interpretation. The difficulty is not that there are differences between the various manuscripts, but that the thoughts are very briefly stated and their meaning is difficult to apprehend.

Paul says in vs. 10: "For all who rely on works of the law are under a curse; for it is written, 'Cursed be every one who does not abide by all the things written in the book of the law, and do them." Then he continues in vs. 11: "Now it is evident that no man is justified before God by the law; for 'The righteous shall live by faith.' (*or*, 'He who through faith is righteous shall

115

live').'' Then finally he says in vs. 12: "but the law does not rest on faith, for [it says in Scripture] 'He who does them [what is written in the law] shall live by them."

In vs. 10 the statement is connected with the preceding with a "for." He has just emphasized that those who are of faith are blessed with faithful Abraham. Faith is combined with blessing, and this is evidenced by the fact that Scripture, according to Paul's interpretation, pronounces a curse upon all who are of the works of the law.

Paul thus unites those who believe in Christ with Abraham. While the Jews drew a line from Abraham to Sinai, which to them symbolized the external precepts of the law which were conducive to righteousness by the law, Paul drew a line from Abraham to Christ who is the true fulfilment of the law.

What Paul means now is that just as Abraham became a father of those who believe in Christ, so it was the Christians who stood in a right relationship to the inner meaning and will of the law. At this point, however, the ambiguity of the word "law" complicates the presentation. What Paul objects to is "being of the law" and seeking one's righteousness by the law. According to Paul righteousness is not obtained in this way. But the law is nevertheless holy, just, and good. But it does not bestow righteousness. According to Paul man can never obtain righteousness by either inner or external observance of the law. The fulfilment of the law comes only through Christ (cf. the exposition of 3:13 below). He himself was the new law. He was the fulfilment of the law. Only by the faith in him which meant living in him, or his living in the believer, did that take place which the law could not bring about because "it was weak through the flesh."

The righteousness, Spirit, and life which the law was unable to provide came in Christ. In him the perfect law became identical with the fulfilled law. Paul's thought that the law was fulfilled in Christ (that he was its *telos,* its end and goal [Rom. 10:4]) implies that it was both perfected and fulfilled through him. But in a certain sense this meant that the law had come to an end. Only in the Spirit who was the presence of Christ in the believer did the will of the law become clear. But now it was not merely concerned with precepts, but involved a new life in Christ, based on his atoning death on the cross and his resurrection, and given to those who had been united with him in baptism. It did not mean that the Christian was given power to observe the law, but that he shared in the righteousness of Christ and that Christ lived in him. The condemnation of the law was removed from those who were in Christ. The law which had been perverted to the use of gaining righteousness appeared now as "refuse" to him who had been won to Christ. Since faith meant "to be in Christ," and since everything the law sought to accomplish was included in his righteousness, the accusing and condemning law could not be the final end; still less could a law demanding human efforts exist for those who lived in faith. Thus Christ was the end of the law. Since Christ himself was present by faith through his Spirit and righteousness, he provided participation in that life whose quality was the life of the fulfilled law, and which was characterized by the love that fulfils the law (cf. Gal. 5:14). The life in the Spirit bore witness to and belonged in the age to come.

According to Paul the true circumcision was not that "made with hands" but that which took place through incorporation into the fellowship with Christ. Similarly in a general sense the real fulfilment of the law was not an external matter but that which took place through Christ. Through him God himself had continued and amplified his revelation given in the law. Paul held that the law was interpreted and fulfilled through that which happened in Christ. For him it was not merely a question of a new theoretical principle of understanding and interpreting the law, nor was it a matter of trying to obey new precepts and rules of conduct. The law was interpreted only through God's continuing, redemptive activity, the climax of which was in Christ.

That the believer participated in the fulfilment of the law through Christ did not mean for Paul that the believer need not do anything after he had received the gift of forgiveness, nor that he had now received power to do the good works which he now had to produce. Later theological thought has often operated with these alternatives. But Paul did not think along those lines. The fulfilment of the law was found in the righteousness of Christ. But participation in that righteousness was also a participation in the life of the Spirit. This life involved a continual growth in which the whole man in his will and work was engaged. The gospel *always* came as a challenge. The life of faith may also be described as a race. But the law was fulfilled not by what the believer did, but through the righteousness of Christ in which the believer participated. But participation in the righteousness of Christ was not a quietistic life, but a life continually active in love to the neighbor. Thus it was evident that the life of the believer shared in the fulfilment of the law, because in love of the neighbor the commandments of the law were fulfilled. Love needs no external commandments. In love both the knowledge of God's will and its fulfilment were given.

What had been written in the book of the law had its fulfilment in Christ. He who was "of the works of the law," i.e., who sought his own righteousness through observance of the law, rejected the fulfilment of the law through Christ. He became the object of the curse which the law pronounced upon him who did not do all the things written in the law. The words in the law about doing the law referred to the fulfilment to come in Christ. Scripture had foreseen his coming. Whoever did not submit to these words and did not acknowledge God's justice as he acted in Christ placed himself outside the fulfilment of the law and opposed his own righteousness to that act through which God brought about the fulfilment. He rejected God's Word and his activity, and thus became the object of the curse of the law. According to vs. 11 righteousness was connected with *faith*. To believe meant obediently to acknowledge God and to turn away from that self-assertion which substituted self-righteousness for that righteousness which God provided through his action. But the words of the law pointed ahead to that fulfilment of the demands of the law which came through the atonement of Christ, through his death and resurrection. The opposite of faith was therefore not the law in itself but that righteousness of the law which involved disobedience to the words of the law.

When this fact was ignored, the words in vss. 10-12 were easily interpreted to mean that the law as such contains a principle in conflict with faith. The idea was that the demands of the law were too severe and difficult. In themselves these demands did indeed constitute a means to attain righteousness, but since man was not able to attain the goal by this way, the gospel had to replace the law. According to this view Paul referred to the way of salvation by the works of the law when he quotes Lev. 18:5: "He who does them shall live by them." This equates law with righteousness of the law. Since Paul, however, clearly rejects the righteousness of the law he had accepted before his conversion, it is incomprehensible on the basis of this interpretation that he should speak of the law as holy and good and hold that it was fulfilled in Christ. Furthermore it is difficult to see how Paul could have held that Scripture demands righteousness by the law.

It is obvious that Paul does not hold the ways of faith and of the law (law-observance) to be two equal and parallel ways to righteousness. According to him observance of the law does not lead to true righteousness at all. Righteousness is not of the law. "If justification were through the law, then Christ died to no purpose" (2:21).

Paul did not regard the law as a means by which man could acquire a righteousness of his own. Such a conception would be a perversion of the most profound meaning of the law. The law had received its fulfilment in the gospel. Paul did not reject the real meaning of the law at all. No, he really gave it a higher place than the Pharisees. For Paul it really represented God's activity, his commandment and word, which governed man, and which man could not control or use for his own purpose. That the law was lord over man could be seen clearly in that it demanded a righteousness man was unable to produce (cf. Rom. 10:2f.). The law in its deepest meaning was an expression of God's own activity. But if the words of the law were rationalized and regarded as finished, it would be natural to try making them a means for man to secure a righteousness of his own. But this was a hindrance to God's righteousness. When the Jews rejected Christ, it was a sign that they were disobedient to *the law,* because God acted in Christ and continued in him the kind of works to which the law bore witness. The law was not simply legal and juridical, it contained God's election and guidance, all of his revealed will and work.

As we have pointed out it is a familiar thought in Paul that man cannot fulfil the commandments of the law so as to secure righteousness through them. Its demands, its *dikaioma,* could not be fulfiled as long as sin ruled over man. The law could be truly in force only after *he* had come who atoned for sin and made the law perfect and operative. Only in the Spirit through which man was united with Christ could the will of the law become realized.

Paul did not place faith and works against one another in such a way that faith would exclude works. What he rejected was "works of the law," i.e., the attempts to secure one's own righteousness through the observance of the law. But for Paul faith was really connected with actions and works of love. Love was the greatest gift of the Spirit. In I Corinthians 13 it is described as the love of God which the Christian receives, and it expresses itself in works.

A familiar argument for interpreting vs. 10 to mean that the cause of the curse is man's inability to fulfil all the requirements of the law has been found in Acts 15:10: "Why do you make trial of God by putting a yoke upon the neck of the disciples which neither our fathers nor we have been able to bear?"

That man has not been able to bear the yoke and burden of the law must be interpreted on the basis of the Christian insight that the yoke of the law did not lead to freedom. It did not provide righteousness and unity with God's will. The yoke therefore involved a real bondage. Those who had received a new conception of freedom could say this. But this word must not be taken to mean that the law appeared to the Jews as a burden, and that *therefore* the reception of the gospel was a liberation and set them free from their burden.

The Jews did not regard the law as a heavy yoke, but as a source of life and joy and a light on the way. The law was a means of helping them to walk on the right way, a means which the Gentiles did not possess. The Gentiles lived in the sins against which the law warned, and from which it wanted to preserve the chosen people. That was the way Paul the Pharisee had understood the law. That Paul as a Christian regarded the law differently was due to the insight and faith he lived in since the event on the road to Damascus. But the difficulty of observing the law was never the motive for his warnings against the righteousness of the law.

We should note that in vs. 10 Paul quotes a word of Scripture (Deut. 27:26) which seems to say the opposite of what he wants to prove. This word pronounces a curse on the one who does *not* abide by the words of the law. It does not seem to say that he who is "of the works of the law" should be cursed. On the contrary, blessing seems to be promised to those who keep the commandments of the law, which according to a reasonable interpretation of Deut. 28:1ff. is obviously possible. But Paul asserts that *Scripture* proclaims that man to be under a curse who is "of the works of the law." He seems to be speaking against the quotation which he cites as authority. In Deut. 30:11ff. (which Paul alludes to in Rom. 10:6ff.) we read: "For this commandment which I command you this day is not too hard for you, neither is it far off." According to the Jewish interpretation it was obvious that the commandments were declared possible of fulfilment. The quotation seems to require being understood as pronouncing a curse on those who were *not* "of the works of the law," on those who did *not* do its precepts.

An easy but misleading interpretation of the passage would be to assume that Paul meant that the Judaizers themselves did not keep the law completely (cf. 6:13), and that they demanded only such a limited observance as was customary among many Jews. Then certain portions of the law may have been regarded as of special importance. Against this conception Paul could point out that the law is a unit, and that he who transgresses *one* commandment is guilty of *all*. Paul could have assumed, we may suppose, that the Galatians wanted to be under the law according to the Jewish interpretation, but did not want to keep it *completely*. But in that case they would be under a curse. Even though this interpretation in general may reflect certain aspects of Paul's thought, the meaning is much more profound. His argument is directed not only against those who did not keep the whole law, but against all those who "were of the law," all those who sought righteousness by the law, even those who were most zealous for its observance. His statement therefore really seems to be absurd. But if we take account of what has been said above, his words appear both reasonable and natural. It is precisely Scripture itself, the word of God in the law, that speaks *against* righteousness by the law. Scripture states that he who does not do *all* that the law commands is under a curse. And according to Paul's interpretation, therefore, the law curses all those who live in the righteousness of the law because they do not submit to the law. They do not permit the *whole* law to speak, but set it aside in favor of their own righteousness.

It is especially important to interpret the word *all* ("all things written in the book of the law"). To the Pharisees *all* meant all the precepts in their most elaborate interpretation. For Paul's Scripture had received a new light through the revelation of Christ. Its deepest meaning was that it bore witness to the righteousness which had now come in Christ. Then to fulfil *all* must mean to fulfil the law in its deepest meaning. The law told how righteousness and blessing were to be given. Then only would the law be fulfilled. What had been spoken before would then be fulfilled, and the law itself would speak clearly. The will of God concealed in the law would then be realized, and the word of the law would

provide participation in that realization. Now Christ had come and
the age of fulfilment was at hand. In Christ *all* in the law had
been fulfilled. Now the blessing promised to Abraham was at hand.
Now the law was completely fulfilled. Observance of the law would
not fulfil the law further, but would place the one who sought
righteousness through the law under the curse pronounced on
the one who did *not* fully keep the law.

We must note carefully the words "blessing" in vs. 9 and "curse"
in vs. 10. For those who knew the Old Testament the quotation
would call their attention to the words about curse and blessing
in Deuteronomy 27 and 28. The curse was pronounced on those
who did not keep the words of the law. Blessing was promised to
those who kept and obeyed all the commandments. Paul interpreted the words in the light of the Messianic hope now fulfilled
in Christ. He gave a deeper meaning to the blessing than what
the ordinary interpretation of Gen. 12:3; 18:18; 22:18; 26:4; and
28:14 had had. The real meaning of the blessing was not earthly
success, happiness, power, and numerous descendants, but a
promise of the blessing to come with Messiah-Christ. And now
that blessing had come.

The state of blessedness connected with the presence of Christ
now in faith stood in contrast to the state of the curse which
because of sin was connected with the law. The law's purpose was
to judge. During the present evil age judgment rested on all men.
The works of the law which never could produce righteousness
or bring in the promised blessing did not save at all from the
judgment of the curse; on the contrary, just because they were
intended to circumvent righteous judgment, they made it permanent. They obscured the promised blessing and the possibility
of receiving it and of becoming free from the curse. Essentially
the works of the law belonged in the realm of the curse and
enslaved men under it. But when the law was not done, it had
to pronounce a curse. It had to do so when the righteousness it
spoke about and served was not at hand. The nature of the law
was such that it could not serve as a means of satisfying man's
desire to be accounted righteous. Righteousness could be given
only in and through the fulfilment of the law in Christ. Only the
man who lived by faith in Christ, therefore, could receive righteousness. *The law itself* cursed all righteousness of the law, because
the law, which in its deepest sense was not contrary to God's
promises (Gal. 3:21), but "holy, just, and good" (Rom. 7:12),

demanded submission to God. Submission was not realized but rather rejected and denied through the works of the law. But the fulness of the law came in Christ, and he who received a share in his righteousness and "lived in him" could not be condemned by the law (cf. Rom. 8:1ff.). In the faith-union with Christ love to the neighbor was realized as well (Gal. 5:13ff.; Rom. 12:9ff.). But this did not take place in order to secure one's own righteousness; it was connected with faith. The law, as long as it was not fulfilled, placed all men under a curse; but the promise to him who kept the commandments and the promise of a future blessing through Messiah-Christ were joined into one.

Paul means therefore that the commandments can never be kept by man's own efforts and free will. The words of the law were and remained true. They contained a deeper meaning. They were rightly fulfilled only in the fulfilment provided by God. Then the law was fulfilled and perfected, and then the law became such that it included righteousness. Then life came from it. Then the commandments were not a means of righteousness in the hands of carnal man. Christ was the Word who fulfilled and represented the complete word of the law. As we shall see further below, the commandment in Deut. 30:11ff. is made to refer to Christ in Rom. 10:6ff.

Because those who were "of the works of the law" did not actually obey the law, the blessing of the law promised to those who kept the commandments did not come to them. Instead they received the curse. All who were "of the works of the law" and had accepted the law as a means through which they sought righteousness were under a curse *according to the law's own words*. For righteousness did not come through the law, and the law demanded righteousness. The commandments were holy, just, and good; and Paul points to the commandments. Rightly understood the commandments *demanded* a righteousness they themselves could not give, and which could not be produced because of the universal rule of sin. It was still true, therefore, that the commandments pronounced a curse.

The blessing which had been promised in Scripture to those who kept the law could be given to men freely only after the fulfilment of the law had taken place in Christ. Now its spiritual power manifested itself through faith. Faith united the believer with the age to come and bestowed that Spirit which belonged to life in the promised kingdom.

The law and its fulfilment are related to one another as the promise of blessing is related to its fulfilment through the Messiah-Christ. Although law and promise are not the same, the fulfilment of the law and the promise were combined in Christ.

A right submission to the will of God in the law involved, according to Paul, an acceptance of the word of Scripture that the blessing was to be given to the Gentiles. From this point of view we may paraphrase vs. 10 with special reference to the position of the Gentiles: "All who seek righteousness through works of the law are under the curse of the law. Works of the law are really contrary to the law in its complete form. To abide by all that is written in the book of the law includes faith in Christ and in the blessing which now through him has been given to the Gentiles."

The real and final fulfilment of the law came through Jesus Christ, through whom the blessing promised to Abraham now was bestowed upon the Gentiles (cf. vs. 14). That Christ should assume the curse belonged also to "all that is written in the book of the law." This had been suggested by the words in Deut. 21:23 about the tree of the curse. Scripture also speaks about the Gentiles receiving the blessings of the kingdom of God. To reject the fact that the Gentiles by faith shared in the gospel and to set up the works of the law as a way of righteousness was certainly *not* abiding in that which was written in the book of the law. The law, *Torah,* made all of life subject to God, but the Jews who sought righteousness through the works of the law were disobedient to and in rebellion against the law.

To seek righteousness through the works of the law or to "be of the works of the law" meant therefore a refusal to submit to the God who spoke in the law. It meant a rejection of the blessing promised to Abraham and of the righteousness reckoned to him by faith. Those who were "of the works of the law" stood in conflict with the words addressed to Abraham in the book of the law and with Abraham himself to whom righteousness had been reckoned when in faith he submitted to God's will and waited for God's act and for the blessing promised to him. There is a decisive conflict between seeking one's own righteousness through the observance of the law and subordinating oneself to God's will expressed in the law. This will of God, revealed in Christ who fulfilled the law, was the foundation of the commandments and precepts of the law. He who refused to submit to this will and who wanted to make himself righteous through works of the law became subject to the curse pronounced on those who did *not* keep the commandments and statutes of the law.

This argument, says Paul in the following verse, is supported by the words of Scripture in Hab. 2:4, where it is stated that righteousness is connected with *faith.* "Now it is evident that no man is justified before God by the law; *for* it says that life and righteousness belong with faith." Scripture proclaims that it is impossible to secure righteousness before God through the observance of the law, and it bears witness instead to righteousness by faith.

b) Scripture bears witness to righteousness by faith (3:11)

It is clear therefore that righteousness cannot be secured through "the works of the law" as the Judaizers thought. Scripture itself substantiates this fact. That no one is justified through the law is stated, according to Paul, in these words: *ho dikaios ek pisteos zesetai,* which most naturally would be translated, "the just shall live by faith," but which also may be rendered, "the just by faith shall live." This passage, which Paul quotes also in Rom. 1:17, may be paraphrased thus: the one who is righteous will receive eternal life, and his righteousness is righteousness by faith.

Righteousness is revealed by God's acts, and man must submit in obedience to this activity of God. Since God permitted Christ to be crucified and thereby provided for man's justification, man must submit in obedience to this act of God and acknowledge his justice; in other words, *believe.* By this faith righteousness was bestowed upon him. In our exegesis of vs. 12 we must return to the statement, "the just shall live by faith." Here we must first consider the meaning of the term *faith.* In Hebrew this is very closely related to the idea of *faithfulness.* Behind Paul's Greek word *pistis* stands the Hebrew *emunah* (faith, faithfulness). The Hebrew words which Paul quotes from Hab. 2:4 means, "the righteous shall live by his faith," or "faithfulness." The Septuagint introduces a slight change and renders it: "the just shall live by my (God's) faithfulness." By dropping "my" Paul comes closer to the Hebrew text. But by the word *faith* he does not mean something that might accrue to man's merit. He does not conceive of *faith* as a human action to be performed, but as a faithful submission to God's promise and deeds. In this sense *faith* stands in contrast to the *righteousness by the law* which really involves a rejection of the justifying act of God. Faith always means for Paul a surrender to God, and the idea of God's faithfulness and man's confident trust is always present in his use of *pistis*. In the idea of justification by faith the word faith does not refer to probability, but to trust in a promise, even though that promise, as in the case of Abraham, demanded confidence in something which seemed impossible. This is emphasized especially in Rom. 4:17ff., "in the presence of the God in whom he believed, who gives life to the dead and calls into existence the things that do not exist. In hope he believed against hope, that he should become the father of many nations." Faith means to Paul that a person faithfully stands by his word. This is God's character. He is true. Man shows the right attitude when he relies on God's faithfulness. Man manifests his own trustworthiness in that he does not doubt God even when it seems impossible that his words could be true and his promises fulfilled.

It is important to understand that the thought of faithfulness both of God and of man is an essential element in Paul's conception of faith. Faith is related to covenant faithfulness. God is true and does not fail, even though men are faithless (Rom. 3:2ff). Man's faithlessness (*apistia*) cannot nullify the faithfulness (*pistis*) of God. In the last analysis God's words will prove true, but man can receive the blessings of his promises only by trusting in those promises. To believe means that having received the promise man lives in confident trust in God's Word, in his election, and in his promise. The believer lives by receiving the fulfilment of the promise in Christ. In faith he submits to God's faithful work, and thus he receives the righteousness which God has provided through Christ. In righteousness by the law man distrusts God and attempts to propitiate him as if he were not faithful to his promise. In faith man acknowledges God's truth and righteousness. Since God has bestowed righteousness in Christ, the believer accepts this gift and is thus united with Christ. Faith is therefore clearly related to Paul's conception of Christ *in* the believer and the believer *in* Christ. (See exegesis of Gal. 2:20. Cf. Rom. 6:5ff.; 8:1; 12:5; I Cor. 1:30; II Cor. 5:17; Eph. 2:13.) Christ is the believer's life (cf. II Cor. 13:5; Col. 3:4). He is active as the Spirit given to the believer. This Spirit belonged to that promised age when the Messiah and his righteousness were to come.

When the word "faith" is associated with ideas regarded as

a part of Paul's mysticism, it is quite likely due to the Hebrew meaning of the word. This may also serve as a warning against interpreting Paul's words about Christ living in him from the point of view of Hellenistic mysticism. Nor can *faith* be rightly understood on the basis of Greek rationalism, where its meaning is primarily regarding something as true. In Greek literature faith has an intellectual connotation, and means to regard something as true or probable. Believing in the gods involves the assumption that they probably exist. But the Hebrew words *aman* and *emunah* (faith or faithfulness), denote an adherence to something with a steadfast and persevering trust. In that sense, as we have said above, faith becomes something especially characteristic of God. The man who believes receives and holds fast to God's faithfulness.

It lies near at hand, therefore, for Paul to think of God and Christ as present and active in faith. Faith is the only attitude which corresponds to God's faithfulness. After God sent Christ and thereby prepared the way for bestowing his righteousness on man, faith constitutes that relation to God through which he is able to confer righteousness and life on man. Faith's reception of the righteousness of God is for Paul therefore a form of God's presence in man through Christ. This is the exact opposite of righteousness by the law in which man seeks to assert himself and make himself righteous before God. In that way man separates himself from God and refuses the gifts prepared through Christ. It is natural therefore that the righteousness of faith goes with *life;* and life in this connection does not mean continued life on earth, but rather God's life, eternal life. What has sometimes been called Paul's mysticism may therefore be said to be a part of his doctine of justification by faith in contrast to justification by works.

Faith, therefore, does not mean a meritorious virtue in man which he could possess independently of God, or an effort by which he enhances himself and makes claims to righteousness. We may define faith by saying that man receives God's righteousness gratis (by grace) and lives in and through its active power. Consequently the Spirit is active in faith, and faith is connected with love. That this faith also contains an element of knowledge is quite clear. It is faith in the God who is faithful. But this faith has a paradoxical character of certainty, and it does not rest on calculations of rational probabilities. It is not connected with claims man makes. Faith can never make God its servant. It exists only in his service, without man's own demands or attempts to enhance himself as if he had any claim on God (cf. Rom. 9:14ff.).

Faith is conceived of as a relation to God's righteousness of which man becomes a partaker through Christ. It may also be described as a state that has come into existence because God caused his Messiah to die and rise again, and made him Lord over all peoples. Then this new state is not primarily concerned with the individual; it is a state founded on an event that is decisive for the whole world (cf. Gal. 3:23, 25).

c) The fulfilment of the law gives life (3:12)

Scripture itself, as we have seen, makes known that no one is justified by works of the law. "The law does not rest on faith." Here the word "law" means that definite law which the Jews made into an instrument of righteousness by the law. The law as understood by the Jews compelled men to seek justification through a pious life in works of the law. The right interpretation and fulfilment of the law came first through the act of God in Christ. That the law does not rest on faith means that the law in its uncompleted form does not provide what is given in faith. It belonged to this age, and although it bore witness to the age to come, it did not possess its power. Therefore it could not provide righteousness. It did not supply the Spirit. Christ was not present in it in such a way that one could receive the Spirit through the observance of the law.

The second part of vs. 12 is usually assumed to be an interpretation of the first part and an explication of the fact that the law is not of faith. In Lev. 18:5 we read: "You shall therefore keep my statutes and my ordinances, by doing which a man shall live." It is this passage which Paul renders freely, "He who does them shall live by them." These words have been interpreted as presenting a principle of righteousness by the law which would stand in opposition to faith. The Swedish edition of 1917 seems to understand it thus, as it translates: "But in the law it is not a question of faith; on the contrary it says, 'He who does them shall live by them.'"

We have already remarked that Paul never quotes Scripture to the effect that what is written there is not valid. He does *not* mean that the Scriptures of the old covenant in themselves taught righteousness by the law, and that they should therefore now be set aside. On the contrary he says that the Jews had a veil over their minds whenever Moses was read (II Cor. 3:14ff.). In Christ the right meaning of the commandments became unveiled and clear. In him the commandments found their explanation, fulness, and fulfilment. In him the righteousness to which the words of the law pointed with their demands, threats, and promises had come.

In reality Paul uses the quotation to indicate that observance of the law is *not* the principle of righteousness in the Scriptures of the old covenant. He notes first of all that the law "does not rest on faith." In itself it does not supply righteousness as faith does. It does not say in Scripture that the law can be made a means of righteousness. It speaks of "doing" the law. According to Paul this presupposes its fulfilment. Only in this fulfilment does the law find its real place and a complete expression of its meaning. The statement that the law promises life when it is fulfilled refers therefore to its fulfilment through Christ. How this takes place is explained in vs. 13.

The commandments in Scripture gave a promise: "He who does them shall live by them," The meaning may be paraphrased as follows. The law itself, understood as precepts which man can observe, is not able to provide righteousness. It does not belong to the age of righteousness and life, and it does not possess the powers of that age. Nor does Scripture say that righteousness comes through the law. Righteousness belongs with faith. What Scripture says instead is that he who *does* the commandments shall live. It is not he who *has* the law and uses it as a means for himself that shall live. Scripture does not say that. On the contrary it says: he who *does* the commandments shall live, or: he who lives in the fulfilment of the commandments has and shall receive the life and the righteousness belonging to the fulfilment of the law. He participates in it already here in this life and later also in eternity.

In order to understand vs. 12 the statements in 12a and 12b must not be combined in such a way that the quotation from Lev. 18:5 is understood as a proof of the assertion, "the law does not rest on faith." In vs. 11 Paul quoted Scripture as a proof of the truth of justification by faith. It would be quite absurd if in the following verse he were to quote Scripture in such a way that it asserted the opposite of righteousness by faith, which immediately before he had declared to be the meaning of the scriptural message. The meaning in vs. 12 therefore is *not:* "the law does not rest on faith, and this is demonstrated by the fact that Scripture says that he who does the commandments shall live by them." In that case Scripture itself would establish the observance of the law as a way of righteousness. The true meaning may be paraphrased as follows: "Righteousness is connected with faith" (vs. 11). "It does not say in Scripture that righteousness comes through observance of the law" (vs. 12a). "It says rather, he who does what is written in the book of the law shall thereby receive eternal life" (vs. 12b). In other words it is not the opposite of *faith* that is demonstrated in the quotation in vs. 12b, but the opposite of *righteousness by the law* as Paul understood its meaning. According to Paul's meaning the doing of the commandments does not take place through the works of the law, but through Christ. The promise of life belongs, not to the observance of the law, but to that fulfilment which took place when Christ fulfilled the law even unto death on the cross.

The usual assumption, which Paul is supposed to maintain in vs. 12, that faith stands in opposition to works, is in general not found in the New Testament. The coming of the Messiah meant the fulfilment of the law. But it was not a question of observing individual precepts. *To obey the commandments must be connected with God's creative activity in the present.* Otherwise obedience would have no contact with present reality. The commandments would then be the commandments of men and would *obstruct God's* work (cf. H. Ljungman, *Das Gesetz erfüllen,* pp. 71ff.).

In general in the New Testament man is confronted with the demand to *do* what the law commands. But this "doing" does not involve at all a righteousness of works. The first thing told to those who asked about eternal life was the injunction to *do* the commandments (cf. for example, Matt. 19:17; Luke 10:28). Then the question of what this doing involved had to be raised, but it could not be answered in the context of asking how eternal life could be attained. The way in which the Gospels deal with this question indicates their complete reversal of the Pharasiac teaching that the observance of the law, "works," was the way to righteousness (cf. Rom. 9:32). The new proclamation of the deepest and most essential meaning of law and righteousness involved a complete reversal of the conception of late Judaism, even though Jewish expressions and methods of presentation were employed. (Compare, for instance, Jesus' attitude to the interpretation of the law in the rabbinical tradition and his understanding and application of the Sabbath commandment.)

To keep the commandments rightly presupposed that life had been given, because righteousness could not be produced by works of the law (cf. the interpretation of 3:21). Life would be given through the fulfilment of the law by the Messiah. Then would come the fulfilment of the law which the law itself could not accomplish because it "was weakened by the flesh" (Rom. 8:3). Fulfilment meant therefore that life was given, and only *then* could righteousness be bestowed and the law be rightly fulfilled. The words, "he who does them shall live by them," were fulfilled through Christ, who came with life and righteousness, and who fulfilled the law by bearing its curse upon the cross. His act of obedient submission to the curse was not the opposite of faith at all; it was rather the climax of faith and made righteousness by faith possible. And in and through the believer who has become *one* with Christ and therefore lives in the Spirit the just requirements of the law are fulfilled (Rom. 8:4).

The verb "do" ("he who does them") may be compared to "he who does" in Matt. 5:19 (*hos d'an poiese*). This "doing" is connected with the coming of the Messiah. His coming involves an activity concerned with the fulfilment of the law. This activity takes place in the Spirit, and through it the law is fulfilled (cf. Rom. 8:4). The time of the Messiah was a time of doing. According to the Gospel of John the Jews can therefore be accused of not keeping the law (John 7:19; cf. John 5:29, 46ff.). None of them *does* the law (Ljungman, *op. cit.,* p. 73). When in Gal. 3:12 Paul speaks about doing what is written in the law and "he who does them," this conception is not in any sense the opposite of faith, but rather just another expression for the faith connected with life and righteousness. "The law does not rest on faith." To rest on the law involves a conception of the law as a means of salvation. Over against this idea Paul places the "doing" that belongs to the Messianic age. When Scripture connects life with law, it is concerned with *doing,* i.e., that activity which belongs to the day of salvation or the day of the Messiah. His work meant primarily taking upon himself the curse of the law, and vs. 13 continues the explication of this idea.

"He who does them" points forward therefore to vs. 13, which

states that Christ redeemed us from the curse of the law, but also
it points back to the words in vs. 10: "every one who does not
abide by all the things written in the book of the law, and *do
them*." This "doing" meant to abide in *all things* written in the
book of the law. To do *all things* means to complete and fulfil
everything in the way it should be when in the day of salvation
men shared in the Messiah's fulfilment of the law.

To *do* the things written in the book of the law, *poiein ta en to biblio
tou nomou gegrammena* is the language of the Septuagint. To Paul
the fulfilment of the law in this connection is essentially equivalent to
fulfilling it in its entirety (vs. 10, "Cursed be every one who does
not abide by *all things* written in the book of the law"). Complete
fulfilment meant for Paul the Pharisee a zealous obedience to all the
statutes. In general the law had to be fulfilled *completely*, because he
who fails in *one* point has become guilty of *all*. After Paul's Damascus
experience the fulfilment of the law meant that the law was brought
to its climax and goal (*telos*). *To do the law* (*poiein ton nomon*) thus
came to mean the same as to fulfil it (*telein ton nomon*). To keep the
law in the ordinary sense may also be expressed by this latter verb
(cf. Rom. 2:27).

We may understand Paul's thinking in principle if we remember
his conception of the function of the law. Its function was to include
all under accusation and judgment. Only he who submitted to the
law and accepted its judgment in complete obedience stood in a right
relation to the law. Even though Christ himself was righteous, he
had accepted the conditions and judgment of the law (cf., below,
3:13ff and 4:4ff.). He was righteous and could therefore rightly obey
the law. He did not seek to be justified through the law, and he did
not use it as means for his own advantage. He was obedient unto
death, even death on a cross (Phil. 2:8). Just the fact that he submitted to the will of God even to the extent of going the way of the
cross was the complete fulfilment of the law. The function of the law
was to condemn, and all humanity with which Christ identified himself stood under the judgment. By his fulfilment of the law he brought
it to its climax and goal, to its *telos*. Thereby he redeemed those
who were *one* with him from the curse of the law. *The final goal* of
the law became its *end* for those who were in Christ. Nor could the
law drive them any more to seek righteousness by the law.

It was to this fulfilment of the law that the scriptural promise of
life was to be applied. When Lev. 18:5 states that he who does the
law shall live by it, this word, according to Paul, must be understood
as referring to Christ's fulfilment of the law and to the life received
by him who is *one* with Him.

The complete doing of the law means that the law is brought to its
fulness and perfection, and thus becomes so entirely determinative
for man that it ceases to be an external rule. Jeremiah said about the
new covenant that then a law would be given which one man need

not teach to another because the Lord would write it upon their hearts (Jer. 31:33). This complete doing of the law was identical with the fulfilment of the promises. The promises concerned a coming righteousness. The function of the law was to serve righteousness, to judge and to keep under restraint until righteousness comes through the Messiah (cf. below, 3:23). Everything, both promise and law, was fulfilled through Christ. The prophecies of Scripture (cf. Acts 1:16: *edei plerothenai ten graphen hen proeipen to pneuma to hagion,* "the scripture had to be fulfilled, which the Holy Spirit spoke beforehand"), the fulfilment of the promises (cf. II Cor. 1:20: "For all the promises of God find their Yes in him") and the fulfilment of the requirement of the law (Rom. 8:4: *hina to dikaioma tou nomou plerothe en hemin,* "that the just requirement of the law might be fulfilled in us") all had the same purpose. The *promises* were to be fulfilled when *the requirement of the law* was fulfilled; and vice versa, *the requirement of the law* was to be fulfilled when *the promises* were fulfilled. The law's demand for righteousness and its judgment on sin were brought to their climax when *he* came who in himself represented the fulness of God's righteousness. He accepted the law's inevitable judgment on sin. At the same time he could make man a participant in God's righteousness and the love contained in it. He blotted out the sin and took the curse of the law upon himself. In his action the law was fulfilled in such a way that the promise of life to those who met its demand could be redeemed and life could be found. In that same action the promises of that Messiah who came with righteousness were fulfilled. Thus all the promises of Scripture and all the demands of the law were fulfilled. According to the prophecies the law was to be fulfilled in the new covenant (cf. Heb. 8:8ff., where Jeremiah 31 is quoted). From the point of view of the ancient church it was a question of the same reality when the law was fulfilled through Christ and life thus arose, and when the predictions of the prophets were fulfilled (cf. Acts 10:43).

It is customary to distinguish between the commandments of the law as objectively given and obedience to and doing them. This indicates a view of the law different from that of Paul. He cannot conceive of objective and prescribed rules apart from obedience to them. The law in its deepest meaning did not consist of definable rules to which man could adjust himself more or less readily. The law was a unit which a person did not really know as long as it appeared as an entity in itself foreign to man. Man's inability to do the law fully implied also that he did not really theoretically even know the law. Real knowledge of the law came only through Christ who in his work fulfilled the law and made its demands effective. Only the complete *doing* could bring the content of the law to its perfection and fulfilment. The law became new at the same time that it remained the law once given. Thus the doing of the law created the perfect law in the person and work of Christ, and God's will was thus perfectly expressed. The love of God, wherein forgiveness was found, and wherein was contained the righteousness the law bore witness to and served, could now be brought near to men. The blessing promised to Abraham, which for Paul included the fulness of righteousness, could now become available to the Gentiles (3:14), because by taking upon himself the curse of the law Christ took away their sins as well. Thus life could come, the life whose presupposition and content was full righteousness. Righteousness and life belong so closely together, according to Paul, that they may designate the same thing, because life is the life of righteousness, the life given in union with God. The words of the law in vs. 12, therefore, that the doing of these precepts would give life, find their profound fulfilment in Christ. The blessing which according to vs. 14 was to be given to the Gentiles was that same life which according to vs. 12 Scripture promised to those who do the law.

Who is it then that receives the life promised to the one who does the law? The just requirement of the law is fulfilled "in us, who walk not according to the flesh but according to the Spirit" (Rom. 8:4). Christ fulfilled the law. He was in reality the one who brought the law to perfection, and who altogether represented the righteousness of God himself. Only *the righteous* can do works of righteousness. Efforts of man to keep the law cannot produce righteousness. When man turns the commandments into achievements, he no longer permits them to serve as his lord, as the Word of God which accuses and condemns him. Instead he makes the commandments his servant and a means to obtain his own righteousness (Rom. 10:3; Phil. 3:9). He uses the law as a means to enhance himself with regard to salvation and to appear righteous. The law becomes a servant of sin. Then man does not rightly keep the law but trangresses God's will. The right attitude to the law is to submit to its judgment in *faith* and to *believe* in Christ. The law had spoken beforehand about him and had promised his coming. He submitted to the law's condemnation and thus canceled it. The law was set free from its service to sin, whereupon its purpose could be fulfilled. Those who lived in him and in whom his Spirit dwelt shared in his righteousness and in that life in which the fulfilment of the law was a reality. They could acknowledge the justice of the judgment and at the same time be free from it.

Paul interprets the quotation from Lev. 18:5, therefore, as a reference to the promised righteousness. The new life in faith is a life in Christ rather than in conformity to law. The meaning of this, as we indicated in our discussion of 2:20, is seen in the fact that life in Christ is put in opposition to works of the law. Christ himself is righteousness, and this is the sum of it all. The Christian is not understood as a person who through Christ has obtained the

ability to produce an obedience to the law of which he was
incapable before. He has his righteousness in Christ through whom
the law has been fulfilled, and his new life is a life in Christ. This
life takes the place of all observance of the law. When the believer
has received righteousness, the Spirit, and life from Christ, the
demands of the law are thereby completed and fully met. What the
Christian must do is not to turn again with new strength to the
demands of the law, as if these were in addition to the gospel,
but rather really to live in Christ in whom the law has been fulfilled. Herein is included the love to the neighbor in which the
whole law is summarized.

In the context of vss. 10-12 the meaning of vs. 12 becomes
clear. In vs. 10 Scripture points to the curse on everyone who
does not abide by the commandments. In vs. 12 it is said that he
who does them, *ho poiesas auta,* shall live. "Shall live" repeats
the words of vs. 11: "The just shall live by faith," or, "He who
through faith is righteous shall live." The righteous one shall
receive what had been promised to the one who kept the law.
Behind the Greek phrase, *ho dikaios ek pisteos,* stands the Hebrew
text: "the righteous shall live by his faith (faithfulness)." (In
Greek usage it may seem strange to combine "the righteous,"
ho dikaios, with "through faith," *ek pisteos.* If that were the sense,
we should have expected *ho ek pisteos dikaios* or, *ho dikaios ho
ek pisteos.* Not the arrogant man but the one who lives in faithfulness and righteousness shall find salvation and life. This means
to Paul that the righteous shall participate in life, and that
righteousness is given through faith. The statements, "he who
through faith is righteous shall live," and "he who does them shall
live by them," should *not* be regarded as opposites, as is often
done, but as expressing the same truth. This is clear from vs. 10,
where we read that he who does not abide in all things written in
the book of the law is cursed. This is applied to all who are "of the
works of the law," who therefore are not righteous and consequently have not done what was written in the law. The context contrasts
being of the works of the law with being of faith. Life comes of
faith, and life had been promised at the fulfilment of the law which
took place in Christ. Those who sought righteousness through the
observance of the law did *not* keep the commandments in the
fullest and deepest meaning, and came therefore under the curse.
Those who belonged to the faith, which now had come, obtained
righteousness. The works of the law did not result in the keeping

of the commandments or in the promised blessing. Scripture said: He who keeps the commandments shall live. This refers to Christ, who took upon himself the judgment of the law, and to him who through Christ has been redeemed from the curse of the law and lives in the promised blessing.

It is quite clear that according to Paul Scripture bears witness to Christ. But it is important to realize that this is true also of the commandments. When they promise a blessing to those who abide in them (Lev. 18:5; Deut. 28:2; cf. also Deut. 27:26, where those who do not keep the words of the law are threatened with a curse), the hidden and latent meaning of this promise of *blessing* is for Paul the promise of *Christ* and the coming life in him. This life belonged to the age to come and was of the character of eternity. Paul equates the promise of blessing to Abraham, which he interpreted as Messianic and as pointing to Christ and his righteousness, with the promise of life which according to the law was to come to those who kept the commandments. In both of these cases the blessing comes in and through faith. Then the time of the law is at an end and the age of the Spirit has come. In vs. 13 we are told that Christ has redeemed us from the curse of the law. In vs. 11 righteousness is equated with faith. Righteousness and faith belong together. Just as life is promised to the one who through faith is righteous, so life is promised also to the one who keeps the commandments. He who lives in faith says: Christ lives in me and I live in Christ (2:19-20). He therefore participates in Christ's fulfilment of the law.

Summing up we may say that the words "shall live" in vs. 11 and in vs. 12b speak of the *same* life, the promised, Messianic life which came in Christ. Through the Spirit this life is given to the believer already here on earth, and it is connected with the eternal life which eventually shall be revealed. In Paul's thinking, therefore, the words "shall live" cannot be interpreted to mean that the one righteous through the law shall live (receive strength and be preserved in life) through his obedience to the law. Paul in his interpretation of Scripture is concerned with *the Messianic life,* the life in righteousness, the life given in Christ; and that life does not come through the righteousness of the law at all.

In the statement in vs. 12, "but the law does not rest on faith, for 'He who does them shall live by them,' " the word translated "for" should be rendered by an emphatic "but" or "but on the contrary." It should not be taken to imply an *antithesis* between *faith* and the fulfilment of the *law.* For Paul faith and a right keeping of the law (i.e., through Christ) belong together and express the same idea. What Paul has in view when he speaks in vs. 12b about doing the commandments is not the works of the law, but those works which really contain life and righteousness, i.e., the works of Christ, his doing and fulfilling the law.

In Paul's thinking the life in faith always expresses itself in works done in love. We are "created in Christ Jesus for good works, which God prepared beforehand, that we should walk in them" (Eph. 2:10). But these are not efforts under the law, but such works belong to the life in faith. Works done in order to obtain a righteousness of one's own do not lead to the real righteousness. This is emphasized in the passage immediately preceding the words quoted above from Eph. 2:10. "For by grace you have been saved through faith; and this is not your own doing, it is the gift of God—not because of works, lest any man should boast" (Eph. 2:8). When Paul, later in the Letter to the Galatians (chap. 5), admonishes them not to abuse the freedom of faith but to serve one another in love, he adds: "For the whole law is fulfilled in one word, 'You shall love your neighbor as yourself' " (5:14). Here he describes how in the life of faith and in the Spirit the believer participates in the love given through Christ, and how he manifests this love in service to the neighbor.

It could be said that both vs. 12 and vs. 10 contrast the fulfilled law with the law mistakenly regarded as a self-contained entity. In vs. 10 those "who rely on works of the law" are the ones who accept this self-contained law and thereby reject its fulfilment in Christ. In vs. 12 he says that the law does not rest on faith and does not provide righteousness (cf. vs. 11, where life is connected with faith). Only he who participates in Christ's fulfilment of the law has a share in the law's promise of life. When Christ took the curse of the law upon himself, he took away its power to condemn (vs. 13). Thus a way was prepared for all men to the righteousness of God. Thus also the words of the law were fulfilled that the blessing should be given also to the Gentiles (vs. 14). The observance of the law in the Jewish sense separated the Jew who had the law from the Gentiles who had not received it; and also separated men from one another according to each one's ability to follow the letter of the law. Thus one would be approved and not the other. But in Christ the *whole* majesty of the law had appeared, and it had become evident that the righteousness to which the law bore witness could not be realized through the observance of the letter of the law. The Jewish conception of works of the law as a means of righteousness was proved false. But now a relation to the law in the Spirit had appeared. This was a relation to a fulfilment of the law in its deepest meaning, i.e., *Christ's* fulfilment of the law fully and completely, when he took upon himself the curse of the law to redeem the Jews from it and bring the blessing of Abraham not only to them but also to the Gentiles. Christ fulfilled the law completely. He did what no previous obedience of the law and no observance of the letter had been able to accomplish in that he took away sin by becoming sin for us (II Cor. 5:21), that "in him we might become the righteousness of God."

The quotation from Lev. 18:5, which appears in Gal. 3:12, is found also in Rom. 10:5. It is obvious, therefore, that Paul does not refer to it by chance, or on the basis of a casual association. Since, however, his quotation in Rom. 10:5 has been assumed to favor the interpretation of the meaning we have rejected here, we must consider briefly this passage also as an important parallel to Gal. 3:12. "Moses writes that the man who practices the righteousness which is based on the law shall live by it" (Rom. 10:5). In the previous verse he says, "For Christ is the end of the law, that every one who has faith may be justified."

The meaning would seem to be as follows. That Christ is the end and goal of the law is elucidated by a word of Scripture which speaks about righteousness. Paul says that in regard to the righteousness by the law Moses writes that he who fulfils the law shall live by it. It is not true that righteousness comes from the law in the way the Jews understood it in their unenlightened zeal for the law. They had not sought righteousness through faith but as something which was to be gained by means of works (Rom. 9:30). They had not submitted to God's righteousness (10:3). Now Christ had come, and in him was given the righteousness the Jews had failed to obtain. He who has faith will be justified in him (10:4). Scripture testifies through Moses that life shall be given to him who fulfils the righteousness the law demands—the righteousness the Jews sought in vain to secure. This righteousness had now come in and through Christ. He was the fulfilment of the law, its *telos,* goal and end. (We will return to this subject in our exposition of 3:13, where we will further elucidate what Paul means by Christ's fulfilment of the law.)

That the line of thought in Romans 10 is as we have suggested in the above paragraph is indicated also by what is said in the context (Rom. 10:6ff.) about the righteousness of faith. Faith need not look forward to a coming righteousness, because in it righteousness is already present. "But the righteousness based on faith says, Do not say in your heart, 'Who will ascend into heaven?' (that is, to bring Christ down) or 'Who will descend into the abyss?' (that is, to bring Christ up from the dead). But what does it say? The word is near you, on your lips and in your heart (that is, the word of faith which we preach)." Hence the righteousness of faith is present here and now. It has come through Christ. Paul makes the Old Testament promise of righteousness to (and through) the one who fulfilled the law refer to Christ. In the light of the gospel he sees a deeper meaning in the Old Testament text, a reference to the coming of righteousness through Christ. The commandment, which according to Deut. 30:11ff. was not too far off nor too difficult to hear and do, is interpreted as referring to the word about Christ. The Old Testament commandment, which had been interpreted so as to lead to righteousness by works, had in reality a deeper meaning and was concerned with Christ. What men had sought for in vain through righteousness based on the law was fulfilled and completed in righteousness by faith. In Rom. 10:5 Paul can say therefore that according to the righteousness of the law life is to be given to the one who *does* the demands of the law, because the word about the fulfilment of the law had reference to Christ as the *telos* of the law. The fulfilment of the law was not at hand before Christ (cf. Rom. 9:32ff.). In and through Christ had come the commandment (*he entole* [Deut. 30:11]) which was near, and through which the fulfilment of the requirements of the law, its *dikaioma* (Rom. 8:4), was secured. When Christ came, the time of righteousness in which the commandments were to be fulfilled in their deepest meaning was no longer in the future. The day of righteousness had now come. The righteousness of faith imparted precisely the righteousness of which the law spoke. In Christ the perfect content of the law and its fulfilment in life were fused into a unity. The law was no longer an external rule for life, It was now written in the heart as Jeremiah had prophesied about the new covenant. The completion and the fulfilment of the law were included in the righteousness of Christ. Faith meant living in Christ. Good works were no longer achievements of men of which they could boast, but works prepared beforehand by God in which the Christians should walk (Eph. 2:9ff.).

In order to understand the content of the important passage in Gal. 3:10-12 it appeared necessary to compare it to Rom. 10:5 and its context (Rom. 9:30—10:8). We thereby also elucidate one aspect of Paul's conception of the righteousness proclaimed in the Old Testament which otherwise is easily overlooked. What causes the difficulty in Rom. 10:5 is that the righteousness which receives its fulfilment in and through Christ is called *he dikaiosune he ek nomou,* an expression otherwise used to designate the righteousness based on the law. If dogmatically we place the righteousness by the law side by side with the righteousness of which the law speaks, and which was fulfilled in Christ, and assume that these concepts are consistently designated by two different terms, it would be difficult to maintain our interpretation. But Paul does not express himself in logically defined terms, and the concepts he is dealing with are of such vital character that such logical consistency is hardly possible.

In the previous section righteousness of the law and righteousness of faith have been sharply contrasted. The other meanings of the law will be discussed further, as for example in the interpretation of 3:20. The contrast between the law and the righteousness by the law will be further elucidated in that context.

If we therefore posit an antithesis between the righteousness of faith, which permits God's essential will and the whole majesty of the law to appear, and the rigtheousness based on the law, in which man makes the law his servant and a means to obtain his own righteousness, we must not fail to observe that even the righteousness based on the law may in one sense have its origin in the requirements of the law. Just because before Christ came these requirements lacked the elucidation given through him, they could be interpreted in such a way that they became servants of sin. The glory of the law was as the shadow of the coming glory; it was a revelation which became fully clear only when it was superseded and illumined by the higher and more perfect revelation in Christ, who unveiled the innermost and hidden will of the whole law.

It is only through Christ that the law appears as Spirit and no longer as a written code (cf. II Cor. 3:6). We can understand, therefore, how Paul in Rom. 10:5 can speak about the righteousness of the law as something which only now could be rightly interpreted and realized. Rightly understood this righteousness, which the law demanded, and which the Jews in their ignorant zeal had understood as a righteousness based on law and obtainable through an external conformity to the statutes, means a fulfilment made possible because the law is written in man's heart, and man is therefore *one* with the law. Such a fulfilment became a reality only through Christ who is the Righteous One, and who need not fulfil the law in order to become righteous. By faith in him the righteousness demanded by the law became a present reality, because the word about him was no longer far off but present in heart and mouth.

In a purely formal sense the righteousness about which the law speaks can also be designated as "a righteousness of the law," even though this phrase is usually reserved for the false interpretation of the words of the law concerning righteousness. The righteousness demanded by the law drove the Jews to seek righteousness. But according to Paul they went the wrong way and sought for a false goal, because they did not understand the righteousness from God. But it was nevertheless the words of the law about righteousness that drove them on in their search.

We may say that in this passage in Romans Paul endeavors to see the positive element in the activity of the Jews (cf. 10:2). As long as their attitude was one of search and struggle, their contact with the truth of the law was not entirely broken. But by their presumptuous self-righteousness and especially by their rejection of the gospel and faith their zeal for the righteousness based on the law came in conflict with the majesty of the law as rightly understood, and prevented a true and faithful submission to the law. Just as the Gentiles rejected the law, so also did the Jews because of their bondage to the righteousness by the law and their opposition to its real meaning. Consequently they became just like the Gentiles whom they despised because they did not know the law.

Righteousness of faith and righteousness by the law may often be described as standing in conflict with one another. But even though this description is correct, they are not really on a par as independent entities, because the righteousness of the law is a perversion of the true law. Even though erroneous it receives its power from the true law. Paul can therefore use the term "law" even when the context indicates that he means the false use of the law and of its statutes to obtain righteousness. *It is really the same law—statutes and ceremonies—which rightly understood and faithfully accepted constituted a preparation for and a shadow of what was to come, and which in the service of sin became legalism and bondage under powers hostile to God.* If this is kept clearly in mind, it is easy to understand how the terminology may vary and how impossible it is to determine the meaning of a certain term without a thorough investigation of the context in which the word occurs.

In this connection we may refer also to the phrase, "the law of the Spirit of life," in Rom. 8:2. If we were to judge Paul by means of hard and fast terminology, the word "law" in this passage would be difficult to understand. In reality he is talking about the gospel, because the law in question is "Spirit and life" (cf. John 6:63). The term "law" may indeed designate the way to righteousness. The law of Moses in its external form was regarded by the Jews as a way of righteousness and freedom for the people. To them the law of Sinai was comparable to the redemption out of Egypt, a complement of that event and a fulfilment of God's promise to Abraham. God's election appeared in the law. As Paul had come to realize that the law of Moses in this external sense had been meant in the economy of salvation to condemn, destroy, and keep under restraint until the coming of redemption, he could call this realization of salvation through Christ a law which sets men free from the law of sin and death. Christ *was* the new law at the same time that he was the victor over the law. He came with that righteousness which the law of Moses bore witness to and served, but which it could not produce in this world of sin. Paul's presentation is perfectly clear in principle, but there is a shift in the meaning of his terms. Since this is the case the interpretation of "the righteousness of the law" in Rom. 10:5 cannot be confined to one fixed meaning (the righteousness based on law), but the context must also be taken in consideration. "The righteousness of the law" may mean the righteousness based on works of the law, but in this passage where he quotes Scripture he is not concerned with this righteousness in itself but with what Scripture says about it. And according to Paul Scripture never proclaims a righteousness on the basis of law. He quotes the words which by a false interpretation

may be made to support this legalistic righteousness. He can therefore ask: what does Scripture say about the righteousness of the law?
He answers: Scripture says (about righteousness from the law) that
righteousness appears in *the fulfilment*. But this fulfilment is connected
with Christ and faith. The righteousness of the law as the Jews understood it has therefore no support in Scripture. Scripture says about
the righteousness which comes from the law that it is a righteousness
which gives life when it is *fulfilled*. But this took place in Christ. Paul
proclaims faith in his fulfilment, and the word of faith is "on your
lips and in your heart." It is no longer only a promise of a future
salvation; it is now present in faith.

4. The curse Christ assumes prepares the way for the blessing which comes upon the Gentiles also (3:13-14)

On the basis of the interpretation suggested above the connection between vs. 12 and vs. 13 becomes quite natural: "Christ
redeemed us from the curse of the law." The law with its statutes
established a curse. It revealed that man is not his own master,
and it demanded obedience although it did not provide righteousness. Not *everything* in the book of the law was done by the mere
observance of the statutes. These statutes did not bestow righteousness; they revealed rather that man stands under judgment
and is subject to death. Righteousness and life cannot come
through the observance of limited and specific commandments.
Christ redeemed from the curse; he redeemed unto participation
in this freedom from the law and from its curse. Positively stated,
both Jews and Gentiles were invited through the gospel to participation in the blessing.

Paul's words in vs. 10 about the curse of the law are continued
in vs. 13 with a reference to the fact that Christ had become a
curse for us, and the words in vs. 12b concerning the promise
of life to those who do the law are continued in vs. 14 with a
reference to the promise of the Spirit. Thus the righteousness
spoken of in vs. 11 is given, and thereby the real fulfilment of
the law takes place. We may compare Gal. 3:13-14 with Rom.
8:3-4. After the reference to the work of Christ in Rom. 8:3
Paul emphasizes in vs. 4 how the just requirements of the law
are fulfilled in those who walk according to the Spirit. We must
also note that in Gal. 3:2ff. Paul referred to the Spirit given to
the Galatians when they received the gospel in faith. In vs. 14 the
final goal of Christ's redemption from the curse of the law is the

reception of the Spirit. The Spirit had been given to the Galatians
because Christ had taken the curse of the law upon himself. If they
were to return to the way of righteousness by the law, they would
be like redeemed slaves who had so little appreciation of their
freedom that they thought of bondage as real happiness.

We have been redeemed from the curse of the law by Christ,
says Paul. Through him the promised righteousness came. But
the relationship between the sovereignty of the law and the new
creation in Christ was not so uncomplicated that the new simply
replaced the old. In the old aeon the law represented God's will.
The law was of God, good, holy, and just. Since its demands are
God's demands, they must in some way be realized. Its curse
represented something which could not simply be set aside. Since
men had fallen short of the glory of God (Rom. 3:23; cf. Rom.
3:9ff.), the whole world was held accountable to him (Rom.
3:19).

The expression "become a curse" rather than "be cursed" be-
trays the influence of Hebrew usage. Paul evidently intends to
say that Christ became so heavily cursed and so deeply sinful
that *all* curse and sin were laid upon him. In this passage Paul
refers to the subject only in passing. In Rom. 3:24ff.; 4:25; 5:6ff.,
11; 8:32; I Cor. 15:3, and especially in the important passage
in II Cor. 5:20ff., Paul deals again with these and related ideas.

Paul held that the law came because of transgressions (Gal.
3:19). It was not a guide to right living, nor was it, as the rabbis
thought, a light on the way of righteousness. It involved an accusation and a condemnation of sin. Since it had not been given as
a guide to right living but for the purpose of revealing the sin
which held everyone in bondage, the right obedience to the law
was to acknowledge its accusations and submit to its judgment.

But man, entangled in the power of sin, could not acknowledge
the law and submit to its judgment, but was rather driven deeper
into sin. The fact is that he sought to make the law itself a means
of obtaining his own righteousness. Thus the way of righteousness
by the law really involves disobedience to the law. The attitude
of righteousness by the law was the opposite of faith in God who
through the law subjected man to condemnation and through the
promise provided a hope of righteousness.

When Christ came he was, like other men, placed under the
law (Gal. 4:4), under its accusation and judgment. The law applied primarily to the people of Israel, but to Paul the people

represented all men, since all have sinned and fall short of the glory of God (Rom. 3:23; cf. Rom. 3:9). Christ's fulfilment of the law meant that he fully accepted its judgment. He did so in his crucifixion. His fulfilment of the law was therefore connected with his crucifixion. On the cross he submitted completely to the law's condemnation of sinful man, and thus he fulfilled the law and its demands. He identified himself with men in their state of being accused by the law. He did not seek his own righteousness and an escape from the judgment, as the Jews did who in this respect represented all humanity. Instead he accepted the judgment. The fact that he did not seek to avoid the condemnation of the law resting on all humanity revealed that he was righteous. The law's condemnation of him was a judgment which did not apply to him personally, but which came to him because of his identification with those who lived under the power of sin. Because of his love for those who did not submit to the condemnation of the law, but by the power of sin were driven to answer the law's accusation by seeking to make themselves righteous and thus sank deeper into sin, Christ accepted the judgment and thus fulfilled the demands of the law. Through his act the purpose of the law was fulfilled and righteousness attained. Thus the law was fulfilled through the crucifixion. Christ submitted truly to the law's condemnation of sin. The paradox is that the judgment of the law could truly be received only by the One who was not in bondage to sin, and who personally was free from condemnation. The law could be completely fulfilled only when the One wholly righteous vicariously took its judgment upon himself. Only in this way could there be life, because life was promised to the one who kept the law. Christ alone fulfilled the law, and he did so with finality in and through his crucifixion. He who represented God's own righteousness submitted to the righteous words of the law in its condemnation of sin. He did this in the love included in righteousness.

In his earlier days Paul had looked upon the cross of Christ as a proof that Jesus and his disciples were enemies of God. After his Damascus experience the cross represented the curse which God's Son, the Suffering Servant of the Lord, took upon himself and carried on behalf of others. Here in Gal. 3:13 Paul uses the words in Deut. 21:23 to indicate that the cross really was associated with a curse. In II Cor. 5:21 he points out how God reconciled the world to himself through Christ and "made him to be sin who knew no sin, so that in him we might become the righteousness of God."

According to God's plan of salvation the Gentiles participated in salvation as a result of the work of Christ. When the curse was removed, a way was prepared for that blessing which was intended for all peoples. The crucifixion of Christ did not mean simply that he was rejected and executed by the Jews. It was really *God's* curse. It meant that God's law really condemned him, and, since the law was holy, it exercised its function by God's direction. But this judgment was illumined through Scripture. The judgment was directed against the sins Christ took upon himself when he identified himself with those in bondage under sin. He took the judgment upon himself as the Suffering Servant. The significance of the act of Christ, therefore, was far beyond mere instruction about God's love or an indication to men how they were to keep the law. His encounter with the condemnation of the law had cosmic dimensions. It was God himself who permitted this to happen, and who through Christ redeemed men from the curse which otherwise rested upon them. The curse and the judgment must fulfil their task. But in Christ God himself took the curse and the judgment upon himself.

The Law and the Prophets had borne witness to the righteousness which in this way became available (Rom. 3:21). It was not a righteousness which could be attained through the observance of the law. Through the redemption from death, sin, and the condemnation of the law which Christ accomplished he gave righteousness and life to those who were subject to death, sin, and judgment. He was "put forward" as the ark of the covenant in the Old Testament (Rom. 3:25). On the great Day of Atonement in the old covenant the high priest performed the act of cleansing by sprinkling blood on "the mercy-seat." The sacrifices were a remembrance of sin (Heb. 10:3). Now through the blood of Christ a complete atonement for all sin had been made (cf. Lev. 16:13ff.; Heb. 10:1-22). Through the blood of Christ shed on the cross the new covenant prophesied by Jeremiah had been established (Jer. 31:31ff.; Heb. 10:16ff.). These ideas were familiar to those who had heard Paul and his associates proclaim Christ. They were accustomed to the ideas of the Old Testament, and these were interpreted and applied as referring to Christ as the Messiah and the Suffering Servant. This made it possible for Paul to indicate very briefly the significance of the atonement of Christ by the quotation from Deut. 21:23, and to be understood in spite of his brevity (cf. Anders Nygren, *Commentary on Romans,* trans. Carl C. Rasmussen [Philadelphia: Muhlenberg, 1949], pp. 156-62).

When Christ took the curse upon himself, the blessing of Abraham was given also to the Gentiles. When Christ was crucified, he took upon himself the guilt of "the many" (Rom. 5:15-19), i.e., of all men, both of Jews and Gentiles. Thus he made them *one,* and broke down the wall of partition in that by one act he reconciled all to God (cf. Eph. 2:11-18). In and through his blood he brought all together into *one,* because he delivered everyone from the powers that had held them captive: sin, death, and law. He made all to be *one* in himself. The curse had rested also on the Gentiles. They were all under sin (Rom. 3:9, 19, 23). But the curse became revealed precisely to that people to whom the law had been given. They were under the law, but they were unable to distinguish between the real demands of the law and the works of the law. Christ opened a way to freedom from condemnation, from the curse, and from the attempt to find life through the works of the law. Both the curse of the law and the illusion that life could be secured by the observance of the law were evidences of their bondage under the law. When Israel was set free, this act had a universal significance. The redemption came to mean freedom for *all* people, even for the Gentiles. The positive side of this act was a blessing, a revelation of a righteousness which was not dependent on works of the law. In his plan of salvation God took the curse into his service. When Christ redeemed men from the curse, his act became valid for all men, because all were subject under some law and were therefore essentially under judgment, since no one had attained to righteousness.

According to Paul, when the curse of the law was laid upon him who as the Messiah represented the promised blessing, this condemning power of the curse was abolished. In Christ it was changed into a blessing. Through the abrogation of the curse of the law, which took place when Christ took the curse upon himself, the real purpose of the law became clear. It had had the task of accusing, condemning, and keeping under restraint until the coming of Christ. It was a *paidagogos,* a custodian, until Christ came. Thereby also it became clear that the commandments of the law were perverted when they were used as a means of obtaining righteousness. In that case the commandments separated the Jews from the Gentiles.

In Col. 2:14 Paul says that Christ has "canceled the bond which stood against us with its legal demands . . . nailing it to the cross." When this accusing power was removed, those powers which had obtained their dominion under the pressure of guilt were robbed of their authority. When Christ took upon himself the just accusation of the law against men's sin, he also "disarmed the principalities and powers" (Col. 2:15). Israel's righteousness of the law, into which they had been enticed under the accusations of the law, meant to Paul not only a subjective mistake in the interpretation of the law, but also that Israel had entered the service of "the elemental spirits of the universe" (cf. Gal. 4:3, 8ff.; Col. 2:8, 20). Christ redeemed men from bondage under the law. The law was indeed given by God, but it had become a servant of sin. The real task of the law was to pronounce judgment. But through the act of Christ this judgment was changed into a blessing, just as the death of Christ on the cross was transformed into life in the resurrection.

The curse which Christ took upon himself was of course primarily the curse of the law on *Israel.* Instead of letting the righteousness to which the law really bore witness judge the people and bring them to faith in Christ, Israel had changed the law into a means of justification. The Gentiles of course served gods who by nature were no gods, and they had a share in the perversion of faith in the true God into law-righteousness (cf. Rom. 2:14; 1:18ff.). It was the task of the law to make sin appear as transgressions and to condemn them. Everyone was subject to this condemnation until Christ redeemed him by taking the curse upon himself and fulfilling what had been said about the Suffering Servant of the Lord. Now both Gentiles and Jews were invited to faith in this act. A similar thought is expressed in I Peter: "He himself bore our sins in his body on the tree, that we might die to sin and live to righteousness. By his wounds you have been healed" (I Pet. 2:24, with an allusion to Isa. 53:2).

In vs. 14 Paul placed Christ's act of reconciliation in the context of his conception of God's plan of salvation according to which the gospel is to be brought to the Gentiles. It is clear from Romans 9-11 that Paul brooded over the fact that the Jews had rejected their Messiah who is also the world's Lord. He finds an explanation, however, in God's hidden plan of salvation, which Scripture if it is rightly understood illuminates (cf. the scriptural quotations in Rom. 9:25ff., 33; 10:16-21). God's ways are inscrutable to men's mind (Rom. 11:33). He also incorporated the hardening of Israel into his plan of salvation. But after the salvation of the Gentiles Israel, too, will participate in that salvation and righteousness which they themselves had failed to attain because of their mistaken zeal and their persistent adherence to righteousness by the law (Rom. 10:2ff.). Their sin of self-righteousness was brought to its climax by their rejection of Christ who represented the promised righteousness himself.

But because Christ vicariously took upon himself all sin and
became a curse, "he made him to be sin who knew no sin"
(II Cor. 5:21), Israel was redeemed from the irrevocable curse
of the law. Israel's rejection of the righteousness in Christ had
revealed clearly that their legalism had brought them to an im-
penitent hardness of heart. But this very fact became a means of
bringing the gospel to the Gentiles, and the gospel could now be
proclaimed as being intended also for them. Now the curse that
rested on them, too, was removed, now Israel was redeemed from
the curse of the law, and now the blessing promised to Abraham
could be available also for the Gentiles. Finally Israel itself, pro-
voked to jealousy (Rom. 10:19; 11:11), would be brought to
faith and the new age would come.

It is evident that Paul's presentation of his conception of God's
plan of salvation in Gal. 3:13 is intended as a complete refutation of the error into which the Galatians had fallen. That the
Gentile Christians should accept circumcision and law in order
to make certain of their righteousness appeared on the basis of
Paul's presentation as a denial of the faith. It meant that they
accepted that conception of the law and became servants of that
evil power through which Christ had been rejected. By so doing
the Galatians refused to accept the fact that Christ had taken
the curse upon himself in behalf of man. In addition their action
involved a rejection of God's plan of salvation, in and through
which Israel was to attain salvation and come to faith through
the acceptance of the gospel by the Gentiles—and also by the
Galatians. Thus they eliminated themselves from participation
in God's redemptive work and became its enemies. From this
point of view we can easily understand Paul's passionate words
to the Galatians (e.g., Gal. 1:6; 3:1ff.; 4:19ff.; 5:2, 7ff.) and
his bitterness against the seducers (1:8ff.; 5:12; 6:12ff.).

The new people of God who succeeded the people of the circumcision had baptism as their distinctive mark, as Paul says later in
vs. 27. Through baptism they were incorporated into the death and
resurrection of Jesus. Baptism meant that the Christian through the
cross of Christ had been delivered from the powers of this age, which
also included the law. The Christian had died to all of this through
Christ. The law had therefore no authority to condemn him. Those
who were baptized into Christ were baptized into his death (Rom.
6:3ff.). He who was baptized lived in the new life of the Spirit. For
him there was no condemnation (Rom. 8:1). Through the crucifixion
of Christ God fulfilled the promise of righteousness, and prepared
a way of righteousness for the world in bondage under the curse. The

crucifixion could not therefore be viewed as the martyrdom of a holy man, or as a final heroic act of a great prophet. Only the crucifixion of *Christ* could mean that through him life and righteousness came to all men. Only *he* who was righteous could fulfil the law and rescind the judgment resting on humanity. Only Christ's voluntary death on the cross and God's judgment involved in this act could effect a complete fulfilment of the law. According to Paul, the same is true of the resurrection of Christ. He was not an individual man who escaped death. He was the Son of God who brought in the victory of life and righteousness (Rom. 8:1; I Cor. 15:17, 26, 56).

We must note carefully that Paul did not understand the crucifixion chiefly as a physical martyrdom. Its real meaning was that the whole curse of the law was laid upon Christ; a curse which in the deepest sense excluded him from the communion of the chosen people and the law. The Letter to the Hebrews expresses the words of Paul in 3:13 differently when it points out that Christ suffered "outside the gate" (Heb. 13:11ff.), just as according to the law of Moses everything from the animals that was unclean should be burnt as a sin offering outside the camp (Exod. 29:14; Lev. 4:11, 21; 16:27). This signified that the curse and condemnation of the law was present, and the crucifixion meant that Christ took the curse upon himself.

According to the New Testament conception of the suffering, death, and resurrection of Jesus it was the righteous who was made sin, the holy One who was brought out to the place of all uncleanness, and the One who came with the promised blessing was placed under a curse. On this account his work had a reconciling effect. And therefore the connection between the crucifixion and the resurrection becomes evident; both belong together in God's act with and through Christ, and both are on the same level. Both are physical and consist in something that has happened here on earth at a definite time and place; but the real significance of each extends beyond the physical and historical sphere. As the power of death was gathered together and vanquished at the cross, the whole power of life was made manifest in the resurrection. Death belonged with sin and signified condemnation, while life belonged together with righteousness. In the resurrection life there appeared the victory not only over physical death but also over eternal death. And the resurrection life was eternal life, created by the God who made the world. Thus in the resurrection of Christ the guilt was removed and the eternal life of righteousness which belonged to the promised age appeared.

Even in the ancient church the words in vs. 13, that Christ had set us free from the curse of the law, had been developed into a theology of reconciliation or redemption. Redemption is a figure setting forth the fact that by taking upon himself the curse of the law (and of God) Christ created a new channel for God's forgiveness and love to men. This act demanded the greatest of all sacrifices. He had to take upon himself the whole curse of the law. Later this was interpreted as the price Christ had to pay for the redemption. The thought Paul presents here was emphasized and sometimes interpreted in a rather superficial sense in the ancient church. The question was asked whether the price had been paid to God or to the devil. Paul never asked to whom the price was paid, whether to God or to the devil. That question goes beyond the scope of the figure and presupposes a less complicated conception of evil than that of Paul. But according to Paul redemption is from the curse of *the law,* and in the idea of the law there is a certain tension. The law stands in the service of God, but in this world it has also been taken into the service of evil. Later, when his figure was used to express more than he had intended, and the metaphor became a rational theory, the question arose as to whether the price had been paid to God or to the devil.

Redemption itself is a figure taken from the liberation of prisoners of war and of slaves in the ancient world (cf. also below the exposition of 4:5). The redemption Paul speaks of here is redemption from the curse of the law. Life under the law may therefore be likened to bondage under an alien and hostile power. Since the commandments of the law stand in the service of sin, they can only lead, as we have said, not to righteousness and life but to death. Thus all of life under the law is a life subject to the power of death.

We must observe that the participation of the Gentiles in the blessing given to Abraham belonged among the events connected with the fulfilment of the promise. This was a promise about a future righteousness. The reception of this righteousness took place in faith, and faith was thus a constitutive factor in the new covenant. To hesitate now about the fulfilment of the promise and to demand circumcision as a condition on which the Gentiles might be received into membership in the Christian congregation would, according to Paul, involve a failure to recognize the present eschatological reality. This new reality meant that the Gentiles were to be received into fellowship with the Jewish Christians, and that the blessing of Abraham belonged also to the Gentile Christians.

B. *The promise and the law* (3:15-25)

1. The law did not annul the promise; the promise had reference to the "offspring" (3:15-18)

In vs. 15ff. Paul indicates the place of the law in reference to the promise. He points out here that according to Scripture the law cannot be the principle elucidating the way and conditions of salvation.

To Paul the law agrees with and serves the promise. In vs. 21 he categorically denies that the law could be understood as contrary to God's promise. But the law cannot bestow righteousness. The law was given because man had transgressed God's will and his purpose with man's creation. The purpose of the law was to make this situation clear, but it was not meant to atone for the transgression, nor was it to bestow that righteousness which man lacked.

The law had been given its task by God. It was a part of his plan of salvation. It could not therefore be arbitrarily set aside by men. There was no hostile antithesis between promise and law. Both were parts of God's work of salvation. They act together in this work. All modern attempts to interpret Paul as being dependent on Gnostic conceptions, making the law something of a lower or even evil power, are doomed to failure. As we shall try to show later, the meaning in vs. 19 is evidently that the law was given by God. This is emphasized further in vss. 21-24.

Sinful man, therefore, does not attain to life and righteousness through the law. To use the law in that sense was to make the promise void. When man does so, he has begun in the name of the law given by God to serve a false law and thereby also a false god. Sin, making the law its servant, drives man to this false conception of and false relation to the law. By his attempts to be justified by the law man increases his sin and comes more thoroughly under the curse of the law. He is driven still further into that state which the law in accordance with God's will must condemn. Law-righteousness is a typical designation for sin. When the law becomes law-righteousness, the result is an absolute antithesis between promise and law. But this is a denial of the words of Scripture. Then, according to Paul, even the law is denied, because the law bears witness to the right relation to God, even though it does not have the power itself to establish that relationship. If the law is rightly understood, there can be no contradiction in principle between law and promise.

The purpose and meaning of the law therefore could not have been to make void what had been promised, or to add conditions on which it was to be received. Paul elucidates this by reference to the status of a will and to the contemporary legal practices familiar to the Galatians. No one, he says, annuls even a man's will once it has been ratified. Much less then can that testament or new covenant be annulled which God established by his promise to Abraham. The Greek word *diatheke* means both testament and covenant. God made a covenant through a promise, and the promise was fulfilled when the announced blessing became a reality. When this happened in Christ, God's promise to Abraham was realized as a new covenant, in which the righteousness of God was found. That righteousness can become a reality on earth depends on the fact, therefore, that now God bestows this righteousness in and through his presence in Christ. Man may receive righteousness and blessedness as an inheritance given to him through a testament (promise). The law can never be rightly understood if it is assumed that it should annul or invalidate the promise. If the blessing were to be attained through observance of the law, or if this observance were a condition for sharing in it, then it is no longer a question of an inheritance. Now, if receiving the inheritance should be made to depend on observance of the law, the promise would have been annulled later and the content of the promise treated as something man must procure for himself. Then also the will on which the inheritance was based would have been annulled. But this would be manifestly impossible. Consequently to talk about the observance of the law as a basis for righteousness was preposterous.

The words in Rom. 11:29, "For the gifts and the call of God are irrevocable," may be thought of as elucidating this conception of a will. God's election is the basis of his attitude. In human practice a man's will becomes valid upon his death. God's election and his promise are just as firmly established as is a man's will after it has been ratified. But God would have nullified his own election if the law had been added as a condition for obtaining grace. This was not the intention, and the law must not be so understood. The Jews thought they could read something like that into the law because they saw it in a false light. They changed the real meaning of the law and came under the power of law-righteousness. But God was *one;* and although his revelation in the law did not have "the same glory" as the revelation in Christ, he was nevertheless the same. He gave the promise, and he gave the law to Moses as an accuser and guardian of the people. Then later he fulfilled the promise in Christ. The call and election of God are irrevocable. If they thought law-righteousness was a condition for participation in the fulfilment of the promise in Christ, they would *not* see salvation in Christ as the fulfilment of a promise or the presentation of an inheritance. Instead they would nullify the promise and the will.

What Paul wants to make clear by his use of the figure of a will is that the real purpose and task of the law could not have been to add conditions which would permit only those who fulfilled them to obtain a share in the blessing. He makes this plain by pointing out that the law of Moses was given long after the promise had been given to Abraham. It could not therefore change the stipulations which had once been established. Paul follows a tradition stating that the law had come 430 years after the covenant with Abraham (cf. Exod. 12:40; the Hebrew text says this was *the time spent* in Egypt). His main concern was to show that the law could not be interpreted in such a way as to nullify the promise. Righteousness was tied to that act of God which, according to the promise to Abraham, was someday to bring life. This act had now been fulfilled in and through the coming of Christ. It was preposterous, therefore, to attempt to base the relation to Christ on the law as the Judaizers did.

The Jewish righteousness of the law had been supported by a metaphysical speculation about the existence of the law prior to creation. But here in the Letter to the Galatians the law becomes a later element in the history of salvation. Here he says that the law was given later than the promise, and in vs. 19, that it was added afterwards. Since it was added in this way, it could not have the power to annul what had earlier been established as valid. According to contemporary thought the older and the earlier word had primary validity. The law, says Paul, must not be so interpreted that it comes into conflict with the promise.

According to a rabbinical tradition Abraham knew the law and was justified by his obedience to it. But according to Paul Abraham was justified through faith in God's Word and promise, in which a coming blessing was promised. If the law was understood as the basis of justification and was given an eternal validity, it would not retain the place God had given it. This would be to nullify the promise and to abrogate the Word of God and the authoritative statements of Scripture. The law had to be seen as a stage in God's redemptive activity. In principle it belonged in the time between the giving of the promise and its fulfilment.

It has often been assumed that Paul wanted to depreciate
and undervalue the law, but this is an inadequate conception
of his thought. When the Jews made the law a metaphysical
principle and an entity which was prior to creation and was to
remain forever, it would seem that they gave it a very prominent
place. But Paul would say that in so doing they greatly dishonored
the law. They did not permit it to be what God had intended it
to be: an instrument for use in the plan of salvation fulfilled in
Christ. Instead they made it an instrument in the hands of man
for obtaining his own righteousness rather than God's instrument
in his work with men. They made the law into an idol which
they worshiped in the interest of their own righteousness. In
reality the law came to occupy a place beside God, so that, as
Paul understood it, God was no longer the only God. If according
to the Jewish point of view this was intended to exalt the law,
to Paul it meant a dishonoring of the law. But when Paul fought
against law-righteousness, he upheld the validity of the law
and rendered it true honor as the word and law of *God*.

According to Paul, therefore, the law could not have been
meant to nullify or curtail the promise once given. The Galatians
had now become participants in the fulfilment of the promise
and in the blessing. If they misunderstood and misused the law,
they would destroy what they possessed and bring to nought that
in which they were supposed to live in gratitude to God. Their
own participation in the blessing was dependent upon their receiving that blessing in faith, not by their attempts to keep the
law. The Spirit had been given to the Galatians. In vss. 3 and
5 Paul asked them whether they had received the Spirit by works
of the law or by hearing of faith, and thus had reminded them
that they had received the Spirit in faith. Therefore the blessing is
likened to an inheritance which has now become available. It
had come in Christ, and it had been given to that new people of
God whose Lord was Christ.

Paul emphasizes here both that the inheritance from the beginning was based altogether on grace and election (a disposition
of a will), and that the reception and use of the inheritance cannot
be tied together with observance of the law. Now since the new
people of God have received this inheritance, they should take
possession of it and not begin to doubt or to claim that they had
made themselves deserving of the content of the inheritance. In
that case they would lose the inheritance, since it was not given

on the basis of human merit. If anyone had been given the inheritance, it was given according to the stipulations of the will, not according to what he had deserved. The very principle on which the will was based was nullified by the reference to merits. If the law is to be rightly understood, it must be clear that its intention was never in any sense to *limit or change* what God had promised later to give. Thereby it became clear that the law was not intended as a condition which had to be met if the promise was to be fulfilled. If man now assumed salvation and righteousness came through observance of the law, he would not be worshiping the God of righteousness and election. Instead of receiving God's gifts in faith man would create and cherish other values to trust in. But what he thus cherished and made his god was ultimately his own self-righteousness. The attitude of faith was trust in the promise; but he who relied on his observance of the law denied the promise and rejected faith. If those who were of the law (i.e., lived in law-righteousness) were to be heirs, "faith is null and the promise is void" (Rom. 4:14).

The contrast in vs. 16 between the singular, "your offspring," and the plural, which might be translated "your descendants," appears as such a piece of casuistry as might be expected in rabbinical interpretations of Scripture. In a formal sense his exegesis here is rabbinical. It seems like an absurdity since "offspring" (seed) is a collective noun. But just as Paul in chap. 4 gives a deeper meaning to the narrative of Abraham's two wives, so he imparts a hidden meaning to this passage, a reference to Christ. In the allegory in chap. 4 there is a profound idea hidden behind the peculiar speculation as also in this passage.

Not the many who kept the law and boasted of being children of Abraham were bearers of God's redemption, but only a small remnant, and ultimately Christ alone. (Cf. Rom. 9:6-7, where Paul adopts the idea of Isaiah that only a remnant will be saved.) Christ was the offspring to whom the blessing should be given; and that this was the meaning of the scriptural word was clear from the fact that "offspring" was singular. According to Paul the physical descent did not insure real unity, and the observance of the law produced disunity, since it caused distinctions between the members of the people of the law in regard to the degree of their obedience. It also separated this people from the Gentiles. Faith, on the contrary, united all into one in that all became members of the body of Christ. That the faithful shared in the promise did not contradict the fact that the promise was intended for only *one,* Christ.

Behind the thought that the offspring was *one* stood the faith in God's creative act as constitutive for the reality of salvation. While the Jews trusted in physical descent and made this complex of ideas the constitutive element for salvation, Abraham had, according to Paul, put his trust in that God "who gives life to the dead and calls into existence the things that do not exist" (Rom. 4:17). The children of the promise, therefore, were those who were united by faith to the one God. In contrasting in chap. 4 the children of Abraham by the slave woman, who were according to the flesh, with the children of promise, who were prefigured in Sarah's son according to the promise, Paul refers to Isa. 54:1, where faith that God creates descendants stands in contrast to the idea of physical descent. God is the source and origin of life and salvation. His creative activity inaugurated a history which indicated the meaning of events and continually discouraged the tendency to worship natural sequences as something divine. (Cf. how Abraham was praised for his faith even though there seemed to be no hope [Rom. 4:18ff.].) The Jews relied on their physical descent from Abraham and on the observance of the law by those who were circumcised. The rabbis combined the conception of the promise to Abraham with the idea of observance of the law as the basis of salvation in such a way that the promise was said to have been fulfilled in the giving of the law at Sinai. The thought of justification by works of the law and the claim to glory through physical descent from Abraham thus went hand in hand. In opposition to these claims Paul maintains that God creates a reality contrary to all human expectations, that he lets the desolate have "more children than she who hath a husband" (Gal. 4:27, quoting Isa. 54:1), and that righteousness comes through God's own intervention in history whereby he reveals the fulfilment of the promise. These thoughts are based on the same fundamental point of view: God creates righteousness and salvation, and these become actual and available to men through concrete events such as the birth, life, death, and resurrection of Christ.

The contrast between *many* and *one* recurs in vs. 20, where Moses stands as a representative of the many while God, the One, has appeared in the one Jesus Christ and has removed the conflict between himself and men.

2. The relationship of the law to sin and righteousness (3:19-22)

a) The law was added because of transgressions (3:19a)

After Paul had emphatically demonstrated in vss. 15-18 that the law could not be interpreted as being in competition with the promise or as nullifying it, the question would quite naturally arise, "Why then the law?" Since the law was not given as a means of justification (this according to Paul involved a denial of God), what was its positive purpose? Why had it been given? In what relationship did it stand to the promise? These are the questions that Paul intends to answer in vss. 19ff. In the previous discussion we have already touched on Paul's view of these problems. It is, we might say, that the law had not been given in order to bestow righteousness, but had been added in order to brand sin as transgression against the will of God.

When in Rom. 4:14ff. Paul takes up again the ideas he has presented here, he emphasizes primarily that the blessing of Abraham was now available to all who receive it in faith. But if keeping of the law were to become a basis for the blessing, the promise (and thereby also the whole of Scripture) would be of no effect. The real function of the law is connected with God's judgment of wrath. It makes man a guilty transgressor. It reveals the nature of sin as guilt.

According to the Jewish conception God made the law great and marvelous because he wanted to manifest his grace to Israel. But Paul wants to show that the law was added after the word of the promise, and that it was added because of sin. Scripture had not given the function and the place to the law which Jewish interpretation had given it. If that interpretation were followed, the law would, contrary to the witness of Scripture, become a god beside God. But God had added the law, not in order that Israel might boast of being righteous by means of the law, but in order to reveal sin and transgression more clearly, and in order to let Israel know more thoroughly than others the truth and the seriousness of God's demands for full and complete righteousness and the gravity of the guilt incurred by sin (cf. also Amos 3:2).

Sin existed prior to the law (Rom. 5:13). Death, which is the sign of this world of sin, also ruled before the law of Moses. But the law came in "to increase the trespass" (Rom. 5:20). The

law had its definite task and time. For those who lived in the
new life of the Spirit (Rom. 7:6) it had ceased to be a condemning law, because they had died with Christ. The law was to be
valid until the "offspring" should come. When Christ came, faith
as a mature faith became possible. It was a faith not merely in
the future fulfilment of the promise, but a faith that lived by the
fulfilled promise and embraced him through whom the promise
was fulfilled. To believe meant for Paul that Christ lived in the
believer and the believer in Christ. The promise pointed to Christ,
and he was the one who redeemed it.

The statement that "the law was added" emphasizes that, contrary to the claim sometimes made by the rabbis, the law did
not exist before the creation of the world. The Mosaic law was
not a part of God's original creation, and it was not a complete
expression of God's nature. It had been added for a definite
purpose, which is indicated in the words, "for the sake of transgressions." In Rom. 5:20 we read: "Law came in, to increase the
trespass." In the context of sin and death the paradoxical function of the law was to increase transgression and to multiply sin.
In Rom. 7:9 we read further: "When the commandment came,
sin revived." Sin and righteousness are opposites. Where there is
no righteousness, sin rules. The law can define sin and make the
transgressions appear as guilt, but it cannot remove sin or substitute righteousness for it. "Because of transgressions" would
seem to mean, not only that the law made clear that the sin
already committed had the character of guilt and was a transgression of God's will, but also that the law incites to sin. The
law permits sin to appear in the form of transgression. The law
can increase sin even though in itself it is holy and good, because
the *demand* for righteousness cannot *create* righteousness. But
when man knows the demand, he is enticed to seek to attain
righteousness by his own efforts, and thus he adds to his sin. But
this fact, too, could be incorporated into God's plan of salvation
as preparation for a future righteousness.

Here Paul does not elucidate further what it means to say that
the law was added. It is clear from the context, however, that
the function of the law is limited to one aspect or one part in
the history of salvation. In the sequence from Abraham to Christ
God had introduced the law, but its rule signified a period when
sin should become more evident. It is exactly the *good* and *holy*
law that under certain circumstances operates in such a way that

evil appears. The Jews thought in terms of a straight line from Abraham to Sinai, but Paul draws the line from Abraham to Christ. The law was an addition, not the end or the climax of the line of revelation. It had a special place in the pedagogy of God, but it was not its goal.

b) The angels and the "intermediary" (3:19b)

Paul declares in vs. 19 that the law was given "through angels." This statement has been quite commonly interpreted to mean that the law was given not directly by God but by lower powers. Reference has been made to Gnostic ideas, according to which the law is not derived from God but from powers of lesser dignity. According to Marcion, the theological reformer of the second century, the law was associated with the creator god, who was not identical with the Most High God, the God of salvation. Some exegetes, who hold that by his reference to the angels Paul wants to emphasize that the law does not derive directly from God, have combined with this interpretation the idea that in general he seeks to depreciate the law as such. As already stated, this is certainly not correct. The mistake is made because the fact that Paul thinks of the law from many points of view is ignored. In its deepest, hidden meaning the law is God's Word and will, and as such it co-operates with the gospel. Its fulfilment and completion was given in the gospel, and through it the law received light and clarification. As a law whose purpose in this present, evil age was to condemn, it had a definite function, until Christ should come and until the power and *dunamis* of the gospel should become completely operative. In this power the law found its true fulfilment. But when misinterpreted as righteousness by the law, it would become the antithesis of the true law.

The Jews regarded the law as the highest element in existence. Paul rejects this view. But this does not mean that he simply moves the law further down on the same scale of values. Instead, as we have shown above, he must have held that the Jewish conception of the law dishonored the will of God expressed in the law. The Jewish interpretation of the law was wrong, and it made the law into a false god, the god of law-righteousness. Paul rejects this view precisely because he wants to follow Scripture and permit the law to appear good and holy, or, in other words, precisely in order to establish the law (Rom. 3:31).

We must not, therefore, simply assume that the mention of the

angels was made to emphasize that the law is not divine. To be
sure, in one sense according to Paul the law is not divine. We have
already emphasized that the law has been placed here in the
world of sin and has to define sin as transgression. But exactly
because it is holy and reveals the transgression of sinful man, it
can also entice man to seek righteousness by the law. Thus it
results in a perverted relationship to God which in reality is
idolatry of the same essential nature as among the Gentiles (cf.
the exposition of 4:3, 8ff.).

When Stephen according to Acts 7:53 speaks about the law,
he says: "you who received the law as delivered by angels and
did not keep it." The meaning here is that the law is high and
holy. According to Stephen God revealed himself to Moses through
an angel (Acts 7:30, 35, 38). Yes, in the reference to how the
law had been given there is a suggestion that the same faithlessness
which the Jews had shown in relation to the law they have now
also manifested by their refusal to receive the Messiah-Christ (cf.
also Romans 2). If they had been rightly faithful to the Scriptures
and the law of the old covenant (in their deepest meaning), they
would not now have rejected Christ (cf. John 5:45ff.). Their
rejection of him recalls their earlier faithlessness to the law and
their earlier slayings of the prophets. They had not received the
law in true faith, nor had they now in faith accepted the promised
Righteous One.

The idea that the law was given through the mediation of angels
is not unknown in the Jewish interpretation of the narratives of
the giving of the law at Sinai. The Hebrew text does not state this
explicitly, but according to Jewish thinking it lies near at hand to
speak about angels since the text states that the giving of the law
was accompanied by a number of natural phenomena. These
phenomena emphasized the holiness of the law. The Septuagint
in Deut. 33:2 states explicitly that the law was given through
angels. The translators of the Septuagint thus understood the
Hebrew text. In the tradition of later Judaism it was assumed that
the law had been given through angels.

When Paul here refers to Deuteronomy, it would seem that the
mention of angels ought not to be interpreted as an attempt to
deny the holiness of the law. When Paul in Gal. 4:14 wants to
indicate with what gratitude and reverence the Galatians had
received him the first time, he says: You "received me as an angel
of God, as Christ Jesus." It is obvious that the mention of an

angel does not at all imply depreciation or indicate a different
influence from that which emanates from God and Christ. Rather,
the expression, "as an angel of God," is a graphic expression of
how highly the Galatians regarded Paul then.

Therefore, although the mention of angels cannot be interpreted
to mean that the law was not divine, the connection with the
following expression, "intermediary," nevertheless suggests that
God's highest revelation was not given in and through the law.
God did not let his full glory appear through the law, as he did
through Christ, the likeness of God (cf. II Cor. 4:6). Paul held
fast to the holiness of the law, but the gospel represented a greater
glory. (Cf. II Cor. 3:11: "For if what faded away came with
splendor, what is permanent must have much more splendor.")
The law represented the dispensation of judgment and death (II
Cor. 3:7), which also to be sure came with splendor. But "the
dispensation of righteousness" had such great splendor that "what
once had splendor has come to have no splendor at all" (vs. 10).
Only in *this* context can it be said that the law represents something "lower." In and by itself the mention of the angels would
seem to emphasize the holiness and the glory of the law; but a
glory which was not of such surpassing splendor as when God
revealed himself in Christ. Only in this way can the law be seen
as holy, although it is surpassed by the light of the gospel. We
may compare the statement made in the second chapter of the
Letter to the Hebrews, that the world to come was not subjected
to angels but to the Son (vs. 5ff.). The message declared by angels
was valid (vs. 2), but now a salvation had come which was
superior to everything that had appeared before.

Here we have emphasized that Paul does not want to depreciate
the law, also because depreciation has a frame of reference
different from that of Paul's way of thinking. In the context of
his thinking the content of the true religion is assumed to be
expressed in eternal and unchangeable truths. The law would then
be inferior to these truths and represent a lower stage in religious
development toward the highest and perfect religion, which would
express these truths. In that case the law represented a lower level
of evolution. This was the typical thinking of the Enlightenment
but not of Paul. In II Cor. 3:7-8 ("Now if the dispensation of
death, carved in letters on stone, came with such splendor . . .
why should not the dispensation of the Spirit be attended with
greater splendor?") the whole argument stands in the context,

161

not of the modern conception of evolution, but of *the history of salvation*. In the context of the history of salvation the earlier epoch was inferior to the period of the fulfilment of the promise in the sense that the former was a preparation for the latter. In the earlier epoch man could not apprehend the whole height and depth of God's message, which was nevertheless present in a hidden sense in the Word. It became clear only in the perfect revelation in Christ. But the same God who spoke in the law provided later the elucidation of everything in the law by the fulfilment of law and promise. He himself appeared in and through the fulfilment in Christ. There was therefore also a connection between the law and faith, between Moses and Christ. There was something in the law which was explained in the light of the new revelation, and then it was shown to have contained more than could previously have been understood.

What has been said above must be taken into account in the interpretation of the word "intermediary" (*mesites*) in vss. 19-20. It says that the law was ordained through an intermediary. "By the hand of a mediator" (A.S.V.) is a Hebraism for "through an intermediary." That this intermediary is Moses is quite certain. It is true that some interpreters from Chrysostom down have suggested Christ, who is called a mediator between God and man in I Tim. 2:5-6. But this interpretation seems to be accepted by very few. However, there have been many different opinions about what Paul means by this "intermediary."

There have indeed been many different interpretations of vss. 19-20. In agreement with what we maintained previously we must emphasize here that it would be contrary to Paul's whole meaning if the law and its representatives (here the angels and Moses) were to be interpreted as something Paul attacks. That freedom from the law which Paul upholds is a freedom which we have in Christ who is the fulfilment of the law. With respect to the law there are always two things which must be taken into consideration. The one is that law-righteousness is a perversion of the law. The other is that the law represents a revelation of God which was fulfilled in the revelation of Christ. That the law given by Moses led to law-righteousness is true, but in and by itself the judgment of the law expressed the righteousness of God. The law was a link in God's act of election which had its goal in Christ, who took the judgment of the law upon himself and thereby also became the end of the law.

With these ideas as a background it is obvious that interpretations making the intermediary representing the law stand in some kind of conflict with God cannot be correct. Nor do we correctly reproduce Paul's meaning when we interpret vs. 20 with reference to Gnostic speculations according to which the law was not given by the highest God but by demiurgic powers to which the intermediary and the angels belonged. Paul's fundamental conception—that the law referred to the faith to come and was a part of God's plan of salvation—is opposed to these interpretations. The law therefore is not contrary to the promise.

c) The "intermediary" and the one God (3:20)

In making the attempt to explicate Paul's conception of the law, *two* factors have generally been considered: Christ (i.e., righteousness by faith) and law-righteousness. The law has then been identified with law-righteousness, or legalism. But in reality we must consider three factors: 1) Christ and the faith; 2) Moses and the law; and 3) righteousness by the law (legalism). When only two factors were considered, the law has always been identified with law-righteousness. It is this which is wrong. The whole section of Galatians in which vss. 19-20 occur points out the real place of the law as distinct from faith. But this distinction is not identical with the contrast between righteousness by the law and righteousness by faith. Here the law is given the position of a custodian until Christ should come. This law is *not* law-righteousness, but God's law given through the intermediary, Moses. The rabbinical idea that the law was eternal tended to make the law absolute. Then it also became a definable and finished entity, and could thus function as a principle for law-righteousness. It became separated from the activity of the living God. But Paul says that the law is a custodian (vs. 24) who takes man into custody in order that the law's judgment on sin might keep him in expectation of the fulfilment of the promise through Christ (vs. 23). Then the law is not conceived of as a hostile antithesis to the faith that was to come, but as a part of that activity of God whose goal was redemption through Christ. We have already dealt with the contrast between righteousness by the law and righteousness by faith. The word of the law that *God is one* would be abrogated through righteousness by the law.

The law and covenant Moses served is said to have appeared in splendor, in spite of its being a matter of judgment and death. Since the law stands in the service of death and judgment, the conclusion is generally drawn that Paul considers the law as something evil which is not from God. But this is not Paul's thought, for when the law judges, it stands in the service of God. The law represents "the dispensation of condemnation" (II Cor. 3:9). The giving of the law did not mean the establishment of law-righteousness, but that God in his just and redemptive activity condemned sin through the law in order to let the fulness of righteousness come through Christ. In this righteousness he was worshiped correctly as the only God.

We might ask why Paul at this point brought in the idea of an intermediary. According to Paul God gave the law because through sin a separation between God and the people had taken place. The law was given to the people that their transgressions might be revealed. Thus it was to be made clear that the right relationship to God had been broken. The law, therefore, testified *against* the people and established their sin. But the law was not given that through it the people might propitiate God. Such a conception of the law would lead to law-righteousness. It is against such a view of the function of the law that Paul protests. Nor was it the function of the law to provide a complete reconciliation which would remove the separation. This was reserved for the fulfilment of the promise. The work of Moses belongs entirely to the time while the separation between God and the people obtained. In this situation he was a mediator. But the final mediation, the reconciliation which was to remove the separation, was reserved for him who was to complete his work, i.e., Christ. He was to nail to the the cross the bond which stood against us after he had taken the judgment upon himself (cf. Col. 2:14).

According to Paul it was not true, as the rabbis claimed, that the promise was fulfilled through the redemption out of Egypt or through the giving of the law. He held that the law must convict of sin, not bestow righteousness. The law, therefore, as is stated in vs. 19, was to remain "till the offspring should come to whom the promise had been made." As it says in vs. 23, it was to keep "under restraint until faith should be revealed." But the connection between law and faith, however, is not simply that the law should rule until faith came. In God's plan of salvation the law was the background of faith, and faith was the goal of the law. The function of the law was to keep under restraint *with a view to* faith in Christ. That the law held those to whom it was given under restraint did not mean that it kept the people until *the final judgment,* as it is said about the angels who sinned (II Peter 2:4). No, the law should keep the people under restraint for that *faith* which was to be revealed. This faith came in Christ. He was "the offspring" of whom the promises spoke.

At this point we confront the question as to what it means for an intermediary to imply more than *one,* when *God is one* (vs. 20). In vs. 16 Christ as the offspring stands in contrast to the many, the physical descendants of Abraham. The many represent the law in the sense of law-righteousness. The law was understood as a means to propitiate God and to produce, in the case of those who had the law, a righteousness of their own. In vs. 20 the law is associated with the many as over against the fact that God is one. The righteousness of the law introduced a difference between Jews and Gentiles; and among the circumcised it separated those who observed the law fully from the others who did not. The righteousness of the law calls attention to the many who had received the law through Moses. But the promise of the offspring does not make salvation dependent upon the righteousness of the many. In Romans Paul quotes the words of Isaiah: "Though the number of the sons of Israel be as the sand of the sea, only a remnant of them will be saved" (Rom. 9:27). He continues with a quotation from Isa. 1:9: "If the Lord of hosts had not left us children [*sperma*], we would have fared like Sodom and been made like Gomorrah" (Rom. 9:29).

For Paul the remnant, the offspring, which stands in contrast to the many, was Christ. The many were not born through the promise but according to the flesh. In reality, therefore, they were not represented by Isaac, the son of Abraham through the promise, but by the son of Hagar (cf. below, 4:21ff.). The promise referred to the offspring, Christ, and he stood therefore as the one over against the many. In reality we find here the same contrast between the one and the many when the law (Deut. 6:4f.) proclaims that the God of Israel is *one;* the idols on the other hand were many. To live in the righteousness of the law was in reality not to worship the one God. Moses had not proclaimed righteousness by the law, but hardened Israel had not followed Moses and the law given through angels, but had remained in law-righteousness. When the law was given, it was given to the many who lived in sin, but they did not receive the law as a judgment to drive them to Christ, the fulfiller of the promise. Instead they accepted it as a

means of securing righteousness by the law. They believed that
they were the bearers of the promise through their righteousness
of the law. They received the law of Moses as a mediator in that
separation into which sin had led them, and in which they continually lived, without understanding the most profound meaning
of the law.

When Paul says that God is *one,* he refers directly to the well-
known words in Deut. 6:4f.: "Hear, O Israel: The Lord our God
is *one* Lord; and you shall love the Lord your God with all your
heart, and with all your soul, and with all your might." These
words of the law, which were a part of the daily prayer in the
synagogue (Deut. 6:4-7 was recited every day), were as well-
known among the Jews as the Lord's Prayer is among us. It was
the solemn proclamation in which the one God of Israel was
placed over against the idols. It expresses as we see the fundamental commandment to love God with all your heart, soul, and
might.

The law declares that God is *one,* just as it also speaks about
the righteousness of God. Yes, what the law is really concerned
about is to maintain the conception that God is *one.* But then the
question is to what extent this fundamental thought came to char-
acterize man's relationship to God. In reference to this question
we may establish an analogy to Paul's thoughts in reference to
what the law says about righteousness. According to Paul the law
proclaims and *demands* righteousness, but righteousness is not
given until through Christ. Likewise it was only through Christ that
the relationship to God became of such a character that it fully
corresponded to the words of the law that God is *one.* He was
the "offspring" to whom the promise applied. And as the promise
applied to him, the One (in contrast to the many), thus also
through his righteousness the words that God is *one* became an
actual reality in the relationship to God. They had not become
real through the many who boasted of the law. But in Christ God
became *one,* and in him all who believed, both Jews and Gentiles,
were comprehended. In faith all distinctions between the circumcised and the uncircumcised were removed (cf. vs. 28). Man
could not make himself good, but in Christ he was born again.

When Moses gave the law and thus fulfilled the task of clearly
revealing the separation between God and man, which sin had
brought about, two possibilities were open to the people: they
could either faithfully submit to the judgment of the law while

waiting for the fulfilment of the promise, or they could seek to make the law a means to propitiate God and thus establish their own righteousness. The Jews had taken the second course and thereby nullified the real meaning of the law. This became clear in the fact that precisely through their righteousness of the law they had strayed away from a right worship of *the one God*. But in Christ right worship of God and love to God were restored.

According to Paul the sin which separated men from God had made mediation necessary, but the mediation Moses had been commissioned to perform had not meant that sin was taken away through it.

The law of Moses had the function to expose sin and condemn it. Israel therefore ought to have permitted the law to reveal sin clearly and to have accepted its judgment. But sin which was a ruling power in the world made the law its servant instead by turning it into law-righteousness. Here God was not glorified, but in the service of sin the law was made into an idol. They sought to establish their own righteousness instead of the righteousness of God which the law itself was meant to serve (cf. Rom. 9:31-10:3). However, their own righteousness was an idol which they worshiped and served instead of the one God. In this perverted sense Paul equated the law with the worship of "the elemental spirits of the universe" (*ta stoicheia tou kosmou,* Gal. 4:3, 9; Col. 2:8, 20). In their righteousness by the law they violated by their whole attitude the words that God is *one*. Moses had given them that law which proclaimed that God is one, but only if they really attained to a life in righteousness could they in truth worship God as the One. Israel had not attained to this righteousness (Rom. 9:31), but had perverted it into its opposite (Rom. 10:3). Moses' proclamation was true and correct, but Israel had not been able to submit to it. The law had not given life (Gal. 3:21), but new life was the prerequisite if the law was to be kept rightly and lead to righteousness. The righteousness one must have to worship God as the one, was not given through the law. This too was in God's plan reserved for the fulfilment of the promise through Christ, and faith in him established not one's own righteousness (cf. Rom. 10:3) but the law itself in its real meaning and intention (cf. Rom. 3:31). (In both of these passages a form of the verb *histano* is used: "Do we then overthrow the law by this faith? By no means! On the contrary, we uphold the law." "For, being ignorant of the righteousness that comes from God, and seeking to establish their own, they did not submit to God's righteousness.")

The presupposition for Paul's point of view is that faith involves a practical relationship, not merely accepting something as true. In faith man is seized and committed; he is not a spectator on the side line. The pattern for faith is God's own faithfulness, and faith can never become mature except by being incorporated into God's life of righteousness. Righteousness by the law, therefore, is nothing less than unbelief and worship of idols, and thus Paul makes it the opposite of righteousness by faith (Gal. 3:11-12a). The consequence of Paul's view is that faith means the antithesis of sin. Sin means idolatry in one form or another. The function of the law was to elucidate this fact, and thus to reveal the sin man by himself did not conceive as sin (Cf. Rom. 7:7, 13; Gal. 3:19). When on account of sin the law resulted in law-righteousness, it could not really expose sin; rather, the significance and depth of sin became obscured. In this perverted sense the law came rather to increase sin and to drive the people further away from that faith in the one God which the law proclaimed. The law itself, therefore, proved to be death (Rom 7:10). But thus it included all, even the people of the law, under sin, "that what was promised to faith in Jesus Christ might be given to those who believe" (Gal. 3:22).

In contrast to "the Righteous One" (Acts 7:52; 22:14) Moses could not be such a representative of the one God that he made the people righteous and thus fulfilled the words that God is *one*. But Moses was sent by God and mediated God's holy and good law. Christ, however, came with the righteousness that made man righteous. His righteousness made a way through unrighteousness and sin, even the sin through which the law had been enslaved and interpreted as law-righteousness. On the cross he bore the curse the law pronounced on those who did not abide by all the things written in the book of the law. Because of this act righteousness could be given to those who were in such bondage under the curse that they could not have become righteous and received life; i.e., those who had not been able to worship God as one. This applied in the last analysis to all men. But in Paul's proclamation the Gentiles stood as a typical example of those who could not imagine themselves having anything on which they could base a claim of righteousness. They could not therefore like Israel seek righteousness on a false way (Rom. 9:30ff.). They were, as the

Letter to the Ephesians expresses it, "strangers to the covenant of promise, having no hope and without God in the world" (Eph. 2:12). When the Judaizers tried to persuade the Galatians to participate in Israel's seeking after righteousness "based on works" and without being enlightened (Rom. 10: 2f.), they led them astray from the worship of the one God and from participation in the fulfilment of the law and the realization of the promise to which the Galatians had been called through Paul's proclamation. They were enticed to look away from Christ to Moses, whose function nevertheless had been to point forward to Christ. To return in this way to Moses meant that they embraced that false conception of the law and that perverted zeal for the law which the Jews had. But this meant that they exchanged the worship of their heathen gods for the idol of law-righteousness, which simply hid even deeper the meaning of faith in the one God and prevented the fulfilment of and obedience to the word of the law that the Lord is *one*. Only in the righteousness Christ brought which is given in union with him can God really be worshiped as the One.

What the Judaizers completely rejected was exactly what Christ had made a reality: a relation to God founded on the righteousness given through him, namely, the relationship in which God appeared as the One man rightly worships when he loves him with all his heart and soul. Then there could be no boasting that separated the one from the other and made the circumcised more important than the uncircumcised. The Judaizers really upheld what was false in the Jewish attitude to the law and denied what the law actually intended. According to Paul the Jews regarded the law as the fulfilment of the promise rather than waiting for its fulfilment through the Messiah. They did not understand that the law had been given on account of sin; instead they believed it was given for *righteousness'* sake; i.e., the righteousness which they themselves were to obtain by means of the law. Thus they had established an insurmountable *barrier* between Jews and Gentiles and in advance excluded the *unity* between Gentiles and Jews through which the words that *God is one* were to be realized. The Jews, therefore, had not properly accepted the mediation of Moses, and they had also rejected Christ who broke down the dividing wall of hostility and created *one new man* in place of the two (Eph. 2:14). In Rom. 10:12 Paul emphasizes the unity between Jews and Gentiles: "There is no distinction between Jew and Greek; the same Lord is Lord of all." And in Rom. 3:29

with a direct allusion to the words that the Lord is one he says: "Or is God the God of the Jews only? Is he not the God of Gentiles also? Yes, of Gentiles also, *since God is one.*"

It is obvious that Paul means that the union of Jews and Gentiles now taking place means the fulfilment of the promise. But this meant also that in righteousness by faith *the word of Scripture that God is one was realized.*

We may assume, therefore, that Paul saw in Christ the fulfilment of the prophecy incorporated as a prayer in the Jewish worship service: "On that day . . . the Lord will become king over all the earth; on that day the Lord will be one and his name one" (Zech. 14:8-9).

We might really say that to Paul's mind the words about God being *one* had an eschatological meaning. Just as the words of the law concerning righteousness were fulfilled in and through Christ, thus also through him came into the world the faith in which God was to be the *one* and *only* God for all men. This implies that he is also the God of the *Gentiles.* Thus the word of the Law and the Prophets that God was to become the one God was really actualized by faith in Christ. Thus, for example, the word of the Lord to his Suffering Servant that he should be a light for the people was fulfilled (cf. Isa. 49:6; 42:6).

We have pointed out above that we miss Paul's meaning if we assume that the law was given by some lower divinity, and that in and by itself it was opposed to God. On the contrary, we may say, what is emphasized here and in the following verses is that the same, one God stands behind both the law and the promise. The one God had given the law through an intermediary, but he had not fulfilled through an intermediary his promise of blessing and righteousness. When the latter came, faith in the one God became a reality for men, because then the law was fulfilled and God became the one God for all and every man. In the law he had included all under sin (vs. 22) in order that the promise should be fulfilled in Christ. That God was one did not mean that he was recognized simply in an external sense. Israel acknowledged God and his law, but the fulfilment of the law was not given at Sinai; and the people were zealous for the law but not according to knowledge (Rom. 10:2-3). On this account they became hardened and like the Gentiles. Their manner of life was not congruous with the fact that God was one. They were like the Gentiles in the worship of idols and "the elemental spirits of the world" (*ta stoicheia tou kosmou*). But through Christ, on the other hand, all were to become *one* (vs. 28) in the worship of the one God. All who were in Christ, therefore, could be said to belong to the "offspring" ("If you are Christ's, then you are Abraham's offspring"), although the offspring is said to refer to only one, Christ (vss. 16, 29). This unity corresponded to the oneness of God. God became the One for men when they all became one, without any mutual distinction whereby one was separated from the other on the basis of greater glory. Christians constituted not only a fellowship having similar views, but a real *unity* with one another and with Christ, as Christ was *one* with God (John 14: 10-11; 17:11, 21-22). This unity, which also manifested itself in baptism and the Lord's Supper, implied a realization of the word of the Law and the Prophets that God is *one,* and that at the time of the promises, fulfilment he would become the one God for all men. In this connection we may see also how far we have come from Paul's thought world when men have feared the doctrine that God is one to be threatened by the idea of Christ. For Paul the faith in God as *one,* the *one* God, became fully realized through God's revelation of himself in Christ. Christ performed the act of God whereby God could be worshipped as the One, because the power of the law to impel men to the righteousness of the law was destroyed when through Christ the condemnation of the law was taken away and sin was atoned for. Through faith in Christ, faith in the one God became a reality. Christ and God constituted a unity which was not destroyed but was contingent upon the fact that God had appeared in the *man* Jesus. When Christ came as a man, his coming was an integral part of God's redemptive work (cf. the exposition of 4:4-5). The righteousness by faith in which God is *one* for humanity was revealed through Christ. The righteousness by the law, on the contrary, through which God cannot be *one,* is overcome.

It can be shown in various ways that Paul's fundamental ideas may be combined with the statement: "God is *one.*" We call attention to this fact and discuss further some of these fundamental ideas, since the exegesis of this verse has been regarded as particularly difficult.

Sin had introduced a separation from God and broken the relationship to him in which he really was the one God for humanity. A mediation was therefore necessary. In the mediation of Moses the separation between God and the people caused by sin

171

was elucidated. It was proclaimed in the law that God is *one* and that he demands a righteousness in which is implicit the fact that he is one. But this righteousness was not given through Moses, who had to proclaim the law that did not *give* righteousness but consigned all under *sin*. If the law *could have given life* and *bestowed* what it pointed toward, then in the law righteousness would have been present and the promise fulfilled (3:21). But now the law had been given the task by God to consign all things to sin, to let sin appear as transgression, and to keep under restraint until righteousness should come (3:22). If the law could have given life and righteousness, Christ would not have had to suffer death (2:21). Life came with Christ, and the commandment became a word that is near, "on your lips and in your heart" (cf. Rom. 10:6ff.). God became through Christ, not an external, commanding power, but a power to whose service man was completely dedicated; the flesh was destroyed and in the Spirit he was *one* with Christ. God's glory shines forth in the face of Christ (II Cor. 4:6), and he in whom Christ lives has God as the only God, not as a foreign master who imposes external commandments. The doing and fulfilling of the law has its starting point in Christ, it is not something toward which one merely strives. As long as it was a question about commandments to be observed, God could not really be the only God, nor could man really love him with his whole heart and mind. An external law can always entice men to law-righteousness. It was only when the words of Jeremiah about the new covenant had been fulfilled, so that God's law was written in the hearts of men (Jer. 31:31-32; Heb. 8:8ff.), that God really became the only God. Only in the establishment of the Messianic covenant did the word that God is one become fulfilled. The law itself, therefore, also testified that the new covenant fulfilled the deepest meaning of the law.

Circumcision, with which the Letter to the Galatians is especially concerned, had become to the Jews the sign of their alleged privileged status and of the fact that the law and thus also righteousness belonged to them. This view of the law, which Paul held to be false, was accepted as correct by the Judaizers, who demanded that the Gentiles be circumcised to share in the salvation in Christ. This would be a perversion of the gospel. According to Paul circumcision was not a means of obtaining righteousness, but a seal of the righteousness by faith Abraham had (cf. Rom. 4:11). When the Galatians wanted to exclude the uncircumcised from the blessing brought by the Messiah, they also denied the word of Scripture that God is *one* for both the Gentiles and the Jews. Through Christ a way was prepared for that relation to God in which he is no longer hidden behind judgment and death, but appears in his love. Thus the relation to God established in creation was restored. It was on the cross that Christ fulfilled the law, as he submitted fully to and assumed the burden of its judgment. Now in Christ God became one of whom the believer could say; "Abba, Father" (cf. 4:6). The unity of God did not fully appear as long as he was hidden behind the unfulfilled law, and the unity was destroyed when sin made the law into law-righteousness. In Christ who had submitted to the law God became the God of the fulfilled law, the God of love. Through the perfect *Reconciler* the *many* became *one* with God. When the separation between them and God had been removed through Christ, and they could live for God through Christ, hostility toward the Gentiles disappeared and the dividing wall between the circumcised and the uncircumcised was torn down. Then God was confessed as the one God; and the words of Moses to that effect were fulfilled through faith in Christ.

By pointing out that the function of the law was not to bring in the fulfilment of the promise, but that it had a place as an earlier factor in God's act of election, Paul in fact elucidates several aspects of the matter. The law is not contrary to the promise; yet it does not bestow righteousness and life, but on the contrary can lead the sinner even deeper into sin.

d) Scripture consigns all things to sin (3:21-22)

Verse 21 emphasizes that the law was good even though it did not imply the fulfilment of the promise. Since the exegesis of the thought in this passage had to be included in the interpretation of the previous verses (cf. the discussion of 3:19-20 and 3:13), the exposition here may be very brief. The conclusion of the previous argument was that the law, rightly understood, was not at all contrary to God's promise. If there had also been given, together with the law, the righteousness, life, and Spirit in which the fulfilment and completion of the law were included, the age of righteousness would have been present. But God had not given this function to the law. If man refused to submit to the will of God and instead made the law a source of righteousness and life, he introduced a contrast between law and promise

which was contrary to Scripture and perverted the law. Instead
of providing righteousness the law had the function of revealing
sin. Scripture, which expresses God's will and intention, had consigned all things to sin. Even he who regarded himself as righteous
on the basis of his observance of the law actually stood under the
power of sin. Righteousness was not produced by works of the
law. On the contrary, these works were an expression of sin,
since they were supposed to provide righteousness for the one
who was circumcised and observed the law. The works of the law
showed how even the commandments of the law were made to
serve sin. Thus all things were consigned to sin, and what had
been promised was not made dependent on anyone's observance
of the law (vs. 22). Instead of directing attention to the nature
and work of man's own self, Scripture (and therefore also the law)
pointed to Christ, through whom God caused the promise to be
fulfilled.

When it was said that the law of Moses cannot make alive, it
meant precisely that it was not a perfect expression for the whole
righteousness of God. Without life the law could not really be
fulfilled. In that case sinful man perverted it into righteousness
of the law, which was a false obedience. But when sin, which had
driven man to works of the law, had been atoned for and life
had been given, then the fulfilment of the law could take place
in the Spirit. Life was a prerequisite for real righteousness (God's
righteousness). Jeremiah says about the new covenant (Jer. 31:
31ff.) that the law was to be put within the heart of the people
so that everyone would know the Lord immediately and without
instruction. This is really saying what Paul said: that (in contrast
to the righteousness in the new covenant, the righteousness of
Christ) the law could not give life. The difference between the
law in the old covenant and the law fulfilled in Christ was therefore, we might say, that the second was connected with life, or
that the prerequisite for a right doing of the law, i.e. life, had
now been given in Christ. This life was qualitatively a seed of the
promised new age, the incorruptible and eternal life. It was given
in and through Christ, who bore the curse the law of the old
covenant imposed, since new life was not associated with that
law. However, when death, connected with sin, was overcome
through the death of Christ, and life was given to the Christian
in and through his union with the risen Christ, then also righteousness, the real fulfilment of the law, is at hand. This right-

eousness was received when the Christian became *one* with Christ
in baptism, so that he himself died with Christ to sin and "flesh"
and arose to live Christ's resurrection life (cf. Rom. 6:3ff.; Gal.
2:19-20; 3:27ff.). Paul therefore says also that the Christian has
become heir and son (Gal. 3:26, 29), and as heir he has received
the Spirit of Christ (3:2-3; 4:6). He must now therefore also
live the new life of the Spirit (5:16, 25). He had come to know
God, or rather "to be known by God" (4:9), which was precisely what was to be the distinguishing quality of those who
had become partakers of the life of the new covenant.

3. The law has been our custodian that we might receive freedom in Christ (3:23-25)

That the law had kept the people under restraint and, as it
were, kept them in prison does not directly refer to righteousness
by the law. Moses had had the task of giving a law to keep the
people under restraint by putting them under accusation. His
office could thus be called "the dispensation of death" (II Cor.
3:7). But there was a connection between this dispensation and
the dispensation of future glory, because the splendor emanating
from Moses' face, which, because the children of Israel could not
bear to look upon it, he had to cover with a veil, was the glory
of Christ. The law spoke in an esoteric way about Christ; yes,
Christ himself spoke in a hidden manner in the law. But until he
himself came and his glory became revealed, men had to be confined under the law. But the goal of this confinement was Christ.
He was the climax, the goal, the fulfilment, the *telos* of the law.

The situation of the children of Israel in confinement under
the law was like that of a slave. Yet the situation was not without
hope, because there was a promise of coming righteousness. The
fulfilment of this promise involved an unveiling of the glory that
had emanated from Moses' face. During their servitude under the
law Israel had a hope of righteousness, because they had been
entrusted with the promises of God (Rom. 3:2). But when Israel
was led astray into righteousness by the law, they came under
real slavery; the kind from which man does not *want* to be free,
but which he persuades himself is something good, something of
which he is proud and in which he wants to remain. When the
people claimed for themselves an advantage in and through the
law, they lost the advantage which was really theirs.

175

There has been a difference of opinion as to whether the words in vs. 23: *"until* faith should be revealed," and in vs. 24, "our custodian *until* Christ came," are to be understood in a final or temporal sense. There is much that seems to favor a purely temporal sense. The words, "before faith came," seem to favor this view, and furthermore Paul pointed to the time sequence between the promise and the giving of the law (vs. 17). But, as our previous exegesis would indicate, we must not emphasize the temporal meaning one-sidedly. The context does not state merely that the law confined those under its authority during the time before faith came. The meaning is rather that the law kept them under restraint with a definite goal in view, not until a final judgment (cf. II Pet. 2:4; 3:7), but that faith might finally give them the righteousness the law did not give them. This interpretation does not of course exclude a temporal sense. When the goal has been reached, the law has completed its function in the plan of salvation (vs. 25). Christ came at the time determined by the Father.

Just as Christ is not only the end but also the goal of the law, *telos* means both that the relationship between the law and faith is not conceived of purely in a temporal sense, with faith coming after the law, but also that faith is the goal of servitude under the law. The meaning of the positive function of the law has often been conceived of erroneously. This may be the reason that the temporal meaning has been so one-sidely emphasized. Thus for example the 1917 edition of the Swedish Bible translates *paidagogos* by "tutor." This readily suggests that the meaning of the word is that the law is to prepare man in a pedagogical-psychological sense. But that is not the preparation in question here. We will return to this point in our exegesis of *paidagogos,* but first we must elucidate the context in which vs. 23 occurs.

The goal of God's activity in and through the law was the final salvation which came through Christ. The law confined the people under its judgment that its demands might be fulfilled in and through the righteousness of faith. Thus the law was not against God's promises; it was a means in the hands of the one God who gave the promise and by the fulfilment of the promise accomplished that which the law served, but was unable to bring to completion. The end of the law came in Christ, because Christ came with the righteousness the law served and *for* which it kept men under restraint by its judgment. Only in Christ has the law fulfilled its purpose. Although the people of Israel were entrusted with the promises of God and chosen as heirs, they had been placed under the guardianship of the law. They were the ones who received the demands for righteousness and judgment on every man. The law had placed the people under its accusation, and they had to wait for righteousness through a new intervention of God. Thus the law made Israel a people who had nothing of which they could boast.

Hence the connection between Moses and Christ, or between the law and faith, becomes in this context both temporal and final. Moses and the law kept them under restraint *until* faith should be revealed. The law was a means in God's hand of moving toward the goal not yet attained, i.e., righteousness by faith in Christ.

The connection between Moses and the law, on the one hand, and Christ and faith, on the other, is conceived of one-sidedly or wrongly *both* if we think of two successive states without any inner relationship between them, *and* if it be asserted that the meaning of the law was that those who had it were to grow and mature under its ministration. All these ideas are of modern vintage. Moses the intermediary gave Israel a law which through its accusations placed them in custody. The people did not mature spiritually under the law; instead they were led deeper into sin. The law is therefore not to be conceived of as a means through which the people matured and became worthy of the Messiah. Thus the relationship between the law and faith might seem to be only negative and the connection merely temporal. There is nevertheless also a positive connection between them, because the judgment on sin provided a negative expression for the coming righteousness. In the reconciliation of Christ God let the accusing law be revealed and at the same time overcome by the righteousness which contained life. It might be said that confinement under the law took place *in order that* later Christ should give life to all who stood under the accusation of the law, under sin and death. The righteousness Christ brought was to appear at first in the form of judgment, but it imposed the judgment with a view to the future fulfilment of the promise.

The relationship between the situation under the law and that under faith is illustrated in vs. 24 by comparing the law to a *paidagogos*. In the ancient world a *paidagogos* was a slave who had charge of boys and used to accompany them on the way to school. He was not a teacher, but he was to see to it that the boys behaved themselves. It is usually said that such a slave was known for his strictness and severity. He was usually not loved, even though some exceptions may be found, and he was a person from whose authority and power the boys longed to be free. *Paidagogos,* therefore, does not have the meaning of our word "pedagogue" which is derived from it. The word may be understood as a figure illustrating the meaning of the previous verse: "before faith came, we were confined under the law, kept under restraint until faith should be revealed," or "until the faith to come should be revealed." The law was like an overseer, a prison guard; its statutes kept people under restraint, limited their freedom, accused them and threatened them with death. The function of the law as *paidagogos* was that of an overseer, a prison guard, who discovers and punishes transgressions. The function of the law, according to Paul, was to reveal sin.

What the figure intends to say, therefore, is not that the work of the law involves a positive instruction and moulding of character that faith might put the seal on the work done by the law. On the contrary, it exercised discipline, deprived men of freedom and accused them. To be consigned under the law is the opposite of receiving righteousness and freedom. The figure is somewhat variable and fluent, and has many associations.

The law kept men under restraint both by bringing them all under judgment through the revelation of God's demand for righteousness, and by driving sinful man deeper into sin, into a false and imaginary righteousness of his own, because he could not endure the judgment, but wanted to make himself righteous by seeking to conform to the demands of the law. But even the hardening of Israel was incorporated into God's acts of election, the goal of which was Christ (cf. Rom. 11:11ff.).

The best translation of *paidagogos* is therefore not "tutor," as the Swedish edition of 1917 renders it (and as the American Standard Version also has it). The earlier rendering, "chastiser," is better because it stresses the severity and compulsion. The best rendering would seem to be "custodian." The law is likened both to the stipulations which limit freedom and to the custodian who enforces them. We might think both of the walls which enclose a prisoner and of the prison guard. But the imprisonment had a meaning, a purpose, namely to serve a freedom from all that caused the imprisonment; not only freedom from the law, but also from the sin and death existing before the law. The road to freedom went by way of a deeper servitude which the law had brought about.

The word *paidagogos* occurs also in I Cor. 4:15: "For though you have countless guides in Christ, you do not have many fathers." Here it stands in contrast to *father*. Paul was the father of the Corinthians; he had become their father in Christ Jesus through the gospel. In Galatians 3 the law is said to have been a *paidagogos*, and its service lasted until Christ came. It could enforce obedience with severity, but it could not give life. Using the expression in I Corinthians we could say that it did not have the position a father has. The gospel came with the life connected with the Creator, the Father, from whom and to whom are all things. As a *paidagogos* the law could pronounce accusations, it could punish, threaten, and judge. But the really proper and complete demand of the law could never be met by the attempt to follow its precepts or conform to a pattern. The only condition on which the will of God hidden in the law could be realized was that a life became available in which the law could be fulfilled from within. This could happen only when God through the Messiah made atonement for all sin and gave righteousness to those who became one with him. Children could of course be reprimanded by a custodian, who prevented them from taking a freedom to which they were not entitled, "a freedom of the flesh." But a custodian could never give what only a father can give. The law could indeed accuse and judge, but it could never assume the position of man's origin and goal. But on the contrary, after a son had spent a period under a custodian or hard and severe taskmasters, the life once given by the father could then be bestowed on the son in a new and more perfect sense as he comes of age. He would be raised to equality with the father and share in all his possessions.

Paul turns away from those *paidagogoi* who had sought in their own way to continue his work in Corinth, and points to his own work through which the Corinthians had become partakers of the life of the gospel. Here in Galatians 3 the law is called *paidagogos*. It must not be equated with Christ who himself represented the life of God the Father. The idea of the *paidagogos* is supplemented in 4:1ff. by a comparison between the servitude of the heir as a child and the freedom he has after he has come of age.

C. Faith gives to everyone an equal share in the inheritance (3:26—4:7)

1. Baptism makes all one in Christ (3:26-29)

"In Christ Jesus you are all sons of God, through faith," says Paul. The sonship of God was not established through circumcision so as to give the circumcised precedence before God. The faith proclaimed in and with the gospel involved as incorporation into the body of Christ. It was such a participation in the church of Christ and such a unity with him that the believer could be said to have been crucified with him and united with him in his death and resurrection. Through his Spirit Christ was now the active power in the believer. Thereby also the real goal of creation had been restored, because Christ was the origin and goal of creation, the first and the last (cf. Rev. 1:17). All things were created through him and for him (Col. 1:16). The new man who lives in Christ and in whom Christ lives (cf. Gal. 2:19-20) was "the image of its creator" (Col. 3:10). Through the gospel everyone is called to this life in which the relationship between God and man has become what it was intended to be from the beginning. Here all differences between Greek and Jew, circumcised and uncircumcised, barbarian and Scythian, slave and free man have been removed because Christ is all, and in all (Col. 3:11). This comparison is developed in vs. 28; in vs. 27 he points first to baptism through which the Christian has "put on Christ."

The Christian faith is characterized by baptism, just as the law, understood in the Jewish sense, is characterized by circumcision. All Christians were baptized, while circumcision could be applied only to males. Even if circumcision came to epitomize all Israel as a collective, there is a suggestion of the difference between circumcision and baptism in the fact that in the church everyone is baptized, while only men could be circumcised. Baptism meant that a man entered into the kingdom of Christ and became a citizen in it. The dominion of faith was to permeate the whole life of the Christian. Every man, consciously or unconsciously, was governed by the powers of this age, unless Christ had liberated him from them. In baptism man died to the law (cf. Rom. 7:6) and to sin (Rom. 6:3ff.). He became a participant in the death of Christ. In faith and baptism there was also a connection with the resurrection of Christ. He who was baptized was raised with Christ "through faith in the working of God, who raised him from the dead" (Col. 2:12). Baptism meant, therefore, that the baptized person was dead and buried with Christ, and that he participated in his resurrection (I Cor. 15:20ff.). The law, therefore, had no validity for the Christian (Rom. 7:1-6). In baptism a person put off the old man and put on the new. The expression "to put on the new man," means really the same as to put on Christ (cf. exegesis of 2:19-20 above). Belonging to Christ was a reality which demanded as a result that the works of the old man be put away more and more, and that the Christian conform to the new reality into which he had come through faith and baptism. The law which ruled in this age had no longer any authority to judge the baptized person who lived in the power of baptism, and who through it had been united with Christ and through him had received an inheritance in the age to come (cf. Rom. 8:1ff.). "To put on Christ" becomes the same as "to be in Christ."

When Paul says that those who have been baptized into Christ have put on Christ, he uses the verb *enduo,* "to put on." This verb means also "to cover oneself with," "to penetrate," "to submerge oneself in," "to dive into." The baptized person had become completely united with Christ and one with him. We may also think of putting on the heavenly robes of salvation for which the baptized person was destined. These robes characterized his union with Christ; they were held in readiness for him, and even now he could look forward to them as something promised him and which in faith he possessed.

In this act the baptized had also become united with one another. It is stated very emphatically thus: In baptism there can be no question about the differences which are important in this present age, such as between Jew and Greek, slave and free. Neither is there in baptism any distinction between man and woman. The difference between Jews, the circumcised, and Greeks, the uncircumcised, was of course definitive for religious fellowship from the Jewish point of view. But this difference was removed through baptism into Christ. The same was true of the difference which in Paul's day was determinative for social life, the difference between slave and free. The baptized slave was "a freedman of the Lord;" he who was free when baptized was "a slave of Christ" (cf. I Cor. 7:22).

In reference to man and woman we read in vs. 28 not, "neither

181

male *nor* female," (as the other statements: "there is neither Jew
nor Greek, there is neither slave nor free"). It says instead, "there
is neither male *and* female."[1] Linguistically this may not indicate
a deliberate difference. In Gen. 1:27, however, the Septuagint
has the same expression as here, "man and woman" (*arsen kai
thelu*): "So God created man in his own image, in the image of
God he created him; male and female he created them." The
words *arsen kai thelu* mark the difference between the sexes:
"Male and female he created them."

But this division into male and female established in creation is
not relevant in reference to baptism into Christ. No one is baptized to be either man or woman. As we have noted above, circumcision could be applied only to males. According to the
command given to Abraham in Genesis every male should be
circumcised (Gen. 17:10, cf. Lev. 12:3). Baptism on the contrary
included everyone.

Baptism was a baptism *into* Christ. The goal was complete
union with him, which could be experienced in this life by faith,
but which in its finality belonged to the age to come. Through
baptism the baptized person was destined for this goal. But this
destiny did not preclude at all that he would have to "work out
his salvation with fear and trembling" (Phil. 2:12). He had to
strive toward the goal set before him, and therefore he could not
be conformed to this world (Rom. 12:2). The old man who
belonged to this age had been crucified with Christ. Baptism into
Christ meant a baptism into his death (Rom. 6:3-4; 6:6). But
for this reason the baptized person had to be exhorted to "be
renewed in the spirit of your minds" (Eph. 4:23). The goal was
the complete unity with Christ obtained upon entrance into the
new age. The baptized were to walk together toward this goal.
This orientation toward the goal was independent of the differences
separating the uncircumcised from the circumcised, or the slave
from the free man. Yes, not even the two sexes in which man has
to live here on earth in accordance with God's creative act are
relevant to baptism in Christ. We may recall the words of Jesus
in Luke 20:34ff.: "The sons of this age marry and are given in
marriage; but those who are accounted worthy to attain to that
age and to the resurrection from the dead neither marry nor are
given in marriage, for they cannot die any more, because they are

[1] The RSV ignores the *kai* and translates all three "neither . . . nor."—Trans.

equal to angels and are sons of God, being sons of the resurrection." The baptized person is on the way toward this goal.

Even though the figure "to put on Christ" easily suggests the baptismal ceremony in the mystery cults, where the one initiated put on a new dress at baptism, Paul's thought is completely intelligible in its own context. He who in baptism had received a share in all that Christ possesses and had become a member of his body, had been fully united with him. He had become one with him. He had, as it were, assumed a new form and found a place in a new context. When the Spirit worked in him, he stood in contact with that age in which the risen Christ ruled. He had "put on the new man" (Col. 3:10). Those who had thus been united with Christ constituted a unity together with him. The unity was determined by the reception of righteousness from God. This unity existed even though men lived under different social conditions. Such differences did not dominate life when full equality and fellowship, and even unity, obtained on *one* level. The difference for instance between slave and free had lost its absolute character through equality in Christ. The iniquity and injustice which belonged with inequality could not continue for those who lived in faith.

Through faith all are sons of God, we read in vs. 26. Thereby an equality was created between Jew and Gentile, slave and free, man and woman. Since no one had anything to boast of before God, the reason for a separation between Jews and Gentiles no longer existed. Even differences such as that between slave and free men, which in the ancient world created a tremendous social stratification, disappeared as far as righteousness and salvation were concerned. The righteousness of God is for Paul the foundation of life, and because all without distinction have become participants in this righteousness, there was created on life's most essential level equality among all those who share in the righteousness of Christ. There was no reason why anyone who according to contemporary standards was superior to the others should regard this as something significant. The righteousness of the law showed that it belonged to the nature of this present age by the fact that it created differences between people. When that which was essential for the relationship to God was attributed to qualities of men, certain external differences between them were also indirectly encouraged. On the most essential level all Christians were equal, and the actual differences were therefore not humiliating. Although the question is not about the emancipation of either slaves or women in the modern sense, the equality in faith, which Paul says belongs to the gospel, operates nevertheless in such a way that the most serious reason for differences between people, such as free and slave, man and woman, disappeared.

In later theology the abolition of the differences spoken of in vs. 28 (cf. Col. 3:11; I Cor. 12:13) have been interpreted in two different directions. On the one hand, it has been emphasized that the abolition of the difference between Jew and Greek, slave and free, man and woman, who have been baptized in one and the same Spirit and united in one body (cf. Rom. 12:4-5), must directly and immediately lead also to the abolition of social differences between them. On the other hand, interpreters have maintained a very definite separation between two points of reference. In reference to God, righteousness, and salvation there could be full equality; but in reference to social life the external differences could be retained. In the second case it has been pointed out that Paul in I Cor. 7:21 does not seem to have regarded it as of any essential significance what kind of social position a man had.

It is quite right that for Paul equality before God does not immediately involve social equality. But we must be careful not to interpret this distinction as if equality before God in faith had no effect on the inequalities present in social life. Indirectly it must be of immense significance that these differences are stripped of their absolute meaning.

Although it would therefore be a false modernization to read modern striving for equality into the words of Paul, it is nevertheless obvious that such a message as his has actually removed the sting of the differences between Jew and Greek, slave and free, man and woman. As long as the gospel in the Pauline sense was a living power, these differences could not become the basis for arrogance, conceit, brutality and oppression. Wherever unity and equality in the most profound sense, before God and with respect to righteousness, are not present, inequality becomes a starting point for an absolute difference between the privileged and the unprivileged. The ruthless exercise of power by the privileged appears then as something right, good, and natural, and can take place without objection. But this becomes impossible because of equality in faith and on account of the righteousness on which faith rests.

When equality in faith (in Christ) prevails, the way is open for a division of labor based on natural differences, which does not, however, imply that some exercise dominion in their lust for power, and others submit in bitter enviousness. It means rather a mutual service, as the various members of the body serve one another. This does not mean that any part of the body is depreciated, but those parts "which we think less honorable we invest with the greater honor" (cf. I Cor. 12:12-26).

The social differences which characterized the communities in the ancient world, the differences between slave and free, male and female, were consequently overcome from within through the Spirit who created faith. Social equality was not put forward as a program. On the contrary, Paul admonished them to remain in the state in which they were called (cf. I Cor. 7:20ff.). But this was due to the fact that differences had been overcome from within. He who was a slave was a freedman of the Lord, and he who was free was a slave of Christ (cf. Col. 4:1). Through faith a new reality had become determinative for life, and thus every state became an opportunity for service in this reality. No one needed to think of himself seriously as unfree when he was free in Christ.

In the relationship between man and woman, too, the decisive fact was that both could share fully in salvation. Women participated from the beginning in Christian worship, while in the Jewish synagogue they were permitted to listen to the service but could not participate as actively as men. In the family the strongest and most enduring bond became the love revealed through the self-sacrifice of Christ. The husband's position as lord was replaced by his obligation to be toward his wife what Christ was for his church; i.e., to give himself even into death for her in perfect love. Although in accordance with the general opinion it would have been natural to emphasize *only* the woman's position as a servant to her husband, Paul stresses emphatically the duty of the husband to emulate Christ in the family; i.e., to serve and give himself. In this sense the man may be said to represent Christ in the family (cf. Eph. 5:25, 29). All such human ordinances in which the stronger or the socially superior might be thought of as standing closer to God was destroyed when service and the giving of one-self for others became the way in which a person represented Christ. The difficulty the disciples and the early church had in realizing this fact is reflected in the attitude of the disciples as recorded in the Gospels (cf. Mark 10:42ff.; Luke 22:25ff.; Matt.

20:25ff.; 23:11). In discussing marriage in the Letter to the
Ephesians (Eph. 5:25ff.) Paul remarks that the words in Genesis,
that a man is to leave his father and mother and cleave to his
wife, that the two shall become one flesh, have a hidden meaning
and reference, namely that Christ was to forsake his divine glory
(cf. Phil. 2:6ff.) and become man. His life and death were to
serve men, and thereby he would become *one* with those who received him. Thus the unity of Christ with his church became the
pattern of marriage in this interpretation of the Old Testament
words which occur in the Pauline writings. The bond of unity
became in the last analysis the love revealed in the incarnation of
Christ and in his sacrifice of himself in his vicarious suffering and
death. The woman may be said to be man's glory (*doxa*). At the
consummation of redemption, too, she will be for man's glory
and honor.

The difference between man and woman given in their nature
and functions became irradiated through the reality of a salvation
which creates unity and makes mutual service the highest good.
Just as in the relationship between God and Christ one could
speak of a difference in functions and at the same time of a
complete unity between them, and as Christ in his self-sacrifice
appeared as one with the church, so the difference between man
and woman, which seemed to be fundamental and insuperable
in the ancient world, was overcome through their unity in Christ.
The difference in rank and honor in social life was in the unity
with Christ exchanged for the many tasks which appear when the
one serves the other. The give and take which characterizes the
life in God's love, in *agape,* becomes the proper and natural mode
of life.

Where it was said in vs. 20 that God is *one,* we pointed out
that Paul also emphasizes the unity between those who receive
righteousness by faith. They are one in Christ. They would receive the inheritance. Christ was the offspring (seed), and since
those who received righteousness by faith were one with him,
true faith in the one God became a possibility. By faith in Christ
man entered into the true and new covenant. Then God was one,
and all who believed in him had his law in their hearts. The
righteousness of God, given in Christ and realized in him, incorporated all who received righteousness by faith into a unity.
In vss. 28-29 we find again an allusion to what had been stated
earlier, namely that God is *one* and that Christ is the offspring

of Abraham. When he says in vs. 29 that "you are Abraham's offspring," he is not introducing an idea different from that found in vs. 16, where he said that the offspring was *one*. By physical descent Abraham had many offspring, but according to the Spirit his offspring and heir was one, Christ. But those who in faith received the righteousness of Christ were gathered together into one real unity in that they became members of the body of Christ. Through baptism they died with Christ. In his church they became members in the new people of God. Among them there were no degrees of righteousness to be secured, nor different qualities on which inequality before God could be based. They were all one in Christ. This unity was far more profound than a fellowship between those who hold similar views, or who think alike, or who are brought together because of social fellowship and equality. The unity in Christ was a unity which remained in spite of external inequalities, just as the unity of Christ with God remained and did not in any way become less when Christ emptied himself and became man, "born of woman, born under the law."

2. Faith in Christ makes man a mature heir (4:1-7)

Here Paul continues to explicate in new figures what he has discussed in the previous section. He uses the figure of an heir who receives the inheritance at a certain time before which he had no right to it.

The rule of the law is likened to a situation in which in the ancient patriarchal household the position of a minor was like that of a slave. Paul seems to be thinking of the stipulations which obtained in Hellenistic courts. At the time set by the father the heir was to become the lord of all the estate, even of those guardians and stewards who had exercised authority over him, if, as often was the case, these were slaves. The situation was the same as with the guardian ("custodian" or "tutor") to whom Paul had likened the law. A steward was quite often one of the more trusted slaves. Under any circumstances the situation of the heir would become entirely different after he received the inheritance. Paul likened the condition of the heir before he becomes of age to that of a slave. The emphasis is on the fact that he lacks the freedom the inheritance will give him. Later he becomes lord over the inheritance his father has bequeathed to him. In the earlier figure the law as a custodian kept all under restraint. In the present figure the situation before Christ is compared to that of a child or a minor before he comes of age, or before the time which, in accordance with common Hellenistic practice, the father had set for him to assume control in his own right over his inheritance. The figures which Paul uses here were natural to the readers of the letter. Existence under the Old Testament law in its Jewish application is here equated with the situation under the ordinances of heathen religions. The period under the law is compared with a period of such bondage as an impotent slave lives under. The son of a rich man, however, will be delivered from his bondage when he comes of age and enters upon his inheritance. He himself becomes free and the lord over those who previously were equal with him in the state of bondage.

According to Paul the time for the heir to enter upon his inheritance had come in Christ. Now the time of freedom had come. When Paul applies the figure, he uses the first person: "So with us; when we were children, we were slaves to the elemental spirits of the universe." Paul is one of those who had been subject to the rod of a jailer or a "custodian," or had been supervised by guardians and trustees. The Galatians, who were mostly Gentile Christians, are counted among those who had been subject to the law. Instead of "the law" Paul uses here the concept of "the elemental spirits of the universe," which are thus equated with the law.

There has been a great deal of discussion about the meaning of the expression "the elemental spirits of the universe" (*ta stoicheia tou kosmou*). Though "element" (*stoicheia*) can mean the rudiments of a subject, the fundamental rules on which knowledge is based, this meaning is hardly appropriate here, although some ancient and modern interpreters have understood it in this sense. The word may also designate the fundamental elements of the universe and the spiritual powers connected with them. It may also have an astrological meaning and stand for those constellations and heavenly bodies which were supposed to influence the lives of men. It may possibly suggest spiritual beings which were supposed to control the movements of the stars in the heavens (cf. exegesis of vs. 10 below). In general it may mean angelic powers.

Paul suggests that a false insight may manifest itself in the assumption that a life regulated by all kinds of rules and com-

mandments is more honorable and meritorious (cf. Rom. 10:2ff.).
This Paul regarded as servitude under "the elemental spirits."
These ideas had a false appearance of wisdom (cf. Col. 2:20-23).
What is emphasized here, however, is not primarily the false
knowledge connected with the slavery under "the elemental
spirits," but rather the contrast between the status a man has in
the freedom in Christ and the slavery and fear under "the elemental spirits" who must be propitiated and appeased by observance of the law. In Col. 2:8 the expression seems to be equivalent
to "the tradition of the elders," or that false tradition against
which Paul contends. Here he equates it with a false and legalistic
attitude found in other religions. The Hellenistic religions fostered
faith in demonic powers which ruled the world. Paul has in mind
the bondage in which man is placed by his faith in these powers.
His attack is not like that of a modern man concerned primarily
with superstitious *conceptions*. Paul calls attention to the religious
attitude involved. Christ had conquered all such elemental spirits
who enslaved men under observances of the law. In following
Christ the Christian must strive "against the principalities, against
the powers, against the world rulers of this present darkness,
against the spiritual hosts of wickedness in the heavenly places"
(Eph. 6:12). Through Christ the victory over those powers was
assured.

The meaning of the expression "elemental spirits" (*stoicheia*)
is elucidated by the words in Col. 2:14-15, where he speaks first
about the law, "the bond which stood against us with its legal
demands," but which God nailed to the cross of Christ. Then
he continues: "He disarmed the principalities and powers and
made a public example of them, triumphing over them in him."
Consequently he warns against living in an anxious observance
of statutes regarding food and drink, festivals and new moons,
all of which is only a shadow of what is to come while the substance belongs to Christ. They must not revert to the worship of
angels and to forms of legalistic piety. The Christians had died with
Christ and had thus been set free from "the elemental spirits"
(from *ta stoicheia tou kosmou*). The passage in Col. 2:14ff. seems
therefore also to teach that subjection under "the elemental spirits"
is equivalent to righteousness by the law. In Gal. 4:10 Paul cites
examples of bondage under these "elemental spirits." He is
anxious because the Galatians observe days, months, seasons,
and years. Here he uses common expressions which suggest that

religious observance and legalism which may be found in both Jewish and heathen cults. Not only was the sabbath surrounded by restrictions of the law, but the Day of Atonement, new moons, the sabbatical year, and the year of jubilee were similarly regulated (cf. Exod. 23:10ff.; Lev. 23:23ff.; 25:1ff.; Num. 28: 16ff.; 29:1; Deut. 15:1ff.; 31:10; Amos 8:10). Paul did not specifically mention circumcision. He picks out characteristics which are common to both the earlier heathen cult of the Galatians and Judaism. He has in mind that attitude in and through which man seeks to protect and save himself from the influence of dangerous powers and seeks to find for himself a safe way by propitiating the "powers," or by living in the observance of the law.

Later in vs. 9 Paul states that a return to the Jewish observance of the law or to worship of "the elemental spirits" ought to be impossible for those who have learned to know God through Christ and who therefore also should know the inner purpose, task, and meaning of the law. The Galatians had, of course, not simply attained a better religious insight, they had also become incorporated into a historical sequence of events which had a cosmic and redemptive significance. They had not only *heard* about this, they themselves had been chosen to participate in it. What was happening belonged, as far as Paul was concerned, to the events of the last days. Through these events God bestowed the promised life and righteousness. Not only the Jews but also the Gentiles could belong to the elect. Those who were members of the church of Christ and were incorporated into his "body" became participants themselves in the events of the last days and instruments of God's activity.

The most significant point in this context seems to be the way in which Paul equates the law with "the elemental spirits." He regards existence under the law as a bondage which does not express the final, true, and right relationship to God. From this point of view Paul equates the Jewish way of showing their relationship to God by observance of the law with the cult worship of other religions. In these observances man is surrounded by powers which can be prevented from hurting him only by the observance of a multitude of regulations. He thus identifies the religious attitude under a law interpreted as in Judaism with the attitude found in heathen religions.

It is possible that the word *stoicheia* might best be translated divine beings on which man is dependent until the truth has become revealed in Christ. Thus far Paul is thinking of Gentile Christian readers. But essentially the Jews are in the same situation as these Gentiles had been. "The elemental spirits" seem to be identical with those "beings that by nature are no gods" (vs. 8; cf. exegesis of this verse below). What Paul has in mind is, therefore, that religious attitude which man has when he is not set free by Christ. This attitude of bondage, the compulsion to buy and secure religious certainty by works, rites, good conduct, or one's own sacrifices, and the need to propitiate the elemental spirits and render them favorable, are to be found both within Judaism and in pagan religions. These attitudes are in line with faith in the powers that rule in this present evil age. It was precisely at this point that the Jewish attitude to the law became similar to the religion of the pagans because it involved service to the powers of this age. It made the law something which belonged to this age. It deprived the law of its connection with the promise and thereby also with the salvation of the promised age. On this account the law and "the elemental spirits of the world" were equated. As we have already pointed out Paul does not reject faith in the elemental spirits in a way that would seem natural to a modern man by calling it an illusion and a false conception. According to Paul a false faith was concerned with objective powers, and overcoming a false religious conception was for him the same as the conquest of these objective powers. But this conquest can take place only through such a divine intervention as in Christ. Through him the elemental spirits have been overcome in an objective sense, and by faith in him false faith in these elemental spirits is likewise overcome.

Paul asserts that no person who knows what truth means can now voluntarily go back from freedom and light to servitude and darkness. It was for this reason that he addressed the bewildered Galatians as foolish and bewitched (3:1). He had also pointed out that the desire to be under the law and to obtain righteousness from it involved being under a curse (3:10). Darkness, ignorance, servitude, and condemnation are the essential characteristics of that realm where the knowledge of God did not obtain. But this knowledge has now been revealed through Christ. Only after the light has been revealed can man fully understand that the previous situation without Christ was total darkness. Only then can the darkness be known as darkness.

It must be remembered that in this passage Paul does not interpret the old covenant in its entirety. In it were found also the promise and faith in the promise. But here he has in mind righteousness by the law and the desire to seek and find one's own righteousness by observance of the law, contrary to the most profound meaning of Scripture. It was this attitude which was equated with pagan belief in angels, demons, or elemental spirits, which were supposed to be the cause of certain natural phenomena and exercised influence on the life of men. The expression "the elemental spirits of the universe" (*ta stoicheia tou kosmou*) occurs again in vs. 9ff. We will return to the interpretation of it in our exegesis of vss. 8-10.

What Paul urges on his readers is not a new, self-assumed attitude. They are not to develop a new spiritual position, nor are they to reject religious conceptions on mere rational grounds. Nor is he talking about a new psychological or religious method. What Paul proclaims is an objective fact which alone makes an entirely new spiritual attitude and a new religious understanding possible. This objective fact he presents to the Galatians. This alone was the basis on which they could be free from those powers in whose service they had been bound, and thus receive a new religious attitude. This foretold and eagerly awaited time which involved the fulfilment of the promise had now come, and thereby the time was past in which men were compelled to live under the rule of the powers of this world. Christ was precisely the Redeemer Israel had waited for. For people in modern time it might appear as if Jesus were simply a religious genius, and that "faith" meant merely to attach oneself to him by accepting a point of view similar to his. But for Paul it was a question of the fulfilment of the promise of righteousness through which the whole world was changed. As certain church fathers who stood relatively close to the New Testament point of view declare, the coming of Christ was of the same cosmic significance as the original creation; it signifies in a sense a new creation of God, or such a renewal of the first creation that it can now be restored to its original meaning and significance. For this reason the light of faith can be compared with God's original creation of light in the world by his word: "Let there be light" (cf. II Cor. 4:6). The coming of Christ was for Paul entirely different from the birth of an ordinary man. It was possible for him, therefore, to speak of the preexistence of Christ with God and of the creation of everything in heaven and on earth through him (Col. 1:6-7; Rom. 11:36;

I Cor. 8:6). What had come through the reconciliation of Christ and through his life and death was not something which could be produced through the genius of man. It was a work divine. With him came God's own righteousness and life, namely that which the law could not give (cf. 3:21), although the law in itself was holy, righteous, and good. And since man was created for righteousness and life, Christ restored him to that for which he had been created.

What Jesus was and did can be understood, therefore, only in the context of the biblical perspective of salvation. He brought what only God can give: life and righteousness. By this very fact he reveals his "divinity." His coming meant that the promised age was breaking in; its powers were already at work, even though they will be fully revealed only at his return. All the thoughts about Christ, that he who was rich became poor for our sake (II Cor. 8:9), and that he emptied himself (Phil. 2:6ff.), can be understood from the same point of view. The same applies to the words in Colossians: "In whom we have redemption, the forgiveness of sins. He is the image of the invisible God, the first-born of all creation; for in him all things were created, in heaven and on earth, visible and invisible, whether thrones or dominions or principalities or authorities—all things were created through him and for him. He is before all things, and in him all things hold together" (Col. 1:14-17). Life and salvation were to belong to man according to God's creation, but after man had fallen into sin they had to be restored to him through an act of God as significant as the first creation. The fulfilment of the promise came exactly in this way. Righteousness through Christ was made available not only in such a way as when a man comes with a new message and spiritual power, but rather in the way that God creates something entirely new whose profound and universal significance is revealed by the fact that it completes and restores the original creation.

When Christ came, his solidarity with the created world was demonstrated by his being born of a woman. "Man that is born of a woman is of few days," we read in Job. 14:1. Since he was born of woman, Christ belonged to this perishable life and was subject to death. Christ assumed this perishable state whose sting and power was sin and separation from and rebellion against the God of creation and life. He shared the situation of other men by being made subject to the authority of sin and death. Although he knew no sin he was made to be sin for our sake, "so that in him we might become the righteousness of God" (II Cor. 5:21). He was made subject to the law and its judgment, and thus shared the external conditions of other men. But his commission was to redeem those who were under the law. This action is described here and in 3:13-14 as the redemption of a slave. (For a discussion of the figure of redemption see the exegesis of those verses.)

As we have pointed out previously, the redemption could not take place through a proclamation which caused men to set aside the law. The law had divine validity. It could be annulled only because God the Giver of the law caused it to be fulfilled and attain its proper goal. Christ took upon himself the curse of the law, as stated in 3:13, and thereby he secured freedom from the authority of the law; a freedom which became available to both Jews and Gentiles. This meant at the same time that those who were under the law were set free for a life in which the law had no right to command and condemn. That religious freedom which men imagine they attain by accepting a new system of thought is not real freedom according to the New Testament way of thinking. It means rather that they come under a new bondage, even though they do not realize it. The freedom *in Christ* who is the fulfilment of the law is the only true freedom.

When the time had fully come, God sent his Son (vs. 4). The expression, "when the time had fully come," shows clearly that the "redemption" of Christ is seen in the context of the biblical perspective of salvation. The fulfilment of the time corresponds to the expression, "until the date set by the father," in the figure of the inheritance in vss. 1-2. The fulfilment of the time means that the amount of time set aside in God's plan of salvation had now run its course. The idea of the fulfilment of the time is closely related to the end of time. Now the measure of time was fulfilled, and something entirely new was to come. Now the last days had begun. The idea of the fulfilment of time is therefore eschatological; indeed Paul regarded all his work in the service of the gospel as belonging to the work God wanted to have done in the last days. The powers bestowed upon both Gentiles and Jews through the gospel belonged to the powers of the future, promised age, the age in which God's righteousness could be given and the law fulfilled through the life in the Spirit.

The idea that God sent his Son "in the fulness of time" implies that Paul thought of Christ as "pre-existent." Christ appears in God's plan of salvation in such a way that although in himself he was not under the law, he nevertheless became subject to the law. In and through this fact a settlement with the law was effected. God's revelation in Christ eclipsed and fulfilled the revelation in the law. Through the revelation of Christ the righteousness of the law was destroyed. Before Christ the law could be used to secure law-righteousness. Now man was placed before an absolute alternative: either he must submit to the law as fulfilled in Christ and thus be set free from the bondage involved in law-righteousness, or he could reject the law as now fulfilled. In the first case, man would submit in faith to that God who had given the law and had also provided its fulfilment (and its end) in Christ. In the second case, he would reject this faith and instead make himself a slave under the requirements of the law, which thus occupy the same position as the elemental spirits in the pagan religions.

Christ has redeemed men from these powers, but in order to do so he had to become obedient to the law. He became one who came through a woman; he became one who was under the law. The statement might be translated literally: "he was from a woman; he was under the law." Paul has not said therefore that God made use of a man in his service, or that he entrusted a great mission to a man. He speaks rather of Christ as of one who became something new by becoming man, by coming to earth through a woman and by being placed under the law. The import of his words is not merely that God was active in the whole life of Christ. He is concerned with the whole divine drama, which was not limited to the earthly life of Christ. Christ *became* man on earth, he *became* subject to that law which ruled there on account of sin. This thought assigns to Christ a different place in the divine drama from that of any other human being. But at the same time his "human nature" is emphasized by stating that he came from a woman (*genomenos* [to come from] includes also *gennomenos* [to be born]. Cf. Matt. 11:11. In the phrase *genomenos ek gunaikos* the word *genomenos* is given a specific connotation by *ek gunaikos* so that the meaning becomes "born of a woman". Christ the Son of God became the son of a woman; Christ who was not subject to the law became subject to the law.

That Paul here uses the verb *ginomai,* to become, and not *gennao,* to be born, may be due to the fact that he speaks of one who was not only born as everyone else but who came into the

world through a new creation of God. The genesis of the *world*
has its counterpart in the genesis of *Christ* (cf. Matt. 1:18). The
verb "to become" has a wider meaning than "to be born of." It
implies a birth, but it could also suggest that the reference is to
the birth of him who was God's Son and his agent for the regen-
eration of creation. He who was of God was born of a woman;
he who represented righteousness was made subject under the law
that demanded righteousness. "Born of woman" says therefore
something more than that Jesus was an ordinary human being.
His birth is a link in the divine activity. Christ came into the world
by being born of a woman, but he who by birth shared in the
mortality of human flesh was raised from the dead (cf. Acts
13:30-37). His entry into the world was the entry of God's
chosen Messiah. He was the Son of God, "the first-born of all
creation" (Col. 1:15). The words "come (being) of a woman,"
"come (being) under the law," indicate both that according to
Paul Christ came from God and that he was a man. He existed
in the form and appearance of God, but he did not selfishly
retain his likeness to God, but emptied himself and assumed the
form and appearance of a slave (Phil. 2:6ff.). In the words, "born
of woman," there is a suggestion of what in Matthew and Luke
is expressed by the stories of the virgin birth. The incarnation of
Christ is referred to here in dogmatic terms which later became
common. The doctrine of the two natures of Christ developed in
the ancient church uses somewhat different terms, but behind the
Greek formulations of this doctrine there lie thoughts appearing
in this passage of Galatians and elsewhere.

Christ was made subject to the law, but since according to his
nature he did not belong under the law and did not seek righteousness through it, his submission under the law became a fulfilment of the law, through which the meaning and purpose of
the law were brought to its goal. What God did through Christ
was done "so that we might receive adoption as sons," and this
meant the same as saying that the promised "inheritance," the
righteousness from God, came through him. The word *huiothesia*
means sonship (adoption). The task God had given Christ was
"to redeem us" from the law, i.e., from the realm where the law
condemns and where, because it operates in the service of sin, it
incites to law-righteousness.

The positive factor, which replaces slavery under the law after
Christ has set men free from it, is the adoption. Christ redeemed

both Jews and Greeks from their bondage. To receive the adoption expresses the same reality Paul earlier described under the figure of the inheritance and the heir. Adoption means becoming a son. It may seem that coming of age with the privileges of an adult and becoming a child are contradictory figures, but they serve here to illustrate the same reality viewed from two different points of view. Both figures are intended to show how a person who by baptism and faith has been united with Christ receives the life and righteousness promised to Abraham's children who are the heirs of God and belong to him. The word child may of course be used to designate either a descendant of a certain parent or simply a minor. Paul used the word first in the sense of a minor in contrast with one who has attained the privileges of an adult. Since these privileges, however, were dependent on being an heir, he switches over to the primary meaning of the word child. When he enters upon the possession of the inheritance, the difference between the one who is son and heir and the one who is not appears. The mature heir proves to be a son, a child of the one from whom the inheritance came. In this way the emphasis comes to be placed on the sonship that suggests the relationship between an adult son and the father. "Sonship" does not refer then to the child's status as a minor but to the privileged status of the son and heir. It is precisely as mature and in the possession of the inheritance that the heir becomes in a real sense "a child" and proves to be the son of a father in whose riches he now participates.

This sonship or this fellowship with Christ is manifested in the reception of the Spirit. The Spirit belongs with faith. He certifies that God himself has appointed the one who lives in faith (i.e., in Christ) as son and heir, destined to receive a share in the righteousness promised by God. The Spirit is the Spirit of Christ, who enables the Christian to cry, "Abba, Father." Since Christ through his work has secured our adoption as sons, his Spirit can be sent to those who belong to him. Faith, baptism, and the Spirit belong together in Paul's thinking (cf. 3:26ff.).

The change from "you" to "our" in vs. 6 has caused some discussion. "Because *you* are sons, God has sent the Spirit of his Son into *our* hearts." The emphasis is on the word sons. In the second part of the sentence Paul includes himself among them. He means: "You as well as I, all of us as sons have received that Spirit of adoption in whom we cry: 'Abba! Father.'"

This last phrase is made up of an Aramaic and a Greek word with the same meaning. The two languages in which the Christians of that day worshiped God as Father have become fused into *one*. According to Paul no one can really call God Father except through the Spirit. Man's previous situation could be spoken of as a worship of "the elemental spirits of the universe." Among these "elemental spirits" Jewish bondage under the law was included, because by encouraging works of the law and righteousness by works the law was reduced to the level of "the elemental spirits of the universe."

The Spirit God had sent into the hearts of the faithful was the Spirit of his Son. The outpouring of the Spirit belonged to the promised, Messianic time (cf. Joel 2:28-29; Isa. 44:3). These promises were now fulfilled, and believers were permitted to call God "Abba." It appears that Jesus is the one who originated the use of this Aramaic word as addressed to God (cf. Mark 14:36). He addressed God as Abba because he was the Son of God who stood in an immediate and intimate relationship to God. He was the promised Messiah, the Son of God. When Peter confessed him as the Messiah, the Son of the living God, Jesus called him blessed, since flesh and blood had not revealed it to him but the Father in heaven (Matt. 16:16-17). He to whom Jesus has been revealed as the Son and who in faith belongs to him addresses God as "Abba! Father!" This title of God belongs to the time of the fulfilment of the promise, the time of the inheritance, the time of freedom and sonship.

The fact that Jesus called God "Abba" enables us to see a fulfilment of those words in Scripture which speak of God as Father, and which evidently were interpreted in a Messianic sense (cf. Jer. 3:19; 31:9; Ps. 89:27).

In the seventh verse Paul summarizes his exposition of the new factors brought in by Christ. Here he places side by side the figure of the inheritance which the heir receives at the time appointed by the father (vss. 1-2) and the conception of the Christian as one whom Christ has redeemed to become a son and a child of God (vss. 3-5).

To live by faith in God meant to receive the inheritance. It was God's decision that he who in faith received Christ and the Spirit should become an heir. God had appointed as heirs those whom he had called to faith (cf. Rom. 8:29-30). The call of the gospel was a call to receive the Spirit of Christ. This Spirit, the

Spirit of adoption, was the sign that they had been called as heirs of the blessing promised to Abraham. The gospel called them to fellowship with God's chosen people of the last days, of the true Israel, "the Israel according to the Spirit," "the Israel of God" (Rom. 2:28; 9:6; Gal. 6:16). The Spirit of adoption was the sign of freedom from bondage and fear. When law and death ruled, the result was fear. The freedom from fear given in and through the Spirit had now replaced the spirit of slavery which inspired fear and compelled men to seek to propitiate the powers they feared. This meant also that those who had received the spirit of adoption were heirs and would receive with Christ the glory God had prepared for those who belonged to him (cf. Rom. 8:14-17).

He who has received that Spirit in whom he prays: "Abba! Father!" has no reasons to worship those powers under whom he was previously in bondage. Freedom means among other things that man does not need anxiously to seek security through the observance of various customs and regulations. He who has everything need not try to earn anything by his own efforts. He does not need to seek a reward through what he does, and he cannot differentiate himself from others as having a greater claim to a reward just because he has followed the way of the observance of the law.

III. A Relapse into Righteousness of the Law Leads to Bondage (4:8—5:12)

1. A redeemed person, "known by God," ought not to return to bondage (4:8-11)

This paragraph, 4:8-11, is in many respects closely related to the preceding section. These verses continue the exposition of vss. 1-7, and the expression "the elemental spirits of the universe" appears again. Many exegetes in outlining the letter combine vss. 8-11 with vss. 1-7. The fact that Paul seems to make a new start in vs. 12 is in favor of this combination. Some have even assumed that there was a pause in the dictation between vs. 11 and vs. 12.

There are also, however, reasons for taking vss. 8-11 as an introduction to a larger section extending to 5:13. In this section the discussion is concerned with the Galatians' relapse into a state which Paul considers to be of the same kind as the pagan religion they had practiced before they became partakers of the gospel at his first visit. In this large section (4:12—5:12) Paul appeals personally to the Galatians, reminds them how enthusiastically they had received him at first, explains by an allegorical-typological exposition of a well-known Scripture passage what a relapse would mean, and places before them the necessity of decision by showing them what the consequences of their being circumcised would be. The emphasis in this whole section is on the point that the demand for circumcision and observance of the law does not constitute a more complete gospel. This demand meant rather a return to the bondage under the elemental spirits in which the Gentiles lived, or to that covenant of bondage which was prefigured in Abraham's slave concubine Hagar and her son Ishmael, who were driven away from the fellowship with Abraham and the son of the promise. To institute circumcision meant nothing less than to renounce participation in the grace of Christ. Paul even uses violent words in wishing that those who agitate for circumcision would mutilate themselves.

The content in 4:8-11 serves admirably as an introduction to this section. After his explication of how faith in Christ has made man a true heir, free and in possession of the promised blessing, the inheritance which was to come to the children of promise, Paul goes on in 4:8-11 to emphasize how absurd it would be for the Galatians to return to the bondage from which they had been liberated, after they had once attained to the full status as heirs (and were free in the possession of the riches of the gospel).

The transitions between the different sections, however, are so vague that one section in the outline may sometimes be referred either to what precedes or to what follows. In general Paul's letters are not

written as systematic expositions with strictly separated chapters. A
theme which he takes up may have been mentioned earlier in passing.
Thus for example the section 2:15-21 may be taken as a solemn
conclusion to the discussion of his relationship to the older apostles
and a kind of prelude to the melody taken up in the next chapter.
In the beginning of chap. 4 it may be said that vss. 1-7 conclude
the previous discussion with a new figure (the heir and the inheritance, through which the complete change in the situation of the
world, realized through the coming of Christ, could be elucidated
by the idea of how Christ redeemed us from the curse of the law,
alluded to already in 3:13). The material immediately preceding could
have been used in 4:8-11 to illustrate the absurdity of a return to
the old status. That it is a question of such a relapse is evident in
the whole of the following section up to 5:12. Thus also the section
4:8-11 ends with an expression of Paul's personal anxiety that he
may have labored in vain among the Galatians.

Although there may be reasons for taking verses 8-11 with the
previous section, it seems as though the course of the argument becomes clearer if it is taken with the following section dealing with
the danger of a relapse into the bondage under the righteousness of
the law.

It was not the law in itself that Paul regarded as a part of the
"elemental spirits of the universe," but righteousness by the law.
The judgment of the law was not accepted as the judgment of
God, but was evaded by means of righteousness by the law. From
one point of view this was a perversion of the law, which might
appear as something merely subjective. But Paul regarded it also
as an objective power. From Paul's point of view a false religion
represented powers which operated as false gods. Paul's view of
the law is therefore very difficult for modern man to understand,
since in and by itself the law represents God's will, but by a false
use it comes to represent an objective power from which Christ
must set us free. In this false attitude to the law man becomes
a servant of powers which stand in conflict with God and his truth.
These powers could then be spoken of as gods, while at the same
time they are described as being in their very nature *no* gods at
all. They did not represent God's truth, nor those powers which
were to endure and could give life. They were non-beings and
false imaginings, but at the same time also objective powers which
really held men in bondage.

Paul evidently holds that the attitude to the law appearing as
law-righteousness involves worship of powers which are a perversion of God's power and stand in opposition to it. As we have
already stated, however, this does not mean at all that the law

given by God at Sinai in itself really was such an evil power. Nevertheless it did not represent God's clearest and final revelation. It was given because of sin, and its task was to accuse, condemn, and keep men under restraint until the promised righteousness came. Life under the law was thus a life under judgment, but because righteousness had been promised, it was not without hope. But instead of submitting to God's judgment in the law and believing in the promise, the people who lived under the power of sin perverted the law into law-righteousness. They sought to escape the righteous judgment of the law instead of submitting to it. They sought to obtain a righteousness of their own instead of admitting God's justice and looking to the promise of a righteousness which God would send in the fulness of time. *Faith* is precisely this: to acknowledge God's righteous judgment and to trust in his promise; and the opposite of this faith is to seek to enhance oneself before God by one's own righteousness. Men who used the law had fallen away from God and had come under the power of sin. *This* was the reason why the law, in itself good, became a means of law-righteousness and could be placed on a par with "the elemental spirits" and false gods (cf. Rom. 7:7-25).

That God had spoken in the law and had revealed his will through it was for Paul an irrevocable and self-evident truth. But the law had to be accepted in the obedience of faith, and had to be rightly understood and applied.

Through Christ it became evident that the external requirements of the law did not possess any value as means of righteousness. What the requirements of the law contained was "a shadow of what is to come; but the substance belongs to Christ" (Col. 2:17). He who lived in faith, therefore, ought not to let anyone pass judgment on him "in questions of food and drink or with regard to a festival or a new moon or a sabbath" (Col. 2:16). If service under these requirements of the law was regarded as a means of obtaining righteousness, it became service under gods "that by nature are no gods" (Gal. 4:8). These "gods" are evidently the same powers mentioned in vss. 3 and 9. Here it becomes evident how, according to Paul, a false interpretation and use of the law somehow creates false gods. We must not think of these conceptions, however, in the modern sense as mere superstitious notions. The power men served in righteousness by the law was to Paul also a reality in life. In a certain sense the gods who by nature are no gods were real powers, but they had been disarmed through Christ (Col. 2:15). They were therefore indeed real powers for those who did not share in the victory over them through Christ. But for those who lived in faith they were nothing, and their nothingness appeared clearly in the light of faith. Their unreality meant that they lacked the powers which they were believed to possess, and that they led men to unrighteousness rather than righteousness. This very expression, "beings that by nature are no gods" (or "that according to their nature are no gods"), illustrates the difference between Paul's way of speaking about the reality men worship and the way in which we conceive of it today.

It is evident that to Paul the worship of false gods is not something we can dismiss by saying they do not exist. To believe in them involves not only a certain conception but also a practical religious attitude. This attitude is not removed by changing conceptions: it is then simply attached to other notions. We cannot say, therefore, that Paul regarded the Jewish understanding of the law which led to law-righteousness as *merely* a false conception of the law. By the very fact of believing in the law in this sense, man placed himself in the service of a concrete power. Freedom from slavery under the law (in the sense of righteousness by the law) could not therefore be attained, as we might imagine, by simply adopting another conception. The difference between the understanding of the law in righteousness by faith and in righteousness by the law involved, as we have pointed out above, service to different powers: the power of God in the righteousness by faith, and a divinity belonging among "the elemental spirits" in righteousness by the law. Righteousness by faith meant serving God and not self. As long as man serves self, of which service the righteousness by the law is a typical expression, he cannot rightly *comprehend* God. On the whole Paul maintains that a right *knowledge* of God and salvation is connected with a right *religious attitude*. This applied also to the very understanding of Scripture.

There is a formal similarity between the tendency of both Paul and the rabbis to seek for a deeper meaning in Scripture. But to Paul insight into the deeper meaning is not the result of studies or of a tradition received from a teacher. A new understanding of the law and Scripture such as Paul presents could be obtained only through the reception of a revelation which changes completely the manner of the religious life. The revelation would be not only in the nature of an impartation of theoretical knowledge but the acceptance of and participation in an act of God. Only in this way could the new knowledge of Scripture and the new understanding of the law and of God's actions be obtained. Christ must "redeem us" from slavery under the law (or under "the elemental spirits") in order that the new knowledge might become a reality. Servitude under these powers was connected with the wisdom God makes foolish (I Cor. 1:20). On the other hand Christ is the power of God and the wisdom of God (vs. 24). The knowledge connected with the deeper understanding of Scripture and the law is at the same time a power from God, and it was this knowledge that was given in and through the redemption from bondage which came through the work of Christ.

Christ's redemption of man is the prerequisite of the knowledge corresponding with righteousness by faith. At the same time it could be said that this knowledge was latently expressed in Scripture. Righteousness by faith was already given in advance through faith in the promise, especially as exemplified in Abraham, but only as a looking forward to that which was to come. Servitude under righteousness by the law, or under powers and gods who are no gods, involved for Paul always a false knowledge. But this false knowledge cannot be overcome and replaced by a true knowledge except by the attainment of a new religious attitude. But this presupposes that a divine action has been accomplished in and through which redemption takes place and a new power becomes available. Faith and the deeper understanding of the law are therefore always connected with the reception of the Spirit who is the power of God given to men.

Since the power of Christ represents God's own truth, the powers of the world which men serve in righteousness by the law can be said to be nothingness. In spite of the fact that they rule over men in righteousness by the law, and that man can be set free from them only through the work of Christ, they really represent nothingness. They are "beings that by nature are no gods." In Paul's thought about man's redemption through Christ it is never implied that the powers engaged in conflict stand on the same level, nor is the one power stronger in a material sense, as when one nation proves to be stronger than another. On the contrary, God and his truth are revealed through Christ. When this truth is revealed and disseminated through the gospel, which represents the truth (Gal. 5:7), God's power through which man was created has taken possession of him and has redeemed him from the alien power. What we have discussed above may be expressed also by saying that to be under the power of righteousness by the law involved an attempt to make the self master over the law and thus obscuring the revelatory character of the law. In doing so the law was at the same time made to serve powers who are hostile to God and keep men imprisoned in self-righteousness. This means rebellion against God and the divine truth. A true service to God, therefore, meant always a service of righteousness and truth, and to fall away from him meant to fall victim to unrighteousness and falsehood. Through the fall man's mind became "darkened" (Rom. 1:21). That men's falling away from God, appearing as wisdom (cf. also Col. 2:23), was in reality foolishness could be seen clearly in the fact that they acquired "a base mind" (Rom. 1:28).

The worship of alien gods was thus an expression of a lie, because man worshiped a power which in reality was nothingness. It led to bondage, and for a while it may appear powerful. Under the illusion of freedom it kept men from the service which really made them free, i.e., fellowship with Christ.

The expression in vs. 9, "to be known by God," has sometimes been taken as a proof that Paul was dependent on Hellenistic piety. The expression occurs, for example, in Hermetic writings. But in Paul this expression must be understood in connection with his other conceptions. In the mystery cults to be known by a divinity meant in general the highest revelation of the deity and the acceptance of the one initiated into the divine fellowship. In a formal sense it might seem that Paul meant something like that. But his whole conception of the content of the revelation is entirely different from that of the mystery cults. To be known by God is a thought explicated in Rom. 8:29-30. It is closely related to Paul's view of election, and its background is the Old Testament. To know God means to have a God-given understanding of everything that God demands and gives. It involves not only knowledge but also a personal relationship to God. Moses and the prophets knew God and his ways. This knowledge belonged to those specially chosen. But in the enunciated time of the new covenant everyone was to know the ways of the Lord (Jer. 31:33-34). The idea of "being known by God" occurs sometimes in the Old Testament together with the expression "to know God" (cf. Exod.

33:12-13; I Kings 8:39). If to know God was something which belonged to the elect, fellowship with God could be even more strongly expressed by the words "to be known by God." The Lord knows the way of the righteous (Ps. 1:6) and gives them life, while the way of the unrighteous shall perish. The Lord is said to know David. He had chosen him to be king (For example, II Sam. 7:20ff.) over Israel whom he had redeemed in order that they should be his people. A similar thought about election is found in Jeremiah, where the Lord says that he had chosen him before he formed him in the womb (Jer. 1:5). In the servant songs the Suffering Servant of the Lord is said to be the chosen one (Isa. 42ff.). The idea of election is connected with the words that God knows whom he has chosen. Paul himself had been "set apart before he was born." Christ had been revealed to him (cf. exegesis of 1:15-16).

As far as Paul is concerned the expression to "have been known by God" means that man has been chosen to become a partaker in the action of the gospel. Now the Suffering Servant of the Lord had come in Christ, and now he had been declared to be the Son of God in power. Now righteousness was given through the gospel. Man's participation in the action of the gospel and his justification were dependent on God's foreordination and election. God had foreknown those he had called, and he had destined them to conform to the image of his Son (Rom. 8:29-30). He who belonged to God was destined to belong to that spiritual reality which came in Christ, and in which the believer was united with him. The Galatians had been elected and chosen to participate in the righteousness and life Christ bestowed. Thereby they had learned to know God, learned to know his law fulfilled in the life in the Spirit, and had experienced what was involved in the work of Christ. They had been included in God's last and greatest act, that act of revelation in which he not only promised but actually bestowed righteousness. Thus they had seen and been admitted into that new covenant, the new Israel, to which the people of the old covenant had looked forward, and as heirs they had received what had been promised. They had not only become partners in the election of Israel; they had experienced the fulfilment of the promises. Thus they were in the deepest sense known by God. They had become the chosen ones who shared in the final revelation of God as he made himself known through his Son, the only one who could fully make him known.

Now if they left this election and returned to their former state, it would be a most foolish step. The Galatians who wanted to be circumcised acted like persons who had received an inheritance but failed to claim it, or as slaves who had been freed but wanted to return to bondage.

As an example of the bondage to which the Galatians had begun to return during Paul's absence he mentions that they observed days, months, seasons, and years. Some exegetes point out that these words could have a wider reference than merely to Jewish legal requirements. The Ethiopian Book of Enoch holds that astronomic relationships have special significance for human life. Months and seasons are assumed to depend on the authority of definite powers. It is suggested that Paul's "elemental spirits of the universe" refer to astrological powers of nature which are assumed to control human life. Certain exegetes (for example, Schlier) have interpreted vs. 10 in this direction and rejected the commonly accepted assumption that "days, months, seasons, and years" refer to regulations contained in the law of Moses, e.g., the Sabbath, the Year of Jubilee and other matters in the Jewish calendar of festivals.

If by the expression "the elemental spirits" Paul refers to religious, astrological conceptions, it means nevertheless that he equates the bondage under these powers with the attitude to the law of Moses appearing in righteousness by the law. The same religious attitude is involved in both. It is from the point of view of righteousness by faith that this becomes clear. From a practical point of view the result is the same whether Paul in vs. 10 thinks of the regulations of the law of Moses or of astrological conceptions. (See further the exposition of vs. 3 above and the exegesis of "the elemental spirits of the universe.")

Even if the Jewish festival calendar played a minor role outside Palestine, the custom of observing certain seasons may have been strengthened through the Judaizers' way of interpreting the law of Moses. Both the Jews and the Christians talked about righteousness. According to the Judaizers' interpretation righteousness could be obtained by the observance of certain legal requirements. It would then be natural for ancient rules and customs in the observance of months and days of both Jewish and Gentile origin to become of greater importance. The words in vs. 10 may therefore allude both to requirements of the Jewish law and to conceptions found in Hellenism. But we ought not to draw such extravagant conclusions from these words, as some (like A. Oepke) do for instance when they claim on the basis of this verse that the letter was written during a Jewish sabbatical year, and suggest the year A.D. 55 as the most likely.

For anyone who knew what the gospel meant it must have been shocking that those who had received the Spirit would want to seek security in self-assumed works of the law (cf. 3:1ff.; 1:6) and in their own piety (cf. Col. 2:23). Paul expresses his anxiety for the Galatians in a moving, personal address. They would be insane if they permitted themselves to be led astray and lost everything they had received. If they indulged in such folly, there was grave danger that they were lost to the gospel and that Paul's work had been in vain.

2. The Galatians' attitude to the gospel now and at the time of Paul's first visit (4:12-20)

The words in vs. 11 serve as a transition between the previous section and what follows. The present section contains personal appeals and allusions to common experiences. It is very difficult to decide with any degree of certainty what is the right interpretation of the various statements in this section. It is more difficult to know what Paul refers to in these personal appeals than in his theological discussions.

Verse 12 constitutes in a certain sense a new start, but not as definitely as in 3:1. Paul addressed the Galatians directly in the preceding verses also. But in 4:12-20 Paul brings the situation at the time of his first visit into the discussion. In reality this section is a part of the theological argumentation, since it touches on how the Galatians earlier had reacted to the gospel and to him as its apostle. Here, however, it is more a question of their personal relationship to him as the apostle of Christ. In vs. 21 he returns to his exposition of the freedom of faith in contrast to the bondage of righteousness by the law as he begins his formally allegorical exegesis of the story of Abraham's two wives in the Book of Exodus, i.e., in the law. Thus he returns also to the exposition of the law as a witness to faith and to righteousness by the law as a state of bondage; a state which is outside the sphere of election and of that Israel which God had chosen.

a) A personal appeal (4:12)

The meaning in vs. 12 is not immediately clear. It contains a personal appeal. "Become as I am, for I also have become as you are," he says. This has sometimes been interpreted as an appeal for mutual consideration. But in view of the whole content of the letter there can be no question of a real compromise. Rather, what Paul says is that the Galatians ought to follow him in the way of the gospel. Just as he had become as a Jew to the Jews, so he had become as a Greek to the Greeks (I Cor. 9:20). The note of personal appeal is unmistakable. Paul frequently admonished his disciples to become imitators of him (I Cor. 4:16; 11:1; Phil. 3:17; II Thess. 3:7).

When Paul admonished the Corinthians to become his imitators (I Cor. 4:16), he pointed out to them in the previous verses how God had placed him and his helpers as the last of all, as men sentenced to death, as fools for Christ's sake and as weak, while the Corinthians and those whom they imitated were "wise" in Christ and strong.

The idea of imitation as it has appeared in the later history of theology has commonly involved seeking to obtain a greater degree of holiness, virtue, and strength. The imitation that Paul recommends is an imitation of being nothing in oneself and of looking away from self, which cannot be accomplished by merits and "works of the law." Paul, in admonishing the Galatians in 4:12 to become as he was, is urging them to cease their attempts to obtain their own righteousness. He points out that it was physical weakness and sickness that caused him to preach the gospel to them the first time. He had not appeared to be strong and remarkable as men usually judge; he had been a weak and sick man. Nevertheless, then the Galatians understood that he was a true messenger of the gospel. It is in this sense that he admonishes them to become as he was. They were not to seek that self-righteousness the circumcised assumed which separated them from others so that they could imagine themselves strong and holy. They were to receive the gospel in their own weakness. They ought not to build up their own exclusive holiness and trust in it.

The tone in this whole section (vss. 12-20) is intimate and bears witness to Paul's intense union with the Galatians in love. He calls them brethren (vs. 12) and "my little children" (vs. 19). But the fact that at his visit with them he had been as one of them, although they were uncircumcised, was not due to a concession in weakness but was in accordance with the nature and content of the gospel. The gospel was meant for the Gentiles. As pagans the Galatians had stood outside the Jewish law. They had been slaves to "the elemental spirits," and from *one* point of view Paul equated these "spirits" with the law of Moses insofar as this law became a means of righteousness by the law. In admonishing the Galatians to become as he was, Paul refers to the freedom he himself had "in Christ." Only "in Christ," in the gospel, was there real freedom from all righteousness by the law. Paul had become one with the Galatians through the gospel, and in that sense he had become like them. He begs the Galatians now to receive the fellowship of the gospel in that same freedom which he had in Christ, and not to destroy the unity of the gospel by drawing up new limitations for it.

It is difficult to say what the words, "you did me no wrong," refer to. Primarily they seem to mean that Paul's zeal is not due to any personal affront or injury. He did not speak because he had been insulted. It was not a question of personal prestige, and no personal ambition drove him to an exclusive demand on the Galatians' obedience and affection (cf. vs. 18). Possibly the reference is not only to the fact that his zeal was for the cause of the gospel, but more concretely to what he develops in the following verses, that the Galatians had not despised him because of his bodily ailment during his first visit. Then they had understood very well the riches contained in the gospel, so that they had not drawn away from him at all, or regarded him as demon-possessed, and thus humiliated him. On the contrary, they had received him as an angel of God, yea, even as Jesus Christ himself.

It is possible that Paul's words contain another allusion. During his first visit the joy and enthusiasm of the Galatians for the gospel had removed all hindrances of fellowship between them and Paul. *Then* the Galatians had understood how to receive the gospel rightly. Then the gospel had removed not only the fear that Paul's sickness might have inspired (i.e., that he stood under the wrath of God and had been delivered to the demons), but also the fear which the local Jews may have inspired in them, namely that table fellowship among the Christians was wrong unless the regulations of the law were observed. The Galatians had not wronged Paul by separating themselves from him. Neither had they done wrong, however, by giving him occasion to have table fellowship with them without demanding that they be circumcised and observe the law. That he could do so was not because he made concessions in weakness and betrayed the gospel, it was rather the only true form of the gospel.

Whatever Paul may have had in mind, he emphasizes strongly that it was not a matter of an ordinary struggle for power on his part. His words serve to clarify the contrast between the Galatians' submission to the Judaizers and their attitude at the time of Paul's first visit.

> b) *The Galatians' enthusiastic reception of Paul at his first visit (4:13-15)*

Verse 13 refers to Paul's first visit. The words *to proteron* (the first time) do not refer in general to an earlier visit but directly to the first visit. According to Acts Paul visited "the region of Galatia" twice (Acts 16:6; 18:23). If the South-Galatian theory is untenable, the words "at first" would refer to the visit recorded in Acts 16:6 during the second missionary journey (cf. the Introduction).

The Galatians had received Paul as an angel of God, yea, as Christ himself. Proponents of the South-Galatian theory have interpreted these words as reflecting the reception Paul met in Lystra according to Acts 14:11ff. That narrative seems, however, to deal with an entirely different reception from the one Paul talks about here. The homage the people accorded to Paul and Barnabas as Mercury and Jupiter according to Acts 14 was something they emphatically repudiated. In response to this homage they had torn their clothing. But in Gal. 4:14 Paul says that the Galatians received him as Christ himself. They had received the apostle and messenger of Christ as the one who sent him, and had given the same honor to the apostle as to him who had sent him and in whose service he was engaged. He does not speak of this as something worthy of censure, which was the case when the people received Paul and Barnabas as pagan gods. He speaks of it rather with joy and approbation. When he first visited them the Galatians had understood in whose service Paul was engaged. They realized that his gospel was of divine origin and that he represented the Messiah himself. They understood that he came to them with a message which made them partakers in righteousness and life.

The reason Paul stopped and preached the gospel to the Galatians the first time was his sickness. The physical ailment mentioned in vs. 13 was evidently an acute sickness.

There is an extensive literature dealing with this sickness of Paul. Gal. 4:13 has been combined with II Cor. 12:7. It is, however, not at all certain that these two passages refer to the same sickness. It is quite possible that here in Galatians the reference

211

is to an acute sickness, while in II Cor. 12:7 the reference is to a chronic ailment. Some have maintained that the second passage indicates that Paul was afflicted with epilepsy. Other commentators have emphatically rejected this suggestion. There are also some who have held that the reference is not to a sickness but to sufferings caused by his opponents. On the whole it is not necessary to know what sickness it was in order to understand Paul's meaning. What he emphasizes is that the Galatians could easily have rejected him on account of his condition. Paul reminds them that they believed him in spite of his sickness. Many forms of sickness were associated with demons. If the sickness had been of such a kind, it would have been natural for the Galatians to avoid him. Paul points out that they did not follow this obvious course.

The statement in vs. 14 is very compact, as if Paul in his dictation had combined two expressions in one. "And though my condition was a trial to you, you did not scorn or despise me" (despise—really "spew out," which may suggest a gesture of trying to ward off the influence of a sick person suspected of being demon-possessed), "but received me as an angel of God, as Christ Jesus." The two expressions of the same thought seem to mean: You did not despise me in my physical weakness; and: You did not succumb to the temptation into which my physical weakness might have led you. If the two expressions are combined and *peirasmos* is understood as that which causes temptation, the meaning would be: "You did not despise my physical condition, although you might have been tempted to do so."

Instead of avoiding Paul as possessed and unclean the Galatians had received him as a messenger of salvation, yea, even as the Savior himself. Paul's message had made such a deep impression that it had completely overcome their natural reluctance to have anything to do with a person in his physical condition. Paul points to what the Galatians had experienced earlier and reminds them of the satisfaction they had felt. Just as they had received the Spirit when they listened in faith (3:2), thus they had also been filled with thankfulness. But now they were evidently not filled with the same joy. An angel of God comes with a message from God, and the Galatians had understood that the gospel which Paul brought was a real message of joy. They had understood that Paul was in the service of Christ and was sent by him. They received him therefore as the One who had sent him.

The Galatians' devotion and enthusiasm at Paul's first visit must have been tremendous. Paul says that if it were possible they would have plucked out their eyes and given them to him. The statement may mean that they were willing to give Paul their dearest possession. It has also been suggested, however, that the expression is not proverbial or figurative (cf. also Matt. 5:29; 18:9; Mark 9:47), but indicates that Paul's physical ailment was some kind of eye sickness. In that case the meaning would be that if possible the Galatians would have given their own eyes to replace his diseased ones. The words "if possible" might seem to favor this interpretation. The statement does not seem to be a proverbial expression.

c) The Galatians are willingly led astray (4:16-18)

The conduct of the Galatians now and at his first visit was quite different. What was the reason for the change? Was it, he asks, possibly in bitter sarcasm, that he had become their enemy by telling them the truth? What the words "telling you the truth" refer to has been variously interpreted. Some have assumed (thus A. Oepke) that during Paul's second visit he had warned them against apostasy (cf. 1:9), or against abuse of the freedom of the gospel (cf. 5:21), or that he was afraid he had become their enemy by the way he was now writing to them (Zahn). But *aletheuein* (to speak the truth, to maintain truth, to be truthful) very likely refers (as Schlier holds) to the proclamation of the truth of the gospel (cf. 2:5, 14). It was for the truth of the gospel that Paul fought against its perversion of it by the Judaizers. It was Paul's way of explicating, in opposition to the righteousness by the law, the meaning of the gospel that they had now begun to regard as a false and incomplete gospel to be amended and reinterpreted (cf. 1:6ff.). This was the gospel the Galatians at first had received with enthusiasm, but which later had been subjected to criticism, reinterpretation, and doubt. (Paul, of course, had paid them at least a second visit and very likely had maintained contact with them.) Paul asks if it was his preaching of the truth of the gospel which had caused the Galatians to look upon him with such suspicion that he had come to be regarded as a dangerous beguiler and an enemy against whom they must be on their guard. As Paul ironically suggests, it would be an obvious absurdity that the Galatians should regard Paul in this way because of his preaching of the truth of the gospel. They had not avoided him even when his physical condition could have made them suspicious and fearful. Should they now regard him as an enemy, when no such reason was at hand, and after they had experienced the meaning of the gospel through the reception of the Spirit? Was it because of the gifts Paul had mediated—the truth of the gospel and participation in the Spirit—that they now suspected him as an enemy? Telling the truth seems, therefore, to refer to his proclamation and explanation of the meaning of the gospel. It was for the truth that Paul had fought in Jerusalem (cf. 2:5; 2:14). He had entered the conflict then that the truth of the gospel might be brought unobscured to the Gentiles.

Paul says—possibly still ironically—that the Judaizers make much of the Galatians, but for no good purpose. Their zeal was aimed at isolating them. Paul does not say from what the Judaizers wanted to shut them out. He may have meant that they wanted to shut them off from the influence of others, especially from that of Paul and his helpers. He could also have meant that the Judaizers wanted to separate the Galatians from what Paul proclaimed: grace, faith, and everything included in them. Righteousness by the law always separates those who find therein their honor and merit from others who do not follow that pattern. The expression *zelos* (zeal, to make much of) seems to point to the selfish zeal of the Judaizers. It was their intention to guard the Galatians against the influence of Paul and to keep them from participation in the gospel he proclaimed. Instead they put them in bondage under the law. The Judaizers tried to make the Galatians adhere to their own proclamation with enthusiasm and fanaticism. The word *zelos* is translated "envy" in 5:20 and is listed among the works of the flesh. In that passage it denotes selfish zeal born of envy and party spirit. It is a form of the same word that Paul uses in this passage to describe the envious and partisan zeal of the Judaizers for the Galatians (*zelousin humas ou kalos*). He contrasts this zeal with being made much of with a good purpose (*zelousthai en kalo*).

The statement in vs. 18 is so brief that it is difficult to say with certainty what it means. It is always good to be made much of for a good purpose, says Paul, and not only when he is present. The line of thought in vss. 16-18 seems to be as follows: "Have I become your enemy by explaining to you the meaning of the gospel? These false teachers, who have led you astray, make much of you, but for no good purpose. They want to separate you from all who do not observe the rules of piety they propose, and especially from me and from the truth of the gospel. They do this that you may hold yourselves to them and to the form of piety they claim to be the only means of salvation. They want you for themselves, and thereby they reveal the conceit in their religion and their completely selfish motives. As far as I am concerned I think it well that you are made much of, even when I am not present with you. But zeal ought to be in the interest of a good and proper cause, that is, for the truth of the gospel."

d) Paul's anxiety and travail for the Galatians (4:19-20)

In vss. 19 and 20 Paul expresses his anxiety because the Galatians have fallen away from the truth of the gospel. They had been born to the gospel through Paul. He can truly call them his children. But now they have not been living as his children, and they must again experience such a change that they could be said to have been born again as his children. The words, "My little children, with whom I am again in travail until Christ be formed in you!" do not simply express Paul's own emotions of anxiety and love. They also state something objective, namely that to receive Christ involves a new birth. He who is in Christ is a new creation (II Cor. 5:17). For someone to be born in Christ so that Christ is formed in him is to receive a share in the promised righteousness and the powers of the new age. Circumcision and the law in its Jewish interpretation belonged, according to Paul, to the present age and to the old covenant. To be born anew meant to be born to participation in the righteousness of Christ and in his resurrection life. It was something entirely new, in comparison with which every other religion appeared as religious self-aggrandizement. These religions could take various forms, but they all belonged to this age. As we have pointed out above, therefore, the pagan religious forms, astrological cult practices, the piety of the mysteries, and Jewish legalism appeared simply as variations of the service of "the elemental spirits of the universe." Naturally the decisive element was not that conversion to Christianity appeared psychologically as a new birth. This could be found also in the mystery religions. In reality the Christian new birth was something unique. According to Paul the decisive element was not to be found in psychological experience or in transformation, but in real union with Christ. This union he describes here with the words "until Christ be formed in you."

Everything depends on the actual realization of this union. This makes the circumcised and the uncircumcised equal. Later on in the letter he says: "For neither circumcision counts for anything, nor uncircumcision, but a new creation" (6:15). All of Paul's work had the objective of making men members in the body of Christ.

But to proclaim the gospel in such a way that its transforming power really appeared and that men became partakers of the life, power, and spirit which belonged to the promised age of righteousness demanded effort and travail. Paul had already made the Galatians share in the life of the gospel, but now, since they had fallen away, he must again go through travail in order that they might find and understand the truth of the gospel, be confirmed in it, and thus be able to walk steadfastly without being led astray.

In the expressive figure of travail the relationship of Paul to the congregations in Galatia is thought of as that of a mother to her child. In the beginning of the section (vs. 12) he addressed them as "my brethren," but now he calls them "my children," (*tekna mou*); or, according to some manuscripts, "my little children," (*teknia mou*). In I Thess. 2:7, too, Paul has likened his care of the congregation to the care of a mother for her small children. In other places he compares himself with a father. He does so later in the same chapter (I Thess. 2:11), and likewise when he addresses the Corinthians as his "beloved children" (I Cor. 4:15). "For though you have countless guides in Christ, you do not have many fathers. For I became your father in Christ Jesus through the gospel." Paul knew that this arduous work had been given to him by God himself. It was not a question of winning personal followers. Paul's work was a part of the history of God's redemptive activity. Since his work involved trouble and anxiety, those who received his message could be called his children in the sense that they had become Christians through his work of travail and suffering. Since they now had fallen away, he must be in travail with them again in renewed trouble, toil, and suffering until Christ "be formed" in them. This last expression is unusual in the New Testament. It means the same as "put on Christ" (3:27) and "become a new creature." The same idea is found in the expression "to die and rise with Christ." In principle this death and resurrection took place in baptism (cf. 3:27 and the exegesis of 2:19-20 above), but the implication of it was that they should walk steadfastly in the truth of the gospel.

Verse 20 belongs most closely to the preceding verses. In vs. 18 he said it was good for the Galatians to be made much of not only when Paul was present. But *now* he wished that he were present with them, for his presence was needed. Now he should be there that he might travail with them again to life, as he says in vs. 19. And now he wished to speak to them in a new way.

The words, "I could wish to be present with you now and to change my tone," have been interpreted in various ways. Literally the Greek words mean, "I would wish to change my voice." But *phone* (tone, voice) may also mean language (cf. I Cor. 14:10; Heb. 12:26). Some take the words to mean that he wanted to speak to them in a persuasive and pleading tone. It is possible, however, that the words are to be taken more concretely as an expression of his desire to "speak with the tongues of angels" (cf. I Cor. 13:1). The reference would then be to a heavenly language (Schlier) by which he might convince the Galatians that his message was really from God and presented the truth.

It is, however, more likely that Paul is not thinking of a heavenly language but rather of an exposition directed to the mind of the Galatians, making clear to them what Scripture really says. He would like to be able to change his language so that the Galatians would finally understand the gospel and never fall away from it. Possibly the words refer instead to Paul's desire to present the gospel and make its truth so clear and persuasive that the Galatians would finally become firmly rooted in it. We might ask whether the following exegesis of the deeper meaning of the narrative in Genesis concerning Abraham's two wives is not an example of just such a changed language, and thus an application of the interpretation which would make the Galatians understand the law correctly. The allegory in vss. 21-30 might seem to break the connection and is inserted between the personal appeals ending at 4:20 and resumed in 5:2. If it could be taken as an example of the kind of language (in 4:20) Paul wishes he could use in order to persuade those who perplexed him by their lack of understanding, the allegory would have a legitimate place in the context.

The final words in this paragraph (4:12-20) present a vivid picture of Paul's zeal and of his perplexity over the Galatians' lack of understanding. He had called them his children with whom he must travail again to give them life. His deep human emotions appear also in vs. 20. He appears as a perplexed and desperate father or mother who seeks in every way to save his children, but who feels himself helpless in the face of the children's folly. It is precisely this alternation between moving expressions of personal emotions and the strictly objective and concentrated theological argumentation which makes the Letter to the Galatians a unique document.

3. The old and the new covenant (4:21—5:1)

a) What is written in Scripture? (4:21)

Paul begins this section with a new start ("Tell me, you who desire to be under law . . .") which reminds us of 3:1 ("O foolish Galatians . . ."). In this section he demonstrates the scriptural character of the righteousness of faith. Although Paul has just expressed his feeling that the Galatians were so senseless that he did not know what to do with them, he apparently means that the gospel is so clear that anyone who has once seen it *could not* possibly miss its significance. Scripture is after all completely clear. Now he makes use of a well-known story to show that even through it the meaning of the gospel could be understood. But in doing this he does not stop with the surface meaning of the passage. He maintains that he who understands Scripture can see a deeper meaning lying behind and appearing through the apparently commonplace story. It is like a transparency which lets the light from the inner meaning of the text shine through; the light which, according to Paul, is the message that the narrative really contains. What is told, Paul writes, has a deeper meaning (*hatina estin allegoroumena*). We will return presently to the meaning of the allegorical method of interpreting Scripture, but we must first call attention to the fact that Paul is engaged in elucidating the deepest meaning of the law. He opposes this interpretation to the superficial way in which the Judaizers had taught the Galatians to understand the law.

In this allegorical story Paul addressed himself directly to those who believed the Judaizers: "You who desire to be under law." Their goal was to make Scripture a norm for the whole of life, and they were anxious lest they not follow all the regulations literally. Paul begins therefore with the question: "Do you not *hear* the law?" The Scriptures were *read* in the worship services and gatherings. Therefore it was more natural to ask, "Do you not *hear*," rather than, "Have you not read." In the synagogue service a portion from the Pentateuch, i.e., from the Law, was read.

If the allegory is an example of how Paul tries to change his language (vs. 20) in order to make the Galatians finally understand the meaning of the Judaizers' heresy, it fits well into the context. With new methods and with new elucidations of the deepest and most essential meaning of Scripture he shows that the *law* itself (particularly the Pentateuch) testifies that God's actions pointed forward to the covenant of righteousness by faith. His promise to Abraham, which was fulfilled through the birth of Sarah's son Isaac, had really a hidden meaning. It was to be the sign of the promise of a future blessing and a life in a covenant in which God's grace and election were to be the basis of eternal life and righteousness. This covenant was characterized by freedom, which was indicated by the fact that Isaac was the son of the free woman. Scripture speaks in a different way about Hagar and her son. With her it was not a matter of promise and election, but of a kind of marriage that could be annulled. She and her son were driven out that she might not interfere with the son of the free woman through whom God's promise was fulfilled. This passage tells of the relationship of Abraham to a slave whose state of bondage did not change. Hagar could, therefore, be a sign of a covenant which did not realize God's most profound intention and was not the goal of his action. We may compare this passage with II Cor. 3:11, where the giving of the Mosaic law was connected with something that would disappear, while that which remains (*to menon*), before which the disappearing must retreat, represented the greater glory. That which disappeared was connected with something deeper which would sometime be revealed. But this was hidden from the children of Israel. But if that which disappeared was made out to be something permanent, it became false. Then it came to symbolize a relationship to God such as that which belonged to Hagar, who did not have any Messianic promise connected with her son, and whose bondage, therefore, was made to symbolize a fellowship between slaves.

This whole section, therefore, is intended to bring home anew the fact that Scripture and the law as they are read in the synagogues bear witness to the coming faith. Every time this narrative was read, it annunciated the covenant of freedom which had now come in and through faith in Christ, and which proclaimed the end of the time of bondage under righteousness by the law.

It is important to notice how Paul emphasizes that he is referring to the witness of the *law*. The Judaizers had evidently accused
him of neglecting the law. They wanted to complement the proclamation of Jesus as the Messiah with demands for the observance
of the law. But according to Paul they had never rightly understood
the law.

Paul wants to show them now the real meaning of the law, and
he uses therefore a narrative in the part of Scripture generally
called "the Law," the Pentateuch. In the synagogue services they
read from "the Law" and "the Prophets." The Law was especially the Pentateuch. These five books presented the whole divine
activity in which the giving of the law at Sinai in a special sense
belonged.

As we have indicated above, the real task of the law was to
keep men under restraint until righteousness should come. But
the Jews actually misused the law to secure righteousness. Here
Paul brings together into *one* Israel's bondage (its confinement)
under the law and its misuse of the law to secure righteousness.
While confined under the law, the people of Israel held a position
as slaves, although they were the chosen people and heirs to the
promises. But because of the promise of a future righteousness
they were not without hope. The bondage was limited because
of the hope. But when they sought righteousness by the law, they
took away the hope and made the law, in God's hand a means
against sin, into an instrument of sin in the hands of man. The
hope that God would remove the separation was set aside. Thus
the children of Israel, who before had only *resembled* slaves, became real slaves through righteousness by the law without any
hope to cling to. They did not even know that there was anything
better than the state which Paul designated as bondage. The rabbis
saw in the law itself the fulfilment of the promise, and they completely obscured its real meaning,

For Paul, Hagar and Ishmael stand as symbols of Israel's
bondage under the law. Hagar was not free, and the son was not
born according to promise. Israel concentrated on the law and
did not see the promise of a blessing brought by the coming Messiah-Christ.

While the Jews trusted in their physical descent from Abraham,
they rejected the spiritual relationship with Abraham which was
constitutive for God's covenant with him. They became instead
like Ishmael, who was physically a descendant from Abraham but

had no promise. Ishmael became a symbol of a covenant different
from that made with Abraham. He, the son of the expelled slave,
became a symbol of the Israel which received the law at Sinai
but did not submit to it in expectation of the coming righteousness,
and thus like him was driven out and cursed. Just as Hagar prided
herself on being the mother of Abraham's son according to the
flesh, and therefore despised Sarah who had been barren (cf. Gen.
16:4-5), so the Jews were proud of their physical descent from
Abraham.

Isaac was the first link in the fulfilment of the promise. Hagar
was not satisfied to bear a son to Abraham "according to the
flesh" and still wait for the fulfilment of the promise through
Sarah. She wanted her son to be Abraham's sole descendant (cf.
Gen. 16:4-5). In the same way the Jews claimed to have a preference because of their descent. But after the birth of Isaac Hagar
and her son were driven out. They were a symbol of Israel in
their bondage under righteousness by the law. And if Israel did
not wait in faith for the fulfilment of the promise but claimed
to be righteous on the basis of having the law and being Abraham's
children, they would have to share the fate of Hagar and be driven
out after the son of the promise (Isaac, or Christ) had been born.

The Judaizers understood the law in the false Jewish sense as
a condition and means of righteousness. But Paul makes known
to the Galatians through a typological exegesis of a well-known
narrative from a book of the Law that they had taken Hagar
and Ishmael as prototypes instead of Sarah and Isaac, and that
spiritually they belonged with Hagar and Ishmael.

Paul thus interpreted the Genesis story of Hagar and Sarah and
their children (Gen. 16, 17, 21) in a way entirely different from
that of a literal exegesis. Under the historical narrative he believes
he can trace a hidden, deeper meaning. As we have already stated,
in a formal sense this exegesis is allegorical. But sometimes it has
been pointed out that the presentation is "typological" rather than
"allegorical." This may be correct if the meaning is to emphasize
that the decisive element is the thought mentioned above, that
the stories depict two different covenants of which Sarah and
Hagar are the prototypes. It is not a question of reading arbitrary
meanings into every word of the story.

In order to elucidate the meaning of Paul's thought in this
section, which may appear obscure to a modern reader because
of the allegorical method of presentation, it is necessary to see it

in the context of his general view of Scripture and the law. We will discuss the passage first in its general relationship to Paul's view of Scripture and the law, and follow this with a detailed exegesis in which we will have occasion to note some special difficulties.

The method of allegorical interpretation may be defined in various ways. Because of the capriciousness which has at times characterized allegorical interpretation in the history of theology the method has come into disrepute, and it is easy to overlook the brilliant results sometimes achieved. This attitude would seem to be connected with the difficulty, experienced by those accustomed to a literal and historical interpretation, of understanding the legitimacy of an exegesis in which an attempt is made to see and express God's redemptive activity as it were from within. A historical view may be the basis of and enrich the interpretation of the redemptive event, but the redemptive-historical aspect is something other than the literal-historical. The history of redemption involves an interpretation of God's will and action into which the ordinary, historical view cannot enter.

It is obvious that the interpretation Paul gives to the narratives in Genesis of Sarah's and Hagar's sons is a part of a general interpretation of Scripture and of God's redemptive action. As stated above, Paul's presentation may be said to be typological insofar as he presents the stories of Isaac and Ishmael as types of two covenants. The story had a hidden meaning, in that it suggested two types of covenants: freedom and servitude. One reason for understanding the story (Gen. 16) in this way may have been because it is inserted between narratives of God's covenant with Abraham (Gen. 15 and 17; cf. Gen. 21). The leading principle of interpretation is the idea of God's election, secretly adumbrated and prefigured in the events recorded in Scripture and now fully made known in Christ. These redemptive acts of God were for Paul the red thread in all the events in Scripture, and in this the law, too, had a part. Paul shows the Galatians, who had been influenced by the Judaizers, that the presentation in the law, interpreted according to its inner, hidden meaning, points to a covenant characterized not by bondage to the law but by freedom.

In principle Paul's line of thought is the same here as in 3:10-12, where it is asserted, as we have shown above, that the words of the law bear witness to the righteousness of faith and refutes righteousness by the law. Our interpretation of 3:10-12 is supported by the present passage. From Paul's words here in vs. 21, "Tell me, you who desire to be under law, do you not hear the law?" it is evident that, according to Paul, Scripture itself does not speak of "the law" (righteousness by the law) and its covenant as that which will abide, but points forward rather to a new covenant of faith.

The law that spoke in the Pentateuch had been perverted to righteousness by the law. It was the same commandment which in the light of righteousness by the law led to bondage and which in the light of righteousness by faith proved to have been speaking of Christ and faith. Man's different attitudes of righteousness by law and righteousness by faith correspond to different forms of the law, as a power bringing men into bondage, or as a word of God pointing to Christ.

That the real purpose of the law prior to Christ was to keep men in confinement can be understood in the light of righteousness by faith. Obedience to the law in this sense meant to acknowledge the justice of God's judgment, consequently to believe. Obedience under the law then belonged quite naturally with faith in the promise of righteousness. Both obedience under the law and faith in the promise found their fulfilment in union with Christ, where faith has taken definite form and has resulted in such a new creation of man that Christ has become the center of his life and its governing power.

What Paul emphasizes here with the allegory is that Scripture itself, which contains the law, shows that the election of Israel belongs with faith in Christ. It belonged to the freedom in Christ, while the dependence of the Judaizers on circumcision and legal enactments did *not* correspond to the covenant Scripture—especially the Pentateuch in which the law was contained—spoke about and pointed forward to. The covenant promised in Scripture was the one founded on the promise to Abraham. Its fulfilment was the righteousness present in Christ. Here we see the meaning of the allegory. The promise to Abraham that he was to have a son and become the father of many nations meant for Paul, in the context of the history of redemption, the promise of a time when righteousness was to be realized through the Messiah. Since, therefore, this history-of-redemption view places the emphasis on what the words contain in reference to righteousness and eternal life, the whole point of view involves another interpretation of Scripture than the literal-historical. We must note that this view of Scripture and of the deeper meaning of the law appears wherever Paul quotes Scripture. It is not quite correct, therefore, even if it seems plausible, to claim that Paul has used the allegorical method only in a few passages (here and for example in I Cor. 10:1-11; 9:8ff.; 5:6ff.; cf. II Cor. 3:12ff.). According to Paul's view after his Damascus experience Scripture points to Christ and the new age. Consequently the commandment in the Old Testament is sometimes made to refer directly to Christ (e.g., Rom. 10:6ff.); and sometimes the promise connected with the commandment is made to refer to him (cf. exegesis of 3:12 above).

In considering the interpretation of the story of Sarah and Hagar here we must realize that to the early Christians everything in the Old Testament appeared as words and events in the activity of God which reached its highest point in the coming of Christ and in his work. We should remind ourselves how Stephen before the council started with the revelation of God in the Old Testament which culminated in the sending of Christ (Acts 7). According to Luke's report in Acts Paul in his preaching in the Jewish synagogues presented Christ's act of redemption in the context of the scriptural revelation of God's redemptive acts in Israel (e.g., Acts 13:15ff.). He emphasizes that the inhabitants of Jerusalem and their councilmen through their judgment of Christ have fulfilled the words of the prophets which were read every sabbath, and had thus brought to fulfilment everything written about Christ (Acts 13:27ff.). When Christ revealed himself to the disciples on the way to Emmaus, he explained to them, according to Luke, the real meaning of the Old Testament as a witness to the suffering, death, and resurrection of the Messiah. In the passage in the Gospel of John, "If you believed Moses, you would believe me, for he wrote of me" (John 5:46), the supposition is that the Old Testament is essentially a witness to the Messiah. It may be said, therefore, to be quite natural to interpret the Old Testament typologically, or *in one sense* allegorically—or in a sense that appears allegorical. Paul's interpretation of these narratives in Genesis is naturally more definitely allegorical in form than many other interpretations of Old Testament passages regarded as pointing to the Messiah. But we may say nevertheless that the interpretation is not capricious. He does not read everything into it. He stands in the living tradition of the Old Testament, and he is certain that he has found its real meaning and that he speaks in its spirit. It is not general truths and metaphysical conceptions which the stories are used to illustrate. (One might compare Philo's allegorical interpretation of the Old Testament.) It deals with concrete events and data in the history of salvation. Paul does not see the Old Testament as a dead and completed document, but as God's words and acts, which continue forever and have found their decisive fulfilment in Christ. The key to the Old Testament is, therefore, the revelation of Christ, and in the ancient church is was a common assumption that only the Christians understood the content of the Old Testament correctly. They did not ask about the historical significance in a literal sense but about the meaning of the words, narratives, and commandments in their relation to God's redemptive activity. This fact supplies a guiding principle which guards against the allegory becoming capricious. The narratives were not to illustrate and inculcate some general, moral truths, but were understood as providing instruction concerning God's promise and election.

We ought to observe the similarity between the allegorical interpretation of the story of Abraham's wives and what Paul has written about Abraham as the prototype and father of faith. According to Paul the children of faith are children of Abraham. Physical descent from Abraham is not what is decisive, but spiritual affinity to him. Abraham is the prototype of faith in the righteousness fulfilled in and through Christ. In Galatians 3 and Romans 4 (cf. also Rom. 9:6ff.) Paul shows that the real children of Abraham were the children of promise. Fulfilment of the promise created a new fellowship in the reception of righteousness. Man became a partaker in this righteousness by faith in Christ. Christ was the offspring of Abraham of which Scripture latently spoke. And those who belonged to Christ were the children of promise.

The allegorizing of the story of Sarah and Hagar is of this kind. God had given the promise that Sarah would have a son, even though she was considered too old. The similarity between Isaac and the Christians was, therefore, that *the promise* was the basis of their existence. This was the constitutive element in the covenant between God and Abraham, and in this faith Isaac was born. What made Israel God's people was God's promise by which the people had been chosen and separated from others. But what was therefore decisive for belonging to God's people was not physical descent in itself (or any works of the law), but only this promise.

225

An exegesis similar to the one above occurs in Rom. 9:6-9, where the discussion is also concerned with the promise to Abraham and the birth of Isaac. The fact that the birth of Isaac was connected with God's promise meant for Paul that Isaac himself and the descendents of Abraham owed their existence to God's promise. Therefore, says Paul, it is not physical descent but the promise of God that determines who are children of Abraham (cf. Rom. 9:9). God's promise is complemented by man's faith, and it is this faith which characterizes those who are the spiritual children of Abraham. God's election is the basis for membership in the true Israel and for being counted among Abraham's descendents. This fact is also shown in the following verses concerning Jacob and Essau (Rom. 9:10-13). It was God's choice that made Jacob instead of the older Esau the bearer of the promise so that he was reckoned as the first-born. In this way Paul makes clear that it was God's choice which determined who belonged to Abraham's descendents and the children of God (Rom. 9:7). The Jews combined the physical descent from the patriarchs with their own works of the law and thus looked upon themselves as that elect people above all others who had been given the law as a light of righteousness, but Paul combined God's choice and promise with Abraham's faith. Those who believed in Christ and found their righteousness in him were the true Israel and Abraham's children; they were partakers of the promised blessing. *This fact* is what Paul elucidates by his allegory in Gal. 4:21-30.

The new life in which the law is fulfilled was included in the fulfilment of the promise (cf. Rom. 8:4). The law was not fulfilled by "works of the law," and righteousness was not obtained on the basis of being physical descendents of Abraham. John the Baptist had warned the Jews against claiming righteousness on the basis of being Abraham's children and had urged them to repentance (Matt. 3:9; Luke 3:8). Paul demonstrates through the allegory in 4:21ff. that those who accept faith are the true children of Abraham, and that physical descent and works of the law which produced self-confidence did not procure righteousness. This was the central and constitutive thought in his theology. Righteousness by the law and trust in physical descent from Abraham are similar in kind. Paul continued the work of John the Baptist (cf. also John 8:39), and he defines the content of the new life positively as life in Christ through faith and in the power of the Spirit active in love (cf. Gal. 5:16ff.).

The two wives of Abraham, as Paul developed the theme here, are prototypes of two covenants whose signs are freedom and slavery. He who trusts in righteousness by the law lives a life in bondage. But the sign of the covenant of promise is *freedom*. The promise was a promise of blessing to all people without regard to their own merits. He who had come to faith in Christ had become free from the power of sin, death, and the law. He was free from the compulsion of seeking to obtain and present his own righteousness. The work of Christ could, therefore, be described as bringing freedom (cf. 5:1). But freedom is freedom in the Spirit, not simply freedom from certain restraints and false conceptions, nor yet freedom "giving occasion to the flesh." "The law of the Spirit of life in Christ Jesus has set me free from the law of sin and death" (Rom. 8:2). The opposite of this freedom was partly slavery under the righteousness of the law and partly the life in the flesh characterized by the spirit of this age with its sin and its selfish will and works; a life which is often regarded as freedom, but which in its essential nature Paul regards as slavery. He is certain that he who is "in the flesh" belongs to death (Rom. 8:5-13; 6:13-23). The statement in the Gospel of John (John 8:34), that he who commits sin is the slave of sin, agrees with Paul's view of sin. A life in the freedom of "the flesh" is in reality slavery. The freedom from the law of which Paul speaks is of an entirely different nature. The contrast between freedom and slavery corresponds, according to Paul, to the contrast between righteousness by faith and righteousness by the law, or between the Spirit and the flesh (Gal. 5:16ff.; cf. Rom. 8:1ff.), because righteousness by the law is an expression of life in the flesh. Paul could also ask the Galatians if, having begun in the Spirit, they now wanted the Spirit to be fulfilled in the flesh, i.e., in righteousness by the law (3:3). Thus the allegory of Sarah and Hagar belongs in the general development of the thought in Galatians and expresses in a new way what the rest of the letter contains.

b) Details in Paul's interpretation of Scripture (4:22-30)

We will now examine the presentation in detail. Some passages present certain exegetical difficulties.

Paul emphasizes that Sarah is "the free woman." She is called "the free woman" four times without mentioning her name. It is probable that Paul is thinking in terms of rabbinical presentations in which Sarah may have appeared as "the free woman." With a slight change in the name Sarah has been designated as "princess." Her name has been interpreted as the feminine of *Sar* meaning prince.

In rabbinical literature Sarah occupies a prominent place. She was the mother of Israel. In using her now as the prototype of the new covenant, the Christian church, Paul has given a new content to the Jewish idea of Sarah as the mother of Israel. Sarah, the symbol of freedom, is the prototype of the covenant of freedom and salvation which came in Christ and which is the covenant of the fulfilment of the promise.

The thought of freedom and slavery reminds us of thoughts developed earlier: that the position under the law involved a state of minority, while the life in faith was compared with that state of maturity which gave the heir right to use his inheritance. Faith and the Spirit characterized the fulfilment of the promise. This was freedom. "Where the Spirit of the Lord is, there is freedom" (II Cor. 3:17). In other respects the significance of vss. 22-23 has been discussed in the previous section.

The words translated, "Now Hagar is Mount Sinai in Arabia," are textually uncertain. Some manuscripts leave out the word "Hagar," so that the meaning becomes: "For Sinai is a mountain in Arabia." If the text on which our modern translation is based is genuine, Paul must have somehow detected a certain suggestion of a connection between Sinai and the name Hagar. It is possible that Paul had found a similarity in sound between an Arabic word for stone or cliff (*chadschar* or *hadjar*) and the word Hagar (or Agar in some texts), and that a part of the Mount of Sinai was designated by this Arabic word, or had had a somewhat similar name. Philologically the words Hagar and *hadjar* are not related. The mere statement that Sinai is a mountain in Arabia, as some texts have it, does not seem to have any significance in this context. *One* suggestion made was that Arabia was regarded as a land of an oppressed people, and that the location of Mount Sinai in Arabia referred to the slavery in the land where the descendents of Ishmael were supposed to live. That is, however, an unlikely surmise.

Another conjecture has been that Paul held that a place outside the Promised Land could not have been the location of the covenant of promise. This is not a satisfactory interpretation. "The present Jerusalem" corresponds in the allegory to this covenant at Sinai; and Paul points out, of course, that being a descendent of and belonging to the "present" Jerusalem in an external sense does not guarantee that one belongs to the fellowship and covenant the promise had in view. A reference to the fact that Sinai was geographically outside of the land of promise does not seem to fit as an argument in this context. The text that leaves out the word Hagar does not seem to present a better text than the other. It would seem more probable that a word difficult to explain has been taken out rather than added.

We must ask the question whether the meaning of the text with Hagar retained (*to de Hagar oros estin en te Arabia*) is to be rendered, "Now Hagar is Mount Sinai in Arabia." Hagar is neuter (*to Hagar*—the *word* Hagar, the *expression* Hagar, the *thought* Hagar). The question is whether Paul did not allude to the fact that the idea of Hagar in Arabia played a part similar to that of Sinai in the Jewish view of the Mosaic law. Much later, in the time of Mohammed, it is known that the Arabs claimed to be descendents of Hagar and Ishmael. Although the Mohammedan use of the narratives in Genesis came much later, it is possible that in the parts of Arabia bordering on Palestine there had been legends concerning Ishmael and his descendents. If such legends, associated with cultic usages and religious observances, were known even in New Testament times and in some form had become known to Paul, who had gone from Damascus to Arabia (Gal. 1:17), it is possible that he combined them with his view of the Jewish tradition. In that case the meaning of the comparison between Hagar and Sinai could be first that Israel's custom of glorying in their physical descent from Abraham was on a par with the similar claim of the Arabs who reckoned their descent through Ishmael. What really was the difference between Isaac and Ishmael was the promise, but the Jews rejected the fulfilment of the promise in Christ and thereby forfeited their connection with Isaac. Furthermore, the combination of Hagar and Sinai could point in the same direction as when earlier (chap. 4) the requirements of the law as interpreted by the Jews were equated with the bondage under "the elemental spirits of the universe." Paul may have regarded Hagar and the idea of descent from her as being connected with the same kind of servitude under cultic regulations as the Jewish view of the Sinaitic law had imposed on Israel. In that case the reference of the Arabs to Hagar was the same as the Jewish reference to the law. "The present Jerusalem" belonged with the bondage of the Jews in righteousness by the law and their obduracy before Christ. In this respect the Jews were the spiritual children of Ishmael. If in addition the Arabs also regarded Mount Sinai as a holy mountain, and if the word Hagar was somehow connected with it, Paul could find occasion to associate Sinai and Jewish legalism with religious conceptions of Hagar among the Arabs. It is known that in Mohammedan times the word Hagar has been associated with holy stones, and Mount Sinai is also mentioned in Arabic legends concerning Hagar.

It seems probable in any case that Paul associated the name Hagar with Mount Sinai. Since the rabbis frequently argued on the basis of associations, it is possible that a similarity in sound between the name and an Arabic word for cliff, mountain, or some other name of Sinai which Paul had heard used, may have given him occasion to suggest the Arabs' connection with Ishmael, and that their descent and cult corresponded to the law of Sinai according to the Jewish interpretation and application.

By way of summary we may say that, according to Paul, the Jews by their conception and use of the law of Sinai became similar to those who did not live in the covenant of promise. The prototype of these was Hagar, the slave woman, and her son, who was not born of faith in the promise. Hagar's descendants also showed a similarity to the Jews in their view of the law of Sinai. In principle they had the same self-righteous and legalistic attitude. If they also in their stories about their mother Hagar connected her name with Mount Sinai, the connection between them was given. Even if this direct combination had not been made, it is possible nevertheless that the connection between the righteousness by the law of Mount Sinai and the bondage under the law of Ishmael's descendents had been suggested to Paul by some similarity in sound between Hagar and some designation applied to Mount Sinai. Thus Mount Sinai, which the rabbis falsely regarded as the fulfilment of the promise, had become a symbol of slavery because it stood in the way of the real fulfilment. And then the children of Sinai's law, the Jews, must share spiritually the lot of Hagar and find themselves excluded from the fellowship of the promise.

We should also compare this typology with the words in 3:16 that "the offspring" the promise concerned was *one*. The law of Sinai given to the many was not in itself the fulfilment of the promise; that fulfilment came when the One the promise concerned had come. When the promise is conceived of as being fulfilled by the observance of the law by the many, it is transformed into a likeness to "the elemental spirits" and their bondage. Through the Jewish conception Sinai became a sign of their bondage rather than their freedom, and thus they were revealed as the spiritual children of the slave woman and not of her who was called *the free woman.* Her name found its fulfilment in Christ, who came with the freedom by which the Galatians had been set free. She, *the free one,* was destined to rule; she was the regent, the princess. Her freedom, fulfilled in Christ, was a freedom from the way of salvation by the observance of the law, the way of servitude. It was the freedom to live in the love of God which had come in Christ and in which the fulfilment of the law was given.

The other covenant, of which, as stated above, Sarah and Isaac were the prototypes, was the covenant of promise. Its locale was not the earthly but the heavenly Jerusalem. "The Jerusalem above" was the mother who belonged to this covenant. This Jerusalem included the fulfilment of the promise about the kingdom to come with righteousness and peace. It was a heavenly kingdom in which sin and death were overcome. The citizens of this kingdom were to be born by the Spirit (cf. John 3:5). Most appropriately Paul refers here to Isa. 54:1ff., where it is also the joy precisely of the barren that stands over against natural birth. If lack of children was the greatest misfortune of an Israelitic woman, here the barren one was the object of praise. Thus it was emphasized that she belonged to a world and age other than the present. The promise bestowed children and life even where none were to be found. It was not physical descent but the election of God which made a person member of the fellowship of the promise. That election applied to the Galatians if they remained faithful to their call in baptism. The real descent from Isaac was spiritual; a spiritual fellowship with him who was the son of the promise. Those who were of faith were the true children of Abraham (3:7) and belonged to the true descendants of Isaac. They were the true Israel.

The idea of the new Jerusalem has been developed within Jewish apocalyptic, but it was prepared for through the words in the Old Testament about a new Jerusalem to replace the earthly. This new city was conceived of as both earthly and heavenly (cf. Isa. 54:11ff.; 60:1ff.). Many of the Old Testament apocryphal books speak of the new Jerusalem to be revealed. Paul used the new Jerusalem as a designation of the age which had begun spiritually in Christ and which was to be fully revealed in power at his return. Men belonged to this new age and this new covenant through their union with Christ in his church. The Spirit was the hallmark of citizenship in this kingdom of Christ which someday was to be revealed visibly in power; and those who were true members of it were the children of Abraham and Isaac, because they were the children of the promise.

The words of Scripture in Isa. 54:1, that the barren one should break forth into jubilant singing, applied therefore to the Christians. Although the Gentile Christians were not Israelites according to physical descent, they had all, as Paul says later in the Letter to the Romans, become engrafted into the cultivated olive tree (Rom. 11:17ff.). Although according to the flesh they had been "alienated from the commonwealth of Israel, and strangers to the covenant of promise, having no hope and without God in the world" (Eph. 2:12), they had been accepted as legitimate children and had become heirs.

The two covenants did not, however, stand peacefully side by side. The Jews persecuted the Christian church. Paul seems to have detected a Jewish agitation behind the activity of the Judaizers. A messianic sect could be tolerated within Judaism if its members observed the law and circumcision, but Paul's proclamation aroused persecution. Paul finds this prophesied in the story of Sarah and Hagar. The Old Testament relates that Ishmael was quarrelsome and fought with all his brothers (Gen. 16:12; 25:18). Paul certainly knew also the tradition in the Palestinian Haggadah how Ishmael had playfully aimed his bow at Isaac.

The casting out of Hagar was an omen to Paul that the Jews who now persecuted the Christians would not win the final victory. They fought against Scripture and its prophecies. Instead they themselves would be driven out of the fellowship with God's elect. Because of their enmity against the Christian church and the true righteousness (of which Abraham was a prototype) the Jews who were the spiritual children of the slave woman's covenant must be driven out from Abraham's house, which was the true, heavenly Jerusalem. All this had been stated beforehand in the holy Scriptures to which the Jews themselves referred.

c) The free man ought not to submit again to bondage (4:31–5:1)

Paul of course has already emphasized in various ways that Christians are the true children of Abraham. They belonged to the people to whom the law bore witness and who were to live in the age of the fulfilment.

If this were so, it ought to be farthest from their minds to incur the loss of this freedom and return to bondage. Israel had been proud of the preference they had enjoyed in comparison with others because they were the chosen people who had received the law. Paul has shown that they were not good stewards of the law, but that they had become like the Gentiles because of their misuse of the law, their unbelief in general, and their refusal to submit to God's actions and judgments. But if Israel gloried in their privileges and made themselves important in their conceit, the Christians on the other hand had by grace received a freedom they ought to handle rightly, cherish, and live in with gratitude.

Now that Paul has specially elucidated the meaning of Scripture by his exegesis of what lies behind the stories of Sarah and Hagar, he concludes by repeating personal appeals to the Galatians and warnings against yielding to the seduction of the Judaizers like those he voiced before in 4:12-20. In a formal sense he can tie in these appeals with the idea of the freedom of faith in contrast to the bondage of righteousness by the law. This contrast he dealt with in the allegory in 4:21-30, and he also illustrated this earlier by comparing the age of faith with the mature heir's possession of his inheritance.

After a person has been admitted into the new covenant and into the fellowship of mature sons and heirs, he must make the situation and the consequences clear to himself. To have received the Spirit and righteousness through faith meant that he had been received as a child and heir of the free woman, not of the slave woman. Now he must behave himself accordingly. He must live as one freed from the slavery of the law.

Freedom had come because Christ had liberated the slaves. It did not belong to man's empirical nature. It was not true that by himself man could realize a freedom he possessed by nature. Freedom came through an intervention by God. We can understand Paul's conception of freedom only if we see it as a part of the history of salvation the climax of which was God sending Christ and through him fulfilling the righteousness the law could not produce. In this righteousness was contained freedom from the power of law, sin, and death in all its forms, and especially from the need of seeking to procure a righteousness through the observance of the law. In man's "carnal" and sinful state he naturally seeks to escape his guilt by conduct that will lessen his sense of guilt. Viewed from the perspective of the sense of guilt the Deity appears as an angry and vindictive demon who must be propitiated. Christ sets man free from this whole viewpoint and from this method of making oneself free, which simply involved man in an increased and constantly renewed guilt.

Since there are different textual readings in 5:1, the result has been a variety of interpretations. The best attested text indicates that we should translate: "For freedom Christ has set us free." The meaning is then that Christ has set us free for the freedom discussed in the preceding sections: the freedom belonging to the heir, the mature son, the child of the free woman; and that, since Christ has completed his work of liberation, the task is to behave according to this freedom and live as a free man.

The freedom Christ has secured is described in 4:5 as redemption. A slave could be redeemed by a ransom paid from some temple treasury. Such legal transactions were common and may well be suggested in such expressions as Christ "has made us free." The work of Christ meant freedom from the power of the law to condemn (cf. Rom. 8:1; Col. 2:14; and the exegesis of Gal. 3:13-14 above) and in general from bondage under the law (cf. Gal. 3:23).

Since the work of Christ involved a redemption, the redeemed must live as free men and not act as slaves any more. Now the Galatians must not squander their freedom by submitting again as slaves under those powers (cf. 4:9).

According to Paul Christ had not done his work that the redeemed might again submit to bondage but that they might remain free. The redemption of Christ was not only a liberation *from* a state of bondage but also a liberation *to* a new life. Perpetual freedom could be found only in this new life. Paradoxically this new freedom could also be designated as a slavery—slavery under Christ. But this "slavery" was a father-child relationship characterized by joy. It was the only true freedom, because it restored man to the state for which he had been created and gave him participation in the new age. This "slavery" meant participation in the life of the Spirit and the power of the resurrection, because slavery to Christ meant freedom from the power of death.

The freedom *to* which Christ set men free resulted in joy and peace. That is why Paul compares it to the child-relationship. This relationship involves also the idea of belonging to the Father. Those who had been set free by Christ belonged to him so completely that the relationship could be spoken of as a service of slavery or bondage. "For he who was called in the Lord as a slave is a freedman of the Lord. Likewise he who was free when called is a slave of Christ. You were bought with a price" (I Cor. 7:22-23). The Christian was set free from sin *in order to* become a slave of righteousness (Rom. 6:18). The service of Christ may thus also be spoken of as slavery (cf. also Rom. 6:22; 14:18; Col. 3:24). But this servitude, this "slavery," was a service in which man served God "from the heart" (Eph. 6:6). The freedom of the Christian consisted in serving the neighbor in love. Consequently this service to the neighbor was also "a slave-service" done voluntarily, freely, and joyfully, in which the love of God was active. This was the content of the freedom Christ has made possible.

4. Trust in circumcision means loss of Christ (5:2-12)

a) Circumcision obligates a person to keep the whole law (5:2-4)

The message contained in Paul's preaching implied that the Christian belonged to a new world and received a spirit belonging by nature to the promised new age. The decisive religious difference runs therefore between those who have become new creatures by "putting on Christ" and those who belong to the old life. To set up a line of separation between circumcised and uncircumcised would mean to distort the real line of demarcation and substitute a false and irrelevant line. If those who had received the new life permitted themselves to be circumcised, it would mean that they lost the new state and returned to the old bondage.

Paul turns to those Gentile Christians who had not been circumcised and warns them against submitting to it. It is not a question here about those who were circumcised. They must remember that they could not base their righteousness on circumcision and law, because these do not secure any righteousness.

Christ could be of no profit to those who submitted to circumcision. Paul made this statement as personally authoritative as possible (cf. II Cor. 10:1ff.). "Now I, Paul, say to you." Paul seems to match his own authority with that of others. The word "I" is so strongly emphasized and the tone is so authoritative that we might surmise that from this point on Paul did not dictate but wrote the letter himself. Some commentators hold that the words in 6:11, "See with what large letters I am writing to you with my own hand," refer to the part of the letter beginning at 5:2. In our exegesis of 6:11 we will suggest, however, that it is more probable that the section written by himself begins at 6:11 and that the rest was dictated.

A new section begins, however, with 5:2. It is connected with the preceding by 5:1; and the two verses 4:31–5:1 mark the transition between 4:21-30 and the following section.

The aim of the Judaizers was evidently to convince the Galatians that true Christianity meant circumcision and the observance of certain portions of the law in addition to faith in Christ as the Messiah. This is what Paul declares wrong. Submission to circumcision meant that they had entered the old covenant. They would then be excluded from the new, and would be under obligation to keep all the statutes of the old covenant. The law was indivisible. It could not be observed partially. He who failed in one was guilty of all. According to Paul the Christian could not claim any merit at all for being circumcised and knowing the law. Everything depended on whether the law was really observed. It was possible to be zealous for the Scripture in two ways: that of the Jews and that of Paul. The Jews had zeal although it was not enlightened (Rom. 10:2), but the zeal itself was commendable. The Judaizers, however, did not deserve commendation at all. Theirs was an impossible attempt at compromise. They did not keep the law themselves (6:13). If they wanted to follow the way of righteousness by the law, they ought to be consistent and not straddle the fence. In doing so they destroyed both faith and law (cf. exegesis of 2:18). Christ had overcome the way of salvation by the law, but if they wanted to have a share in his freedom, they must not play with righteousness by the law. Through Christ all shadows had been removed and the real substance had appeared (Col. 2:17). They must therefore be consistent in regard to the new, or else freedom would be lost. The old and the new could not be mixed together. They would incur guilt on every hand and be lost beyond all hope. He who submitted to circumcision assumed the obligation of keeping the whole law according to the way those of the circumcision understood it. According to Paul this would never result in righteousness before God, but it involved nevertheless a consistent *zeal* for the law even though it lacked insight. But adding the observance of the law to faith destroyed everything. Then they became as Jews who gloried in the law but failed to keep it. (cf. Romans 2). He who had been baptized into Christ was dead to circumcision and law, as the Jews understood the law. To him circumcision had no significance (cf. I Cor. 7:19).

To do (*poiein*) the whole law may otherwise mean in Paul to keep the law in its most profound sense, in its perfected form, and would consequently refer to a life based on the fulfilment of the law by *Christ*. The context seems to indicate, however, that here it is a question of keeping the whole law in the specifically Jewish sense. Such an attitude to the law might reveal a commendable zeal, and might be preferable to the attempt of the Judaizers to combine faith in Christ with a *partial* observance of the law. Paul criticises this attitude especially in 6:13.

In the exegesis of vs. 3 many have wondered what Paul refers to with the word "again" (*palin*), "I testify again." Some commentators have held that it must refer to an earlier proclamation of Paul to the Galatians, oral or written, about which we have no knowledge (cf. 1:9). Others have concluded that he refers to what had been said in vs. 2. The word is omitted in some manuscripts, and some have therefore suggested that it should be left out. It is found, however, in the majority of the manuscripts. The word stands without emphasis, and it may mean simply that he wants to repeat an idea connected with his fundamental point of view; namely, that Jewish law and Christian faith must not be mixed together (cf. 2:18).

When Paul emphasized that circumcision entailed the obligation to keep the whole law, he did not mean, of course, that if the law was kept perfectly, it would be a possible way of salvation along with faith. Eventually the way of salvation by the law always leads to condemnation. In the most profound sense the law cannot be fulfilled by attempts to conform to it. The law bears witness to a deeper righteousness to come through faith, but it does not give righteousness. Only when righteousness has been obtained through Christ and has been given in faith, was the curse of the law removed.

If they sought to combine faith with such a means of salvation as righteousness by the law, faith would no longer be active. In that case they had forsaken faith. Being united with Christ meant *not* to seek righteousness through the law. Whoever sought righteousness and life through the law, therefore, had forsaken grace and faith.

b) In Christ neither circumcision nor uncircumcision avails anything, but faith working through love (5:5-6)

"We" in vs. 5 is emphatic and refers to the true Christians who live in righteousness by faith. They hope for salvation through their union with Christ and not through the law. The eschatological aspect of salvation is emphasized here. In contrast to salvation by the works of the law the Christians waited for a salvation they could not provide themselves. They continued the waiting upon righteousness which characterized the Old Testament saints, among them Abraham. In one sense this hope was now fulfilled in Christ, but it could be possessed only in faith; and those who lived in faith must always look forward to the full realization of hope (cf. Rom. 8:24). The eschatological nature of salvation appears both in the fact that it cannot be procured by man but is a gift of God, and in the fact that its consummation lies in the future. The coming of Christ provided a concrete contact with salvation and with the righteousness of God belonging to the age to come. The believer could be said to have received it already in advance, although it would be given fully only at the return of Christ. The participation of the believer was at the same time an expectation that this salvation would someday appear fully and completely. Faith and the Spirit belong together. To belong to the world of faith is the same as belonging to the world of the Spirit. In faith and in the life of the Spirit given to them the Christians waited for the full and complete fulfilment of the hope of righteousness. The Spirit was already an earnest that this hope would be realized.

In Christ, i.e., in the salvation he brought, circumcision had no meaning (cf. 6:15). What was important was the new life, the life in the Spirit, the life in faith, or, as we read in 6:15, "a new creation." True faith works through love. Love is not concerned with self. He who sought greater security through circumcision was actuated by concern for self. He who did so after he had become a part of the Christian fellowship turned from the outgoing attitude of love to a selfish religiosity. When Paul had come to the Galatians for the first time, and they had received the gospel, they had also received the Spirit (3:5). This fact indicated that the powers of the coming age had begun to work among them, because the Spirit was not received through works of the law. Paul had done mighty works among them, and they had listened to him in faith and had been receptive to the power he transmitted to them. They had obeyed the gospel, as Abraham had responded to God's promise. On this account they had been received into the life of faith active in love. The demand of circumcision and observance of the law did not accomplish this, for it was an entirely different obedience. Their reception of what Paul transmitted to them did not mean that they remained passive and inactive. But they did not direct their activity toward the fulfilment of works of the law through which they were tied to themselves, but they became partakers in another activity in love. Faith active in love was the sign of being a member in the body of Christ. Here Paul strikes chords which will be heard more fully in the section of the letter beginning at 5:13. Faith did not mean such a freedom from the obligations of the law that it left room for the works of the flesh (cf. vss. 19-20). Faith was essentially *one* with that love which may be said to be the work of a bondservant; a work which becomes freedom because it means a service in love.

c) The Galatians were not steadfast in the truth (5:7-12)

Paul's address to the Galatians in 5:1-4, through which he showed them by personal appeal that the ways of salvation by faith and by the law were incompatible, ended in vs. 6 with an important theological statement. In vs. 7 he continues the purely personal address which he has also used earlier in 1:6-9; 3:1-6; 4:12-20; and he expresses his amazement and sorrow over their insecurity and confusion.

After all, the Galatians had been on the right way. They had begun to run the race. Sometimes Paul uses terms taken from the race-course to describe the life in faith (Phil. 3:13-14; I Cor. 9:24ff.). Faith can be pictured as a forward advance. The fact that righteousness must be received and that faith is a waiting for the consummation of salvation, implies, as we have said, a constant advance. Salvation is to be received more and more fully and completely, and knowledge is to continue to increase.

The Galatians' advance and growth in faith had been hindered and broken through the Judaizers who had made circumcision and the observance of the law a condition of perfect salvation. We must constantly be aware that Paul did not think of the works of the law as constituting an active life and faith a passive one. It was rather the activity of faith that had been stopped by the agitation of the Judaizers.

The question as to who had hindered them and stopped their advance toward the true goal is rhetorical as in 3:1ff. To obey the truth means to submit to the divine truth of the gospel. Paul asks who has hindered them from obeying the truth, and he adds that this impulse did not come from him who called them. The persuasion of the Judaizers was not from God, but was in conflict with God and the gospel of Christ. The words may be translated: "Who has taken you away from obedience to the truth? Such an exhortation has not come from him who called you" (from God or his apostle). The Greek words for "obey" (*peithesdai*) and "persuade" "power of persuasion" (*peismone*), which also may mean obey, have a similar sound which cannot readily be produced in translation. Who, asks Paul, has shut you out from the truth of the gospel so that it does not *persuade* you any more? This *persuasion* did not come from him who called you. The meaning may also be rendered thus: It was not obedience to the one who had called them to the life in the gospel that had broken down their obedience to the gospel. Or, who has brought it about that you are no longer guided by the truth? You are not led in that direction by the one who called you. Later on in vs. 11 Paul points out the absurdity of the reports which claim that he preached circumcision. The Judaizers could not put the blame on Paul and his helpers.

Paul uses an expression which was probably proverbial: "A little yeast leavens the whole lump." The leaven refers to the wrong attitude which was the result of the preaching of the Judaizers. This may appear as a rather insignificant matter. Yielding to them might appear as a concession in certain minor trifles. It might seem that these would not demand such a massive intervention and such sharp words as Paul employs. But Paul insists that these concessions were by no means harmless.

Paul used the same proverb also in I Cor. 5:6. It has been suggested that it came in this form from some Greek comedy (cf. however, Matt. 16:6; Mark 8:15; Luke 12:1; Matt. 13:33; Luke 13:21). The meaning here is that if a wrong conception of the law and righteousness is brought in at one point, the result will be apparent everywhere. The figure of the leaven is common also in Jewish writings, as is indicated in the above references to the Synoptics.

Paul adds that he has confidence in the Lord that the Galatians will agree with his thought. He hopes that they have not really forsaken his message. He evidently wants to believe that they have been confused in regard to only one point, and that they did not fully understand the consequences of the message from which in reality they would not desire to depart. Consequently the blame was on him who had led them astray, and he would be subject to judgment. Judgment on works belonged to God's righteousness. Seduction away from the gospel always brought judgment (cf. Matt. 18:7; Luke 17:1-2). Paul suggests here as in 1:7 that the Galatians had become confused and had missed the right way of the gospel they had received. Just as in 1:8-9 he now declares solemnly that the one who troubles and bewilders them will have to bear his judgment whoever he might be. The curse will rest upon him.

In verse eleven Paul adds a statement which is very difficult to interpret. His words may be rendered thus: "But, my brethren, if *I myself* still preach circumcision, why am I still persecuted?" Paul seems to assume that there are those who claim that he himself preaches circumcision. But the proof that he does *not* do so is the persecution he has to endure.

It is difficult to understand how Paul could have been accused of such preaching. It is possible that his attitude in the case of the circumcision of Timothy (Acts 16:3) may have given rise to this slander. As we have stated earlier, some commentators, the latest E. Haenchen, are of the opinion that the story of Timothy in Acts belongs among those false reports of Paul which he denies here. There are, however, not sufficient reasons for doubting the historicity of this story. The situation in that case was different from that discussed in this passage (cf. exegesis of 2:3-5 above). The word "still" (*eti*) appears both in the main clause and in the subordinate clause. Its presence in the subordinate clause especially ("If I still preach circumcision") has presented some exegetical difficulties. If both words are authentic, it might be possible that earlier he had been willing to combine circumcision with faith, but had later changed his mind. This interpretation seems to be definitely excluded by his own presentation of his life and teaching. His gospel was precisely the gospel free from the law. A group of manuscripts leave out the first "still." It may not be authentic. If it is retained, however, the meaning would seem to be that he does not preach circumcision as he had done *prior* to his conversion. His meaning might be rendered thus: "I myself have never preached circumcision after I met Christ. If I did so still, I would not be an apostle of Christ but a Jewish preacher of law. But if I, as they (falsely) claim, now continually (*eti*) preach circumcision even as a Christian, why should I then continually (*eti*) suffer persecution? It is the very contrast between the preaching of the cross of Christ and that of circumcision that causes offense and persecution." If Paul could have combined the proclamation of Christ with propaganda for circumcision and law, there would have been no need of further persecution. Then he would have appeared to be enlisting adherents to a special Jewish tendency or sect. Then the Jews would not have found it necessary to continue their violent attacks on him.

The fundamental point in Paul's proclamation is that there is an irreconcilable conflict between the cross, which was the revelation of salvation and was valid for all, even the Gentiles, and circumcision which was the sign of Jewish exclusiveness. The cross broke down the Jewish exclusiveness exemplified in circumcision. But for this reason the proclamation of the cross met with hatred and fanatical bitterness on the part of the Jews. This was, however, inevitable. Paul had found a prototype of the Jewish persecution in Ishmael who was said to have been in conflict with his brethren and was believed to have threatened Isaac. The reason why the Jews were so seriously offended by the preaching of the cross was because he proclaimed it in such a way that Jewish righteousness by the law, which had its center in their conception and application of circumcision, became impossible. It was precisely the preaching of the cross that was always an offense (*skandalon*) to the Jews (I Cor. 1:23).

Paul perceived, then, that faith in Christ absolutely excluded all claims that the Christians should be circumcised and observe the law in the Jewish sense. The result of circumcision could only be that faith became nullified. Sarcastically he expresses the wish that those who unsettle the Galatians would mutilate or castrate themselves. We see how Paul's despair and zeal makes him use almost vulgar expressions. Religious castration was practiced in the Hellenistic mystery cults. If the Galatians lived in the ethnic province of Galatia, such practices may have been known among them, since the worship of Attis and Cybele had its center in that area. The priests of this cult were castrated. This practice was forbidden in Israel. Whoever did so was expelled from the people (Deut. 23:1). To compare circumcision with castration was a drastic way of declaring how baneful was the demand for it was in the present situation. He equated circumcision with that heathen cult which both Jews and Christians must reject with intense loathing. This combination of circumcision and castration must have seemed to the Jews as pure blasphemy. From Paul's point of view, however, there was an actual similarity between them, because in both practices the intention was to make oneself more acceptable in the sight of God by a religiously meritorious act. When circumcision is regarded as a means of attaining righteousness, it becomes, after the way of righteousness has been revealed, similar in nature to those acts by which the Gentiles believed they could make themselves more holy. To turn from faith in the righteousness of Christ to circumcision as a requirement for righteousness meant to become slaves under "the elemental spirits of the universe." When faith came, the proclamation of circumcision as a means of salvation became an antithesis to the preaching of the cross. Now after Christ had come, Jewish legalism and heathen religion must be placed on the same level. To be under the law had the same meaning to Paul as to be under "the elemental spirits."

We may understand Paul's words here as an emphatic expression of an actual situation. He regards as most dangerous a righteousness of the law which might appear as faithfulness to Scripture, and which thus under the cloak of Christian piety would destroy faith. That the Judaizers enticed the Galatians to become circumcised—and by this propaganda thus destroyed their faith—troubled Paul so intensely that he employed these strong expressions. We might compare the words of Jesus that a man should cut off his hand or foot rather than permit them to become a stumbling block. The thought in Matt. 5:30; 18:8 is not the same as here, but a similarity is present in the idea that a mutilation is better than causing offense. The paradoxical intensification of the demand for circumcision to a wish that it would lead to mutilation would seem to imply that to Paul the mutilation itself would be preferable to circumcision which made faith and true righteousness void by substituting righteousness by the law. Just as Jesus according to the Gospels turned against the pious Pharisees who were zealous for the law and used against them the strongest expressions, so Paul has not hesitated to use the most violent and offensive words.

PART TWO

In the Holy Spirit received with the gospel the law is fulfilled, but the works of flesh destroyed (5:13–6:10)

The last section discussed (5:2-12) could be regarded as the conclusion of the first part of the letter which deals with justification apart from the law, and the transition to the second part. Paul has shown how in the gospel the law was fulfilled but the righteousness of the law was excluded. Now he proceeds to show how in the Spirit, given in and through the gospel, the fulfilment of the law manifests itself in love (*agape*) being born and the works of the flesh being destroyed. In this transitional section (5:2-12) Paul begins to discuss this faith that is active in love. This faith excludes the works of the law as a condition of salvation. But in and with faith the love to the neighbor with its works of fulfilling the law is likewise present. With the words in 5:6, "For in Christ Jesus neither circumcision nor uncircumcision is of any avail, but faith working through love," Paul has joined together the first and second parts of the letter. In the first part he deals with the antithesis between righteousness through Christ and righteousness by the law. In the second part he points out how the positive meaning of the gospel appears in life in the Spirit and in love to the neighbor.

1. Flesh and Spirit in life and work (5:13-24)

a) Freedom is a freedom in the spirit, not in the flesh (5:13-15)

The Letter to the Galatians has been called the letter of Christian liberty, because the content deals with faith's freedom from the law. Christ has redeemed us from the present evil age and given us a share in that new life which cannot be gained through law.

The great danger of such a proclamation was that freedom might be abused. For the Gentile who had lived under "the elemental spirits," or the Jew who had been captive under the law, the gospel meant an entirely new kind of freedom. But this freedom could be had only in faith; i.e., a man was free only insofar as he really lived in the new life. He was free from law and sin *in order to* serve righteousness (cf. Rom. 6:18). There was always a possibility that the message of Christ just became an occasion to regard oneself as free *from* the old bondage while continuing to live in the old state. This was "carnal" freedom, in which a person was set free from certain bonds but unconsciously became subject to a new bondage. Carnal freedom was simply a new form of bondage to powers which in reality were of the same nature as "the elemental spirits." Paul held, we might say, that freedom from the law could be gained only through bondage in faith to the God of love who through the Spirit bestowed new life. The presupposition and meaning of freedom was subjection to Christ. Real freedom and joy could be found only in this subjection, so that a person need not seek to free himself from the consciousness of guilt. Only in this freedom could a person become a child of God, the Creator and Giver of all things. Only in union with Christ was a man freed from the compulsion to seek his own righteousness.

There is a mutual connection between bondage under the law and "carnal" freedom. Although these two are in a sense opposites, they both imply a profound bondage of the self and manifest a loveless selfishness. "The works of the flesh" which Paul enumerates in vss. 19-20 cannot be rooted out and destroyed through the commandments of the law, although these commandments condemn them and even prevent certain manifestations of the mind of the "flesh." The commandments do not kill sin but revive it (cf. Rom. 7:7-11). They can create a sense of guilt which produces works of the law and a life whose driving power is fear and the desire to make oneself righteous. The same bondage to self which expresses itself in "the works of the flesh" is the foundation also of the works of the law. These are only a more refined expression of the loveless enhancement of self, and to Paul the opposite of both of these forms is love to the neighbor. Since the first of these forms, righteousness by the law, appeared in the guise of piety and claimed to be more faithful in the application of Scripture than Paul himself, he had to deal with this aspect first and show that this involved a perversion of Scripture and the law. In the second part of the letter he now contrasts love to neighbor with "the works of the flesh."

That Paul had to warn against understanding freedom as "carnal" freedom is perfectly natural. It does not mean that he takes up the argument on a new front, as some have suggested. Some have advanced the hypothesis that after Paul has dealt fully with the error of the Judaizers he now turns to the anti-nomians who wanted to change the gospel into a freedom of the flesh.

This theory is not necessary for the explanation of Paul's admonitions. Just as in Romans 12 Paul admonishes his readers not to be conformed to this world, so he admonishes the Galatians not to use their freedom as an opportunity for the flesh. Not to misuse their freedom is the negative side of the admonition to proceed further on the way in which they had made some progress (Phil. 3:13, 16). If the Christians really accepted the new life they received through the gospel, they must grow and advance (cf. Col. 1:10; Eph. 3:16; I Cor. 9:24ff.). If they did not advance further in faith, but departed from a living and growing faith after being freed from the law, the result could be a freedom "for the flesh." In *one* sense the freedom of faith broke with the old moral forms, because the cultic and moral rules that existed had their strength in the conception that they were conditions for obtaining the favor of the deity. But faith was not proclaimed as a new law in the sense of new regulations for obtaining the favor of God. Salvation was entirely a gift of God through which man receives new life. Thereby an entirely new relationship was established between "religion" and "morality"; a relationship, however, which those who did not fully understand it could misuse and pervert into a freedom of the flesh. Faith was *one* with love and freedom.

Paul presents the antithesis to selfishness of the flesh by citing the well-known commandment in Lev. 19:18, "You shall love your neighbor as yourself." This was the fulfilment of the law which flows directly from faith. It was not done in order to obtain righteousness, but became the result of a true life in faith; yes, it was even included in faith so intimately that it could not be separated from it. Here it becomes evident again that Paul does not abrogate the law of the Old Testament, but rather establishes it. (Cf. Rom. 3:31, where Paul says that he establishes the law through faith; and Rom. 10:3, where he says that the Jews seek to establish their own righteousness because they are ignorant of God's righteousness.) After a man has received the message of salvation and the new life, he must walk accordingly. He could not continue in the life he had lived before he received that message. Then it had been natural to live after "the flesh," but now he must order his whole life in conformity with the reality with which he had come in contact.

We should notice Paul's expression: "through love be servants of one another." The word, "be servants of," is the same as "be slave to" (*douleuein*). To be a bond servant to the neighbor through love is the very opposite of being a servant of the flesh as a slave. The former service is a life in the Spirit, and to do this service and in love belong to the neighbor is real freedom (cf. also Mark 10:41ff.). Paul has already spoken about freedom, and he confirms (vs. 13) that Christians were called to freedom. But this freedom is to be applied in service described here in words that seem to imply the opposite of freedom (cf. also Rom. 6:18; 7:6). Freedom from the law belongs with slavery of righteousness in the new life of the Spirit. It is precisely this paradoxical form that expresses the nature of Christian freedom. Real freedom means to be able to lead a life for which God created man: a life in the service of love; a life in which the self is not the master. Here it becomes evident that the conceptions of both freedom and love have a content in Paul different from that usually associated with these conceptions. Love is not desire and satisfaction, not egoistical love, but a love in service. Freedom is not a freedom to do selfishly whatever one may desire and to maintain oneself and one's interests against others, but a freedom which realizes itself in accordance with its own nature in service to others motivated by love. Love becomes willingness to serve and expend oneself. Here appears the new fundamental conception that the freedom and love proclaimed are not manifested in doing what a man desires, nor in possessing and enjoying, but in serving. But this service is of a very special kind. To be a bond servant of Christ implies freedom from bondage to righteousness by the law and to "the flesh," from the power of sin and death, from the tendency of the guilty conscience to compensate for the guilt or to dismiss it without removing the cause. Freedom means glad service in which a man in untroubled confidence does to others what he would have them do to him. Only in that way can man be what he was intended to be, while the power of selfishness means slavery. The rabbis too did summarize the law in a few commandments, or eventually in only one, the commandment of love. Paul does not regard love as something which can be presented as the fulfilment of a demand. Love to one's neighbor belongs with faith. The Christian must "put on Christ" (Rom. 13:14). Love does no wrong to the neighbor and is therefore the fulfilment of the law. If a man lives in love, he *cannot* injure his neighbor at all (cf. Rom. 13:8ff.); instead he will help and serve him.

According to Paul the whole fulfilment of the law is found

in this service of love to the neighbor. We may compare this to Rom. 13:8-10. "He who loves his neighbor has fulfilled the law." The commandments are summed up in these words: "You shall love your neighbor as yourself." Love (*agape*) itself is the fulness of the law (*pleroma nomou*) and its fulfilling (Rom. 13:10). This love came in its fulness in Christ. This is the climax and the goal (*telos*) of everything in the law. Just as it is stated in I Cor. 13:1ff., love is the greatest, it is the perfection of everything spoken in Scripture.

We have pointed out before that Paul considered a sacred document to have a deeper and hidden meaning. According to Paul the most profound meaning of the Old Testament law could appear as something very simple, namely, the love and freedom mentioned here. At the same time it is evident that the meaning of the ideas of freedom and love contained in the message, "You shall love your neighbor as yourself," was something which in one sense could be understood only through the revelation of God. This love had now been revealed through the death and resurrection of Christ, and it revealed and brought to its completion the most profound significance and meaning of the redemptive activity of God the Old Testament contained. The love which was now revealed and which fulfilled the law had been foretold in the law, but now it had become a reality in the death of Christ. When Paul writes that the fulfilment of the law is found in the words, "Love your neighbor as yourself," his words here (as well as in Rom. 13:8-10) do not imply at all a rationalistic simplification of the law in the Old Testament. His words imply instead a more profound interpretation of the law than was possible before Christ. The fulfilling of the commandment of the law could therefore be described as freedom from the law, which could not be said of any other fulfilment. To be called to freedom did not mean simply freedom from certain restrictive statutes. The right fulfilling of the law could not even be said to consist in works of service, if these were done in order to obtain merit (cf. I Cor. 13:3). That the fulfilment and right fulfilling of the law lie in love to the neighbor is connected with the fact that this love is conceived by Paul as having its basis in the reception of God's righteousness which has appeared in love, in God's love for man— become concrete and incarnate in the cross of Christ and in his death and resurrection—and in the love to the neighbor in which God's love continues to live and move. We have already explained (cf. exegesis of 3:10-12; 3:13-14) Paul's view that the work of Christ was the fulfilment and fulfilling of the law. Christ took the just curse of the law upon himself and made it possible for righteousness to do its work as love. In saying that the fulfilling of the law is love to the neighbor, Paul does not say anything different but only applies to the Christian life what he has already said. The statement that love to one's neighbor is the fulfilling of the law can easily be misunderstood, as we have already indicated. This is done if it is maintained for instance that the law contains "only" the commandment that we must love, as if this were something quite simple, easily understood, and readily accomplished. This is far from the meaning of the love under discussion here. It is something which in one sense is not at all simple. The whole work of Christ was necessary in order to bring this love down to the world and overcome that which retarded, prevented, and perverted it. The Spirit given in faith was the Spirit of Christ, who could be given only through the death of Christ. Paul is perfectly consistent, therefore, in developing the thought of freedom from the law by saying that Christ has redeemed us from the curse of the law by becoming a curse for us (3:13-14) that through his work "we might receive the promise of the Spirit."

What we have said now indicates that it would be a complete misunderstanding of Paul if it were maintained that he, after having rejected the Old Testament law, set up his own ethics of works through his admonitions and exhortations. It has been claimed that Paul adds ethical admonitions to his systematic presentation which do not always agree with his dogmatic argumentation. Though his argumentation was concerned with a proclamation of freedom from the law and salvation through faith in Christ, he is now supposed to be establishing a new ethic of works in and though his exhortations. But whoever argues this way has completely misunderstood both dogmatic reasoning and ethical admonitions. All ethical exhortations in Paul are the consequences of his so-called dogmatic expositions. They make known the new element that has come through Christ, the new freedom and the new love, and they show what consequences must follow because of these gifts.

Paul presents the opposite of a service in love in the next verse, and he does so in a (possibly sarcastic) reproach of the Galatians. They manifested a relationship to one another which was the opposite of love. They sought to hurt and injure one another.

They quarreled, and they needed a warning against devouring one another in this way. The Galatians had, of course, not held fast to the gospel Paul had preached. They had believed it must be complemented with a demand for circumcision and the observance of certain commands and regulations in the law of Moses. But in the midst of this zeal for the law they maintain a mutual relationship which Paul in vs. 15 describes in words reminiscent of wild beasts. The one treats the other in a way that is not at all loving-kindness. This attitude manifests their "carnal" nature. External ethical commandments and cultic regulations cannot prevent men from acting under the influence of such a disposition. Bondage under the law and a "carnal" nature can belong together. When the disposition is carnal in one way or another, there may be need for legal prescriptions with demands and threats, but these cannot set a man free from this "carnal" disposition or make him in Paul's sense "spiritual." It is possible that the inability of the Galatians to understand and apply Paul's earlier proclamation may have manifested itself at first as moral laxity. The defective moral state among the Galatians may have given special force to the Judaizers' demand for the observance of the law. It has been a common tendency in every age to seek to remedy moral laxity with strict external regulations. This may naturally be good and right in regard to public morality, and it may even promote moral behavior. But when ethical rigor and a strict moral attitude are conceived of as decisive by themselves for one's whole personality and relation to God, making them completely dependent on man's own life and ability, the result is an external separation between those who appear good because of their observance of certain customs and laws and those who are not able or willing to do so. Then goodness easily becomes conceit, and eventually it becomes conventional. In addition, the conception Paul proclaimed in his service of Christ becomes obscured and impossible, namely, that humanity belongs to this age and to the powers which rule in it; that redemption comes through God's creation of righteousness through the atonement for all sins, for common "works of the flesh" as well as for sins of self-glorying, and for moral laxity as well as ethical rigor.

When Paul encountered the seductive legalism of the Judaizers which was attractive because of its strictness, he had both to expose the fundamental error of this proclamation of law, which appeared to be a higher and more demanding religion and morality, and also to turn against the moral laxity which may have appeared because of a misunderstanding of his proclamation of justification by faith without the works of the law. After he thoroughly exposed the deceit of the Judaizers' alleged faithfulness to Scripture and zeal for law, morality, and religion, he had to point out the true consequences of justification by faith, which appear in a life of love to the neighbor and in a life in the Spirit and the fruits of the Spirit.

The discussion above is summarized in vs. 18: life in the Spirit means freedom from law. The condemnation of the law does not strike those who are in Christ (Rom. 8:1). As we have explained above, freedom from the law belongs with bondage in love to the neighbor, while bondage to legal requirements, through which a man seeks to make himself righteous and religiously qualified, may in reality go with a life and disposition that expresses itself in what Paul describes as mutually biting and devouring one another.

We may express the meaning of Paul's point of view here by saying that the result of not adhering to the commandment of love is men destroying themselves. Indirectly it is thus revealed that men were *created* to love and serve one another. Christ brought and revealed as something new what in reality was in the most profound sense natural to men and that for which they were created. When all of human society has been taken captive by the powers of evil, man cannot of himself love as he should in accordance with his real nature, the nature with which he was created, but which has been corrupted through the power of evil. After the curse of the law had been taken away and the presence of Christ on earth had become a reality, love could be received. Life in the Spirit was life in love. Faith must continually become incarnate in love to the neighbor. This love leads to the restoration of life on earth; but even more than that, it is rooted in that imperishable life for which man was created, and it must end in the imperishable state. This love is connected, therefore, with God's creation and his providence, and likewise with its redemption and its goal in incorruption (cf. Rom. 8:12-23). Love is essentially the same as God's righteousness. Righteousness and life belong together; where the one is the other will be also. Eternal life can never be given as a reward for the observance of the law. But eternal life follows upon the true fulfilment of the law in the Spirit of Christ, who is also called the Spirit of life (Rom. 8:2).

Life in the Spirit is an earnest of the life which will receive visible form through the resurrection (cf. II Cor. 5:1-5). Then the perishable nature will be changed into the imperishable, and the mortal nature of creation is given meaning by partaking of the immortality which is the inheritance of the children of promise.

b) The conflict between the flesh and the Spirit (5:16-18)

The Spirit of whom Paul speaks here is the Spirit of life, faith, and the promised new age. It is the Spirit given to the disciples of Christ. The giving of the Spirit meant that the Christians were called not to uncleanness but to a life in holiness. Whoever neglects life in holiness, says Paul in I Thess. 4:7-8, disregards God "who gives his Holy Spirit to you." The Galatians had received the Spirit. If they now walked by the Spirit, they would not gratify the desires of the flesh. What "the flesh" means he explains later. Here Paul presents Spirit and flesh as two powers in conflict. "The flesh" is conceived of as a mighty force in *this* age, and paradoxically may be called its spirit (cf. Rom. 8:1-17). What "the flesh" drives men to do here on earth is the opposite of that which the Spirit of God brings. It drives men to unrighteousness instead of righteousness, to hate and envy instead of love. "The flesh" is therefore not conceived of as sexual desire, *libido carnis,* but could be described instead as an evil power in control of this existence which has taken possession of man's body and soul and has perverted their activity. This perversity manifests itself in such doings as he enumerates in vss. 19-20, but it may also appear in such unnatural acts as he describes in Rom. 1:21-31. Man is under the control of a power which has taken possession of him and impels him. He is essentially a slave of sin insofar as he is not set free from it.

The function of the law in this age was to pronounce judgment, accuse of sin, and "to increase the trespass." But he who is led by the Spirit is not under the law (vs. 18). He is not bound and driven by the flesh, but has been set free from its works.

Now after the Galatians had heard the proclamation of Christ, they were to consider its meaning and live accordingly (vs. 16). Even though in this age man is driven by evil, nevertheless when the Spirit has been given to him and thus he has experienced the power of forgiveness and reconciliation, he can listen and cling to the Spirit and turn away from that which had distorted his perception. Although he cannot by himself produce the good, when Christ and his Spirit have come into the world, he can listen to His Word, become incorporated into the body of Christ, and turn away from the evil powers and their enticements. If he would acknowledge the testimony of the Spirit and accept the living Christ, the Spirit could become the driving power in his life (cf. Rom. 7:5-6). If he did so, he was free from the law. On the contrary, if he turned away from faith in Christ and back to the law as a way of salvation, he would be imprisoned in the sphere ruled by the power of the flesh. Under the conditions of this present age the law belonged with the power of the flesh, and it was unable to set anyone free from it, even though it prevented the manifestation of some of its work by commandments and threats.

This discussion elucidates also Paul's thesis that the Spirit gives freedom, but the flesh bondage. The Spirit brings man back to that freedom for which he was created and fulfils the promise of freedom. Freedom, the Spirit, life, and righteousness belong together. Only when man *is* righteous can he act righteously. He who had not received the gift of righteousness and life could not be taught by the law to live righteously. Only when life and righteousness had come to man could he do the works which are designated as the fruits of the Spirit.

c) The works of the flesh (5:19-21)

The powers contending for man, which Paul calls the Spirit and the flesh, disclose themselves through their works. The distinctions between the various vices enumerated as the works of the flesh are difficult to establish, but it is easy to get a total picture of the kind of works Paul regards as typical of "the flesh." A similar list of sins is found in II Cor. 12:20. There is nothing ascetic in Paul's conception. Evil is not one-sidedly characterized as sensuality. Paul begins by saying that the works of the flesh are *plain*. Everyone ought to be able to see that these things were evil and destructive, and that they destroyed both individual and social life (cf. Rom. 1:29-32).

Many discussions have been held about the lists of vices and virtues found in Paul's letters. In addition to those already mentioned we find others in Rom. 13:13; I Cor. 5:10-11; 6:9-10; Eph. 4:31; 5:3-4; Col. 3:5, 8. "Lists of vices" were common in Stoic writings, but they are also known in the literature of late Judaism, especially in the Wisdom of Solomon. Some have assumed that Paul was familiar with popular philosophical and ethical presentations and that he adopted their form of writing. In any case, however, the content and context are different in Paul from those in Greek popular philosophy. The Stoic lists of vices were systematic presentations giving instruction concerning the nature of evil. Paul has no systematic order but picks out a variety of examples of "the works of the flesh," He holds that these are plain to all. No one can refuse to see that they are evil. As Paul says in the letter to the Romans, *the wrath of God* is revealed through these things. When man has exchanged God's truth for a lie (Rom. 1:25), God indeed continues to reveal himself, but then he makes known his wrath. He gives men up to death and destruction. He permits evil to work itself out and show its fruit. Thus men ought to see by themselves that they are evil and transgressors. The revelation of God, which was meant to make men praise and thank God as the Creator, took the form of wrath because of men's depravity, and through his wrath he gave them up to works of corruption and wickedness. These works led to destruction and death. Their real depravity appears perhaps most clearly against the background of love which is the fulfilment of the law, and prevails through the Spirit and appears in the fruits of the Spirit. But Paul does not discuss how we can know that these works are evil. He assumes that *in the presence of* these works everyone must recognize that they are evil.

Just as the law is a revelation of God, which nevertheless in the service of sin has been made a means of righteousness by the law and has been so perverted that it drives men into sin, so it could be said also that the works of God in nature, which should have taught men to praise and worship the Creator, have become corrupted through the depravity and folly that have taken men captive. The natural functions, which should lead to life on earth and in eternity, became unnatural. Man's nature became contrary to nature. Natural love between man and woman became perverse sexuality (Rom. 1:24ff.); natural love and kindness disappeared (Rom. 1:31). All humanity was caught in the worship of the material and the perishable as a substitute for the worship of God (cf. Rom. 1:25). The material and perishable, created to serve man, became his master and god. What was according to nature was in various ways deprived of its functions and became corrupt. Thus death rather than life was the dominant power over man.

As we have already observed, the "vices" which Paul enumerates in vss. 19ff. are examples of the works of "the flesh" and of that wick-

edness which dominates man in this age. What he enumerates is fornication (*porneia*), uncleanness (*akatharsia*) and wantonness (*aselgeia*).
Fornication is mentioned for example in I Cor. 5:1; 6:13, 18; 7:2;
I Thess. 4:3, and has reference to sexual debauchery. Uncleanness
(cf. II Cor. 12:21; Eph. 5:3; Col. 3:5) is the opposite of holiness
(cf. I Thess. 4:7; Rom. 6:19) and is concerned not only with the
physical life but with the whole personality of man. Wantonness and
lewdness probably refer to complete abandonment to debauchery (cf.
Rom. 13:13; II Cor. 12:21; Eph. 4:19). Idolatry (*eidolatria;* cf. I
Cor. 5:10-11; 6:9; Eph. 5:5) is for Paul connected with all these sins
(cf. Rom. 1:23-24). One form of idolatry was sorcery (*pharmakeia*),
which can also mean the mixing of drugs and poisons (for good or
evil). It could refer here to mixing poison, but in this context it would
seem to mean instead sorcery or magic. The word is used in this sense
in the Septuagint (e.g., Exod. 7:11, 22; Deut. 18:10; Jer. 47:9, 12)
and in the Book of Revelation (9:21; 18:23-24).

He also mentions enmity (*echthrai*) which might refer to personal
unfriendliness between the members of the church in Galatia. Quarreling, strife, or controversy (*eris*) is mentioned by Paul for example
in Rom. 1:29; I Cor. 1:11; Phil. 1:15 (cf. also I Tim. 6:4 and Titus
3:9). It occurs frequently, as it does here, in connection with *zelos*
(Rom. 13:13; I Cor. 3:3; II Cor. 12:20) meaning zeal, fanaticism,
impetuosity, hatred, envy. (We are reminded that this last word
has been discussed by Cullmann in his book on Peter. In the First
Letter of Clement, written during the last part of the first century,
there is frequent mention of *zelos,* which Cullmann translates by
Eifersucht (jealousy). Cullmann suggests that this jealousy and fanaticism, which was prevalent in the early church, may have been a cause
of Peter's martyrdom).

Paul also mentions here as in II Cor. 12:20 anger (*thumoi*), which
refers especially to a violent outburst of anger (cf. Eph. 4:31). The
word translated "selfishness" (*eritheia;* cf. Rom. 2:8; Phil. 1:17; 2:3)
may refer to belligerent resistance to the gospel, and may also denote
ambition or rivalry. Plots and intrigues are the result of such an
attitude. The following words also denote strife and quarreling, within
the congregation: *dichostasiai* (dissension) (cf. Rom. 16:17) and
heireseis (party spirit, formation of sects, and schisms, which destroy
unity in the church).

Envy (*phthonoi*) closely resembles *zelos* (zeal, rivalry). (Murder
[*phonoi*], which is omitted in some manuscripts, may be an interpola-
tion.) Drunkenness (*methai*) and carousing (*komoi*) belong together
here as also in Rom. 13:13. The final words, "and the like," indicate
that this is a list of examples of the works of the flesh, not a complete
catalog. They are all different works of the same "flesh" which can
express itself also in various other ways.

The works of "the flesh" were a sign of man's opposition to
the Spirit and the fruits of the Spirit. They should not imagine
that those who were controlled by "the flesh" could inherit the

kingdom of God (vs. 21). Freedom from the law by faith was not a freedom "of the flesh." Faith did not open the way to such works as he has enumerated here. On the contrary, such works show that man is subject to a power which contends against faith and against the Spirit. Those who had placed themselves in the service of "the flesh" would lose the inheritance promised to those who received the promise in faith and for whom the light had dawned.

Paul emphasizes also in I Cor. 6:9 that the unrighteous shall not inherit the kingdom of God. Then he mentions a number of concrete sins and repeats that those who live in this way shall not inherit the kingdom.

d) The fruits of the Spirit (5:22-24)

The Christians who had earlier been slaves of such vices as are enumerated in Gal. 5:19-20 (cf. I Cor. 6:9-10) had now been set free from this bondage. They had been cleansed, sanctified, and justified. In baptism they had been cleansed from sins. But this did not imply a doctrine of sinlessness. Whenever suggestions like this have been made, sin has been conceived of as occasional expressions of man's free will. After man has been converted he presumably has no more to do with sin. But Paul regarded sin as a power which rules over man and whose authority manifests itself in man's works. This power was, to be sure, broken through Christ, and the Christian, who had become a participant in the victory of Christ over this power, had been freed from his bondage under sin and had been placed instead under the power of Christ. But as long as man lives in this world he experiences the power of sin. Because Paul conceives of sin in this way, it is natural for him both to proclaim freedom from sin and to admonish the Christians earnestly not to revert to those sins and vices which belong to the realm of the flesh.

Through baptism man had been united with Christ, and he had to take this fact into consideration in his conduct. Paul develops this in detail in Romans 7. But, as we have said, his freedom from sin did not mean that man could live as sinless. Just as the power of sin had been broken, so also the power of death had been brought to nought. But he still lived in this perishable world; and similarly he lived also in the world where sin is found. The body was subject to death because of sin (Rom. 8:10). There is no sinlessness in the sense that a Christian cannot sin, any more than

there is immortality in the sense that man can escape the necessity
of death. Just as every man must die a physical death, in spite of
life in the Spirit and the promise of resurrection, thus also sin
remains a reality in this life on earth, even though man participates
in the victory of Christ over sin. But the power and authority of
sin as well as that of death had been broken through the work of
Christ, and he who belonged to Christ had died from the whole
context of life dominated and ruled by sin and death. Union with
Christ was not simply a theory or idea; it involved an incorporation with him which must become characteristic of life. The
Christian had "crucified the flesh with its passions and desires"
(vs. 24). Although man continued to live in this present, evil age
of sin and corruption, the promised age to come would take over
completely at the return of Christ, so that sin and corruption would
be entirely eliminated. But through union with Christ and the
power of the Spirit sin was already brought to nought as far as
its authority to determine the destiny of life was concerned.

We may note here that Paul's conception of freedom and
bondage differs from that commonly held. A fatalistic view, according to which man lacks any power of decision and is blindly
subservient to an overpowering fate, has often been placed in opposition to a faith in man as free and independent who determines
his destiny himself. In the history of theology there have often been
proposed the two alternatives: either God does everything and
man is passive; or salvation and righteousness are dependent on
man's free action. Paul does not present either of these alternatives.
Although there are powers which hinder man from doing what he
wills (Rom. 7:17ff.), and which impel him in different directions
(Gal. 5:17), the attitude of man is nevertheless of the greatest
importance. It is true that he cannot of himself create the good,
and the evil is a power in which he shares by nature. But he can
walk in what belongs to the life of faith and turn away from everything pertaining to "the flesh."

"The fruit of the Spirit," which in Greek as well as in English
denotes the result of life in the Spirit, whatever this life produces
and gives, may have had for those who first heard the letter a
connotation different from the one it has for us. It may have
suggested something offered to God. The fruits of the earth were
consecrated to him, and that which was offered to him was
sanctified. The Christian's sanctification appeared in the fruits of

the Spirit, and his life was shown to be consecrated to God. Instead of works of the law, which were done to serve man's desire to make himself righteous, propitiate the deity and make the gods favorable, the Christian does God's work for entirely different reasons and motives. If the works of the law were connected with and stood on the same level as the sacrifices intended to propitiate God, the fruit of the Spirit was the result of the entirely new relation to God, realized in and through the sacrifice of Christ, by which the law was fulfilled, its final meaning revealed and all its demands were met. Righteousness had now been given, and the fruit of the Spirit had its matrix in the participation in righteousness given with the Spirit. The Spirit, righteousness, and love were all expressions of God's making man a participant in his own life. Then man's works were at the same time the only proper sacrifice to God, and man himself was in his life an offering consecrated to God. His sanctification was his growth in works of the Spirit. The life in sanctification, in which man was consecrated to God as his possession, was in reality the proper sacrifice. Then it was not a question of propitiating God or of doing works in order to obtain something, but the matrix was the Spirit and righteousness of God, and the conflict and enmity which motivated the works of the law and the sacrifices connected with them had been overcome. Faith active through love and the fruits of the Spirit become a reception of and a participation in Christ's fulfilment of the law. In the love of God and Christ, translated into the activity of man, it is continually apparent that the law is fulfilled. Its condemnation was therefore removed and its task of keeping men under confinement was at an end. The *end* of the law (*telos*) had come, because in Christ it had had its fulfilment. Life in participation in Christ's fulfilment of the law is the Christians' sanctification, in which they grow more and more and become united with one another and with God. Thus sanctification became the sacrifice associated with the life in the new age. Just as Christ brought the law to fulfilment and completion by assuming its condemnation so as to give life, so his sacrifice was the perfect sacrifice which fulfilled and canceled the previous sacrificial service. For the one baptized into Christ the life in Christ became a life consecrated to God. This had the character of a true sacrifice in which he himself became more fully consecrated to God.

In Gal. 5:19-20 Paul had not been concerned with the fulfilment of the law but with the contrast between the fruits of the Spirit and the apparent wickedness of certain works. It then becomes clear that the fruits of the Spirit were not such that they could be subject to the judgment of the law (vs. 23). He who was led by the Spirit was guided by a power other than the law; a power whose works the law could not judge, and which in contrast to the law gave life. He had "crucified the flesh with its passions and desires" (vs. 24). Christ his Master did not stop at condemning the evil; he bestowed new life. He let everyone who believed in him participate in his life, and let him die to the wickedness which appeared in the works of the flesh. These works were clearly shown to be evil; and participation in the life of Christ was also a participation in his death and crucifixion, in and through which guilt was taken away from men so that it did not drive them to continued and greater sin.

The fruit of the Spirit is presented as something which to an unbeliever may not appear as anything remarkable or desirable. To the pagans many of these fruits of the Spirit might appear as weakness. But the Galatians, who nevertheless had been nourished for a time in the Christian proclamation and had been instructed in the Old Testament, needed only to be shown the new disposition and the new spirit which permeated the Christian life, and they would have to admit that these fruits were good and not subject to the condemnation of the law. First he mentions love (*agape*). This is God's love (cf. Rom. 5:8; II Cor. 13:13; Eph. 1:4-5; 2:4; Col. 3:12; I Thess. 1:4; II Thess. 2:13, 16). This means that it is also the love of Christ (Rom. 8:35, 37; II Cor. 5:14; Eph. 3:19; 5:2, 25; Gal. 2:20). It can also be said to be God's love in Christ (Rom. 8:39), and stand in connection with the Spirit (Rom. 15:30). Love is poured out in our hearts (Rom. 5:5) and now works in us (I Cor. 16:24; II Cor. 2:4; 8:7-8; Phil. 1:9; Col. 1:8; I Thess. 1:3; 3:6; 5:8). But it is defined as God's love, which has now been revealed and in which the Christian participates. In and through this love something new has come which belongs to the promised Messianic age. Love defines life in the Spirit. It may be God's love, love to fellow men, or love to God, but it is all of the same nature as God's love in Christ. God sheds abroad his love in the hearts of the believers through Christ. As we are told in I Cor. 13, it is the greatest, the most precious, and the most fundamental factor in the new life which has come in Christ. It belongs with faith and hope, but it is nevertheless the highest expression of what God has given through Christ. The nature of this love belongs to the promised age to come, but it has become real even now, and it is that "which binds everything together in perfect harmony" (Col. 3:14).

Paul also mentions joy (*chara*) and peace (*eirene*). These belong with the new life given through the Spirit. Paul develops this further in other letters. He speaks of righteousness, peace, and joy in the Holy Spirit (Rom 14:17). Righteousness, which came and was given in Christ, belongs with everything said about the fruits of the Spirit. Peace and joy belong to the promised age to come. Joy comes with the Holy Spirit (I Thess. 1:6), joy in the Lord (Phil. 3:1; 4:4, 10). Joy is also associated with hope; "Rejoice in your hope, be patient in tribulation, be constant in prayer" (Rom. 12:12). Joy had its foundation in the salvation revealed in Christ. "May the God of hope fill you with all joy and peace in believing, so that by the power of the Holy Spirit you may abound in hope" (Rom. 15:13). Many of the fruits of the Spirit which Paul mentions in Gal. 5:22-23 are mentioned also in Romans. Joy is not dependent on success and strength; it can prevail in weakness and suffering (II Cor. 13:9; Col. 1:24; Phil. 2:17), and is therefore of a deeper nature than ordinary joy.

Peace is connected with joy (Rom. 14:17; 15:13), and with love (Rom. 14:15ff.; II Cor. 13:11; Col. 3:14-15; Eph. 6:23). That the Spirit comes from the God of peace is a frequent statement (Rom. 15:33; 16:20; I Cor. 14:33; II Cor. 13:11; Phil. 4:9; I Thess. 5:23). The gospel is the gospel of peace (Eph. 2:17; 6:15). "The peace of Christ" characterizes his faithful people; "let the peace of Christ rule in your hearts, to which indeed you were called in the one body" (Col. 3:15). This is a peace whose basis and quality is more profound than ordinary peace of mind. It is a "peace of God which passes all understanding" (Phil. 4:7). We could also elucidate the reality of which Paul speaks by using the words in the Gospel of John: "Peace I leave with you; my peace I give to you; not as the world gives do I give to you" (John 14:27).

Patience, kindness, goodness (*makrothumia, chrestotes, agathosune*) are fruits of the Spirit which show that the believer has been taken up into a sphere in which God works and makes men share in his gifts. Patience and forbearance in the New Testament are attributed to God (e.g., Rom. 2:4; 9:22; cf. also Luke 18:7). Just as God in patience and forbearance forgives sins, so Christians are to do the same. For the Christian to forgive his neighbor is for him to be taken into that sphere in which God's love and forgiveness have become active powers. The Christian's forgiveness is not his own meritorious accomplishment, nor is it weakness or commendable leniency, but is a sharing in God's own forgiving love.

The Christian manifests patience with his neighbor by forbearance (cf. Col. 3:12; Eph. 4:2-3), and patience appears also under all persecution and suffering (cf. II Cor. 6:6). Kindness is often connected with patience (e.g., Rom. 2:4; II Cor. 6:6; Col. 3:12; cf. I Cor. 13:4). Goodness is called the fruit of light in Eph. 5:9, and there is associated with righteousness and truth. Goodness and knowledge are combined in Rom. 15:14. The word occurs rather seldom.

"Faithfulness" (*pistis*) here means trust, confidence, not merely accepting something as true. Behind this conception stands the Hebrew *emunah,* as we have indicated above (cf. the exegesis of 3:11). In the present context the word does not refer to the age of faith or the rule of faith but to the virtues of faithfulness and trust.

Gentleness and self-control (*prautes, egkrateia*) are mentioned last as the fruits of the Spirit. Gentleness is illustrated later in 6:1 as the opposite of trying to apply always a rigid ethical norm and being ever ready in self-conceit to judge the neighbor. The opposite of gentleness is the fanaticism, passion, and contentious zeal in which men always insist on making their own point of view prevail. We may also compare the words in Matt. 5:5 ("Blessed are the meek") and 11:29 ("I am gentle and lowly in heart") where words of similar derivation are used. Self-control is the opposite of fornication, impurity, drunkeness, and carousing. It refers not only to the sexual life but to self-control in general.

Life in the Spirit implies participation in Christ, and therefore also participation in his crucifixion and death. Baptism meant to Paul that man's life in the flesh died and was buried (cf. Rom. 6:4; Col. 2:12). Man could become free from the power of the flesh only through death. But union with Christ is a real participation in his death. This means that it is impossible to assent to "the works of the flesh." Those who belong to Christ have "crucified" these works. His crucifixion was an assent to the condemnation of all the evil in the world. Everything opposed to the life in the Spirit (vs. 24) must be destroyed in those who have become partakers in all that Christ gives. This can take place only through a participation in the death of Christ, who in his death accepted

264

and bore all guilt, and in the life of Christ, which is eternal life and righteousness from God.

It has sometimes been claimed that the relationship between flesh and Spirit in Paul shows an influence of Gnosticism, or sometimes of Stoicism. We have shown above that Paul thinks of flesh and Spirit as personal powers. This in itself may be similar to Gnostic ideas about various spiritual powers which control men. But the context in Paul is different. While the Gnostics rejected the idea that God himself had created the world, Paul's conception of God as Creator appears also in his contrast between Spirit and flesh. Man becomes free when he is ruled by the Spirit. It is not some foreign or unnatural power that takes possession when the Spirit comes to man. The fruits of the Spirit must be acknowledged as good even by those under the law. On the contrary, it is sin and death that represent something unnatural for man. When he participates in the life of Christ, he has that life for which he was created and which had been promised; that life to which in reality the law also bore witness. The Gnostics held that creation and law were entirely foreign to the new life. They could not, therefore, conceive of faith as the fulfilment of the law. In their case freedom could easily become license. When the works of the flesh as enumerated here are overcome, and such virtues as love, joy, peace, patience, kindness, goodness, faithfulness, gentleness, self-control dominate man, he becomes what he was created to be. In that life there is nothing unnatural, nothing that destroys life. We are God's workmanship, "created in Christ Jesus for good works" (Eph. 2:10). The new man is created after the likeness of God (Eph. 4:24). This is the same God who originally created man. In Christ "all things were created, . . . visible and invisible" (Col. 1:16). The new man is to be renewed in knowledge after the image of its Creator (Col. 3:10).

The ideas presented in Colossians and Ephesians concerning the old and the new man are closely related to Paul's conception of the fruit of the Spirit and works of the flesh in Galatians. Paul obviously holds that God has created the world in Christ, and that it will become what it was intended to be through the redemption in Christ. The creation of the new man is not the work of a god other than he who created heaven and earth. Just as this God created everything through Christ, thus also through Christ's work on earth the creation will be perfected. As the gospel fulfils the law, so the work of Christ fulfils all creation. Salvation in Christ fulfils creation; it overcomes its perversion in sin and resultant death, and restores creation to its original state and meaning. The perversion of creation in sin and death is replaced by righteousness and life. This fundamental point of view is not Gnostic, and in spite of apparent similarities there is in his whole point of view a decisive difference between Paul's conception and the various Gnostic teachings.

Paul's list of "virtues" in vss. 22-23 (cf. Phil. 4:8) has also been interpreted as betraying an influence of Stoicism. In addition to what we have already said about this we may add that here, as in the case of Gnosticism, we must go beyond superficial similarities and consider the matter in the context of his whole theological thinking. The fruits of the Spirit are not described as general, human qualities or virtues which can be attained by practice, contemplation, or speculation. The fruits of the Spirit are consistently defined as gifts which belong to the age to come. The greatest gift is God's love, God's *agape,* given to man through Christ (cf. Rom. 5:8; I Cor. 13:1ff.; II Cor. 13:13). Peace is the salvation which belongs to the coming age. All the fruits of the Spirit have an eschatological connotation. They are not virtues which may be acquired by human efforts. It is true, of course, that they may also be considered as the fulfilment of something known before. Love, peace, joy, etc., in the eschatological sense are such that when they are present, or when they are proclaimed, even those who have not received these gifts can to some extent understand them. And man may experience these as something which transforms and fulfils what he has had or has sought after.

We are, therefore, not concerned here with "natural theology" in the sense in which that term is usually understood. Natural theology usually starts with what is given in reason, and this becomes the basis of man's ascent to the higher realm of grace. Life in the Spirit manifests the works of revelation. At the same time this life speaks to the conscience of man in terms he can understand. In the usual presentation of the so-called natural theology God and man are conceived of as two opposite and mutually exclusive powers, so that some actions originate with God, others with man. If in this context certain virtues and certain knowledge were to be regarded as human, and these were to be incorporated into a certain dogmatics and ethics, the result would be a "natural" theology on the basis of this terminology. It is then

assumed from the beginning that this natural theology is separated
from the actions which are fully dependent on God's work. But
such a contrast between the natural and the revealed is foreign to
Paul. Man cannot know himself without knowing God. If man is
completely known, then, according to Paul, he knows God also as
his Creator and Lord. God and man belong together. The result
becomes, therefore, a "natural" theology in a sense different from
the usual meaning of the term. In the deepest sense man becomes
natural in and through the life of the Spirit, and the nature given
to him in creation is restored. Consequently, that which constitutes
the fruits of the Spirit is something which must be recognized as
good by any common, sane man, and not something which we
learn to call good only through propaganda. "The law" is not
contrary to the life that expresses itself in the fruits of the Spirit
(vs. 23). All life recognized as good, therefore, must be acknowledged as connected with the life of the Spirit (cf. Phil. 4:8).

Paul's added remark after he has described the fruits of the
Spirit, *"against such there is no law"* (vs. 23), serves to illustrate
his view of the relationship between the law and life in faith or
in the Spirit. The law cannot produce the good or create life and
righteousness. Its function is within this age dominated by evil,
and it has to threaten, condemn, and demand. Its demands are
righteous, and their complete fulfilment belongs to the promised
age to come. They are fulfilled through the gospel. The gospel
fulfils the law, brings it to its completion and *bestows* righteousness
and life. The relationship between law and faith therefore is such
that the good and the just cannot be adequately defined in reference to the commandments themselves as rationally stated. These
commandments must be brought to a new completion, of which
their fulfilment in the death of Christ is a part. It is not possible,
therefore, to take the law in its literal and rational meaning and
say that the believer has received power to keep its precepts
exactly. The life of the believer has a greater and more profound
significance. It cannot be defined or understood on the basis of
previously determined factors. Therefore, it is not said that the
life of the believer consists in his ability to fulfil the commandments which had previously proved to be too difficult, but rather
that "the just requirement of the law" is "fulfilled in us, who walk
not according to the flesh but according to the Spirit" (Rom. 8:4).
Paul does not say here in vss. 22ff. that the fruits of the Spirit
consist in the observance of the statutes of the law. He describes

life in the Spirit, and then observes that the law is not against it. Paul assumes that this is obvious to everyone. The requirements of the law serve a just and good life; and life in the Spirit cannot possibly be such that the law would condemn it. In reality the fulfilment of the law in its most profound sense appears in the fruits of the Spirit; a fulfilment in which the powers of the promised age to come are active. Since this is so, the law obviously cannot condemn that which belongs to this fulfilment, even if its require-ments as superficially understood may be set aside (cf. the pres-entation of Jesus' relationship to the law in the Synoptics, e.g., the commandment concerning the Sabbath).

The position of the law in Paul throws a certain light on his view of the relationship between the requirement of the law and the coming age. Since it can be said that the coming age includes the fulfilment of the demand of the law, it is not a question merely of a succession of the coming age after the close of the present without any connection between the coming age and life here on earth. There is a connection between this life and the coming age, but it cannot be defined on the basis of the *present* age. Life in the Spirit cannot be defined in terms of the statutes of the law; and the resurrection life cannot be defined in terms of physical life in this existence. But the relationship is the same as that between the fulfilment of the law in the life of the Spirit and the demands of the law. Just as the fulfilment of the law through the righteousness of God both cancels and completes the demands of the law, the imperishable life is both the annihilation and the fulfilment of the earthly life (cf. II Cor. 5:1-5). The connection with the coming age is given in the Christian's life in the Spirit, in regard to both righteousness and immortality.

We get a glimpse here also into the significance of Paul's inter-pretation of Scripture as he finds a deeper meaning in the word and sometimes uses the allegorical method of interpretation. This deeper exegesis refers to God's sovereign election here on earth and to the righteousness to be given in the coming age. This right-eousness is given to the Christian already here on earth in faith and through the Spirit, even though now he must "see in a mirror dimly" (I Cor. 13:12) and have "this treasure in earthen vessels" (II Cor. 4:7). The life of faith is still always concerned with concrete acts and works in this life on earth. Paul really describes the fruits of the Spirit in concrete and vivid terms. As God's acts of election were to be seen in the common events the Old Testament describes, and as these acts are not attributed to some superior kind of men, so also the participation in the powers of the age to come does not involve something foreign to this life on earth. The place and activity of these powers belong among the tasks and events of this life in the world. The nature of the new life must be recognized as good even by those who have no relation to the gospel. It is connected also with everything that from a general, human point of view may be said to be just and good (cf. Phil. 4:8).

2. Walking in the Spirit (5:25—6:6)

a) The life of the gospel is a walk in the Spirit (5:25)

Those who accepted the gospel received the Spirit, and through him they had access to a life of imperishable nature. But if life comes through the Spirit, it is necessary also to walk by the Spirit. If a Christian took part in such works as belonged to the flesh, he would lose his participation in the life of the Spirit, because this was a participation in the cross of Christ through which the flesh was crucified. Christians must continually realize this. That this means some kind of doctrine of sinlessness, as has sometimes been suggested, is a mistake similar to drawing a limit or setting up an antithesis between what God does and what man does. All of Paul's letters testify that he knows very well of what sins the Christians are guilty. For this reason he admonishes them constantly not to conform to the temper of this age but to live in newness of life. The righteousness and life which belong to the coming of Christ are at the same time present and future. This paradox means that life in the Spirit, too, is at the same time something given and something becoming and growing; something which is to take possession of man more and more. He *possesses* salvation, but at the same time he *is advancing* toward the consummation; he participates in the resurrection life, but he must constantly strive to share in it (cf. Phil. 3:10-14; I Cor. 9:24-25). This eschatological point of view indicates that the doctrine of a sinless state here on earth is foreign to Paul. The doctrine of sinlessness really denies that Christ's kingdom is a future kingdom. A doctrine of sinlessness calls attention to what man does, as if he created the new life; while to Paul the new is always the work of God and of Christ. It is a continually renewed liberation from sin. But he knows that, as man lives in this world of sin and

269

corruption, he must constantly strive and contend in order to avoid being drawn into conformity with this age.

In 5:25 Paul admonishes the Galatians to walk by the Spirit since they had received life through the Spirit. This life they had received through their faith in Christ. A new spiritual reality had come with him, and through him the Christian was connected with imperishable life and with that age to be fully revealed at the return of Christ. To live by the Spirit was something more than being inspired. It meant participation in an entirely new life which now had begun working in Christ. He who believed in him had become a new creature. Christ lived in him through his Spirit (2:20). He was a citizen in a kingdom with access to treasures which previously had been inaccessible or unknown. But this did not mean that the will was cancelled out, or that he lived passively submerged in a strong emotional experience without any will of his own. Paul clearly pointed out through his description of the fruits of the Spirit that faith meant a concrete form of living in the world. The Christian must strive to live in conformity to what was given through the Spirit, both in the insight and in the love given to him. He must walk forward with confidence, and in his conduct he must observe closely what belongs to the gospel and to life in the Spirit. To walk (*stoichein*) means here to go in a definite order, straight forward in the direction indicated (cf. 6:16), and being guided by that which one knows belongs to life in the Spirit. Precisely because the Spirit had been given, the Christian must assiduously avoid that which belonged to the flesh.

It has sometimes appeared as a problem that Paul emphasizes so strongly that the gospel means that God through Christ justifies man without the works of the law, and at the same time can admonish his readers to walk in the Spirit. It is, however, precisely *because* the gospel means life in the Spirit, that it is meaningful and necessary continually to admonish and remind Christians of the obligation to walk in this Spirit and live in accordance with the righteousness given to them. The gospel is a power in which Christ himself is active, and the Christian is taken up into this activity and this life. Therefore, in watchfulness, labor, and conflict he must conduct himself in accordance with that which he has received. Now that God had fulfilled his promises through Christ and the fulfilment of the law was realized in a new covenant of freedom in love and service, everyone who became a partaker of it must conduct himself according to this freedom and not live in that which was characteristic of "the present evil age" (1:4). The Christian must die to what Paul has described as the works of "the flesh" (5:19-20), because he has "crucified the flesh" (5:24) and died with Christ. Baptism can of course be understood as baptism into death through which man is buried with Christ in order to "walk in newness of life" (Rom. 6:4). When man has "died to sin" (Rom. 6:2), the result is that he is not to live in sin. To have died means for Paul to die continually, and to have received righteousness means to receive it continually.

The appeal to the Christians not to be conformed to this world, but to be transformed by the renewal of their mind (Rom. 12:2), or to "walk by the Spirit," did not mean, therefore, that they now should develop their own morality by their own will and thus create their own righteousness. It meant rather that they should live in the righteousness God had sent through Christ. Now that God had made reconciliation for sin, and access to God and his grace had been secured (Rom. 5:2; Eph. 2:18), it was necessary to live faithfully in conformity with everything belonging to this context. Therefore the Galatians are exhorted to walk in the Spirit. Although the new life is not produced by the individual through his free will, he needs guidance, admonition, and exhortation (cf. Phil. 2:12). The ethical life is not constructed according to certain theories of what a virtuous life might be, nor according to certain general ideals. The starting point is a life and power already given through a proclamation which pointed to certain facts (the death and resurrection of Christ and everything connected with him). So it was not a question of efforts and works of the law, but neither was it a question of a passivity without a will of one's own. The presupposition of all the admonitions was the new situation created by the coming of the Messiah-Christ; i.e., atonement for sins, access to the righteousness of God, the power of the Spirit, and incorporation into the body of Christ in baptism. The Christian must live consistently with the fact that baptism meant dying to that which usually determined life—the passions and desires "of the flesh" (vs. 24). He had "crucified" all these. To be set free from them meant suffering and toil, and the Christian is not passive but actively engaged in this struggle. In the fellowship of the Spirit, the source of life and power, the Christian must strive and work. No one can produce what this fellowship contains. But once it has been given, the Christian can live in it, receive its power, be renewed, grow, and guard against everything that might hinder and obstruct this process. From this point of view justification by faith and an active life in conflict and work did not appear to be mutually exclusive. On the contrary, Paul's admonitions are rather, as we have said, the natural result of his conception of the gospel of Christ, who bestows righteousness on men without works of the law.

b) The application of the admonition to walk in the Spirit (5:26–6:6)

In vs. 26 Paul gives an example of how to avoid hindering life in the Spirit. A life bent on vainglory and popular recognition leads to envy, strife, and jealousy, to all those things which belong to "the flesh." By the Spirit they must "put to death the deeds of the body" and not live "after the flesh" (Rom. 8:13). It is natural, therefore, that Paul admonishes the Galatians not to seek vain honors. He had evidently heard that they esteemed honors highly, and he warns them against provoking envy among themselves. He who hankers after honors becomes a slave to this desire. Their relation to other people could be impaired by stirring them up to the same desire. A competition for places of honor or other forms of recognition is the opposite of the disposition to "outdo one another in showing honor" (Rom. 12:10).

The exhortation to restore in a spirit of gentleness anyone who by chance may have been overtaken in some trespass is based on the same point of view; i.e., walking by the Spirit. Paul turns to those who are called spiritual. There are different opinions about the meaning of this expression. Does it refer to the Christians in general, or is it a somewhat ironical reference to those free spirits who held that faith set them free from all moral obligations? Some commentators who have accepted wholly or in part the theory that Paul contends on two fronts have interpreted this as an admonition to those who regard themselves superior to all moral claims in and through the freedom of faith. (The theory is that especially in 5:13ff. Paul addresses himself to an antino-mian tendency among the Galatians which combined faith with libertinism.)

The context, however, seems to indicate that the reference is to all Christians, who, according to Paul, live by the Spirit and ought also to walk by the Spirit. "To restore him in a spirit of gentleness" is an application of what was said in 5:23, that the fruit of the Spirit is gentleness and love. The Christians were to live by the Spirit, and they were called to receive the fruits of the Spirit and to live in them. This meant that they should not condemn a brother who had sinned, but endeavor to restore him by gentle persuasion.

The Christians are not pictured as sinless at all; instead they are reminded how easy it is to fall into temptation. But the realization of this ought to prevent them from presumptuously condemning those who failed. In the spirit of "the flesh" men forgot their own faults and condemned others according to a rigid norm which enabled them to regard themselves as righteous. In the mind of "the Spirit" men see their own weakness and are not anxious to judge others. A disposition to judge the erring by a hard and fast norm indicated a lack of desire to understand their situation and temptations. In so doing they placed themselves on a different and higher level above those who were judged. The mind of faith and of the Spirit manifests itself in the fact that each one in humility counts others better than himself (Phil. 2:3).

The real Christian attitude in such a situation was to share the burden of the neighbor caused by his trespass. They were to bear his guilt and judgment with him. A self-righteous rejection and condemnation of those who trespassed did not belong to the mind of the Spirit. Just as Christ bore the sin and guilt of others, so the Christian must do likewise. The word "burdens" may refer not only to trespasses but also to difficulties and anxieties in general (cf. vs. 5). But the context seems to indicate especially the guilt which each one may have to bear. To bear one another's burdens is to fulfil "the law of Christ." "The law of Christ" seems to be used in contrast to the law on which the Judaizers wanted to base righteousness, just as in Rom. 8:2, where Paul contrasts the law of the Spirit of life with the law of sin and death. To share in the difficulties, failings, offenses, and guilt, and not to condemn presumptuously but rather to help the neighbor—this is to live in accordance with the love of Christ. Thus they "fulfilled the law" and will of Christ. Christ fulfilled the old law. His love laid the foundation of a life in which the fulfilling of the law is given. We may compare this with the statement, "that the just requirement of the law might be fulfilled in us, who walk not according to the flesh but according to the Spirit" (Rom. 8:4), and with Gal. 5:14, where it is said that "the whole law is fulfilled in one word,

273

'You shall love your neighbor as yourself.' " The kind of life that bears the burdens of others may be said to fulfil the law of Christ. The Jews believed that when the Messiah came, he would instruct them in a higher law. The law of Christ is the life in love. Paul says that he is not "without law toward God, but under the law of Christ" (I Cor. 9:21). The law of Christ is not external commandments which may be defined rationally and fulfilled by human efforts. It can be rightly fulfilled only in the life of the Spirit. In this life there is a given unity with the neighbor, so that we do not condemn and isolate him when he transgresses, but share with him in his suffering under the burden of guilt.

The opposite of bearing one another's burden is the self-satisfied spirit in which one thinks he is something even though he is nothing. A self-complacent man sees not his own faults but the faults of others; he sees the speck in his brother's eye but not the log in his own. The Pharisee in the temple felt that he was obviously better than the publican. In that spirit it is easy to consider oneself better than others. But this is self-delusion. This is not the kind of life lived in the Spirit. It is necessary, therefore, to test one's own work (cf. Rom. 14:10ff.).

One could reject a person because of his offenses, guilt, difficulties, and faults. This attitude would be an example of the life of the flesh. But if one lived the life in the Spirit, it would be possible to be so united with a person that one suffered with him, accepted his offenses as one's own, and as far as possible lightened his burdens. This attitude would not exclude a moral reaction against the wickedness and offenses perpetrated; but when one feels these things in love as being one's own for which one would suffer that they might not destroy the offender, every possibility of indulging in a moralistic condemnation would be removed, and the commandment to love one's neighbor as oneself would be realized.

If instead of being united with others and bearing their burdens, someone separated himself from them in self-sufficiency, as if he were better than they, he would deceive himself. Paul expresses himself hypothetically, "if any one thinks he is something, when he is nothing, he deceives himself." Anyone who despised others and in his self-sufficiency thought himself better than others did not see the reality concerning himself. What we are in ourselves can be seen only in the light of the gospel. But the gospel excluded self-righteousness and moralistic condemnation of others, and fostered instead love to the neighbor which is the fulfilment of the law.

To find the truth concerning oneself it would be necessary to test oneself and see what kind of work had been done. Everyone is to be judged according to his works (cf. Rom. 2:6; 14:12; Gal. 6:8; II Cor. 5:10).

It is difficult to say with certainty what Paul means by saying that the reason for boasting will "be in himself alone and not in his neighbor." The meaning is probably not that each one is to keep to himself whatever may be to his honor, and not boast of it to others. The idea is rather that false self-esteem, in which a man thinks he is something without having any real reason for it, is nourished by looking at the faults of others and thus appearing better than they. By condemning those who have become guilty of other sins and have manifested other weaknesses than those of which we ourselves are guilty, it is possible to look upon ourselves as perfect or at least superior to our neighbor. Paul urges the Christian to examine himself in order to discover his own faults and take them into consideration, that he might not dwell only on those things in which he may consider himself better than others and thus glory over them.

It seems proper in this context that Paul should add, "For each man will have to bear his own load." The faults and difficulties of one are not exactly the same as those of others. It is necessary, not only to point out the faults of others, but also to realize that each one has his own weakness.

The words, "each man will have to bear his own load," appear proverbial. They fit in here, however, because the meaning is that when a person looks at others and self-righteously compares himself with them, he ignores the difficulties and presuppositions under which each one acts. The words do not, therefore, stand in contradiction to the admonition about bearing one another's burden. Paul means, on the contrary, that due to this exhortation one should be willing to understand and participate in the difficulties of others. The Greek word for "burden" is not the same in vs. 2 (*baros,* burden) and vs. 5 (*phortion,* load), but there seems to be no essential difference between them.

The verb "bear" in vs. 5 is future, and is rendered thus in the Revised Standard Version: "For each man will have to bear his own load." It could also be translated, "each one will bear his own load." We may think of future difficulties during life on earth.

It is possible also that Paul was thinking about the coming judgment, when each one will have to bear the burden of his own guilt. We may compare Rom. 14:12, "So each of us shall give account of himself to God" (cf. Rom. 2:6; II Cor. 5:10). Paul never held that judgment of works could be eliminated through his proclamation of justification by faith. Faith belongs with the new life in the Spirit. In the judgment each one will be responsible for his own works.

It is difficult to decide whether vs. 5 refers to the judgment and the whole responsibility of life each one must assume, or if the meaning is more general, i.e., that in this life each one has his own weaknesses and difficulties to bear. The context seems to indicate that he has in mind the responsibility of each one on the day of judgment. The thought recurs in vss. 7ff.

The sixth verse seems to bring in a new idea, which appears to have no direct connection with the rest of the chapter. The meaning of the words is not obvious or certain. "Let him who is taught the word share all good things with him who teaches." It is uncertain whether the true meaning is, "he who is instructed in the word is to have fellowship with his teacher in all good things," or, ". . . shall give his teacher a share in all good things." Then the question has also been raised as to whether the good is spiritual good in which the teacher is to share with the disciple, or if the good is material good in which the teacher ought to have a share. Paul uses *agathon,* good, frequently about good things spiritual. But it does not seem impossible that it refers here to material goods (cf. Luke 12:18ff.; Phil. 4:15; II Cor. 9:12-13). The idea would then be related to what is said in Rom. 15:27 and I Cor. 9:11. The connection with the preceding would then be that fellowship between Christians ought to appear also in that those who are instructed in the word share their material goods with their teachers. The implication is that those who are instructed have better economic resources than the teachers, so that it would be fair for them to share it with the teachers, since they also participate in the teacher's spiritual riches. If the words mean simply that those who are taught ought to participate with the teachers in all spiritual good things, there would seem to be little point to the admonition.

It seems possible to conclude on the basis of vs. 6 that there was a well-developed ministry of teaching in Paul's congregations.

3. The inevitability of retribution (6:7-10)

a) Judgment according to works and justification by faith (6:7-8)

The expression, "Do not be deceived," in vs 7 emphasizes the seriousness of the admonition not to use freedom as an opportunity for the flesh. Whoever did not live according to the Spirit, but let the flesh dominate him, would have to suffer the consequences. Such a warning against abusing the Christian faith, as if it could be combined with a licentious and generally carnal life, occurs also in I Cor. 6:9-10 (cf. also I Cor. 15:33). He who participated in the life of the Spirit was also to walk by the Spirit and not misuse his freedom from the law by providing "an opportunity for the flesh" (5:13). He would not go unpunished who lived as if the consequences of evil were removed after he had been given freedom from the external commandments of the law of Moses. On the contrary, God's punishment is inevitable. If man does not take God and his gifts seriously, he will inevitably harvest the fruits of his evil life. Man cannot make himself master over God, or believe that freedom from the law means freedom to do evil and that to which his own selfish will and his lust drive him.

Paul emphasizes sharply that God is a just judge. In opposition to the fatal misunderstanding that the new freedom from the law meant that it would be possible to live according to the flesh he emphasizes here that each one shall be judged according to his works. We have shown before that this idea is not contrary to faith in righteousness from God given in Christ, but belongs with it. To Paul faith is certainly not a freedom from doing the good. On the contrary, true faith manifests itself in love and in actively doing good. In one sense the law of retribution ruled inexorably. If a man lived according to the nature of this age and acted as Paul describes in 5:19ff., he belongs to this perishable world and cannot expect eternal life. "The flesh" is associated with death, but life comes through the Spirit. Faith is not an opinion or a conception, but an active power, a faithful adherence to what God has done in Christ, and a life lived in accordance with the significance of that work of God. Life in faith is described, therefore, as a life or a walking by the Spirit. The whole of this section repeats with particular emphasis what was said in 5:13, 22-25. Here he points especially to the inevitable consequences in the retribution. The life of faith was a life in holiness (cf. Rom.

6:19). This means that man continually receives anew and lives in that righteousness which Christ came to give. That righteousness bestows forgiveness and restoration. But it stands in constant conflict with that which belongs to the works of "the flesh."

It has sometimes been asserted that there is a contradiction between Paul's doctrine of retribution and judgment according to *works* and his doctrine of justification by *faith*. If works and faith are conceived of as two different means of securing salvation and blessedness by man's own efforts, both works and faith would then be regarded as being in the service of man's own self. Faith would appear then as an easier way of obtaining salvation than works. Such a conception of justification by faith cannot of course be associated with the idea of judgment according to works.

This whole point of view, however, is entirely foreign to Paul. According to this view faith becomes a human act or effort, but this is not Paul's understanding of faith. Paul holds, as we have already pointed out, that the possibility of faith is given in the coming of the Messiah-Christ. Faith is congruent with that new state in which man realizes these facts and lives in accordance with them. It involves obedient submission to God's will and work, and a grateful acceptance of what God has made available through his work in Christ. In faith man participates in the righteousness, life, and Spirit which were promised and could be given when Christ had accomplished his work. The life of the believer is a participation in righteousness obtained now in and through his union with Christ. This righteousness will be given in its fulness at the return of Christ (cf. II Cor. 5:6ff.; I Cor. 13:12). The life of the believer is like running a race toward the goal. It is obvious that this life in faith does not exclude but rather demands works, i.e., the works of love. It is after all a walk in the Spirit and a struggle against the flesh and its enticements. Baptism was the act of consecration in this life. What was originally given in baptism is constantly realized anew in the Christian life. The union with Christ must continually be renewed in life. The Christian must die to the flesh and rise to a new life in the Spirit. The life of the Spirit is a part of that life which shall be revealed in its fulness at the return of Christ. This means, on the one hand, that "there is therefore now no condemnation for those who are in Christ Jesus" (Rom. 8:1); and, on the other hand, that "the flesh" and its works lead to death. Those who are united with Christ share in his victory over sin, death, and the condemning law, which lost its power when Christ took its curse upon himself. Through his resurrection he himself had received the life of the age to come, and he could now give the believer fellowship in this life. This life, the believer's goal, is never conceived of as something he wants to obtain in order to enjoy, or which he will possess and rule over as his own personal property. In the nature of the case life in the Spirit cannot be of that type; it is rather the kind of life exemplified in Christ's action of giving himself for men. Thus Paul, too, because he loved his "brethren according to the flesh" who had persecuted him and caused him constant suffering, could say that he would wish himself accursed and cut off from Christ, if that would in any way help them (Rom. 9:3).

On the basis of this conception of faith and righteousness there obviously can be no contradiction between the statements that righteousness belongs with faith and that nevertheless there must be a judgment according to works. The difficulty arises when we think of salvation according to an egocentric scheme, look only to ourselves, and ask about the requirements for salvation. According to Paul judgment according to works is as inseparably connected with the gospel of grace in Christ as his admonitions are to the struggle against righteousness by the law. It is precisely because the Christian has been born anew to a life in union with Christ that he must work out his own "salvation with fear and trembling" (Phil. 2:12); not as if this were his own accomplishment (then the result would be law-righteousness and hypocrisy), but because righteousness had been given to him, and righteousness is an active power. Only because God works both to will and to do can man's intense activity be good and meaningful. Only he who is righteous can do righteousness. Salvation is not because of works (Eph. 2:9), but "we are his workmanship, created in Christ Jesus for good works" (Eph. 2:10).

Here in Gal. 6:8 the inevitable retribution is presented in a figure of sowing and reaping. "Whatever a man sows, that he will also reap." The life and works of the Spirit and of the flesh had been illustrated in 5:19-23. The result of the works of the flesh would be destruction (*phthora*) and death, and this would be revealed at the coming of Christ. The result of life in the Spirit, on the other hand, was eternal life, which would also be manifested at the return of Christ. The argument here that the works of the

279

flesh and of the Spirit resulted respectively in destruction and life is completely contrary to the idea that man can earn righteousness and life by works of the law. But it is easy to confuse these ideas. In the works ("fruits") of the Spirit man is engaged in a struggle to live in accordance with the gospel which has been revealed and in which love realizes itself. In that life man does not seek his own advantages, because love, the first and greatest fruit of the Spirit, does not seek its own (I Cor. 13:5). He does not seek to gain eternal life in order selfishly to enjoy it for himself, just as Christ did not count equality with God a thing to be grasped (Phil. 2:6). Yet by inner necessity eternal life *follows* upon a life lived in accordance with the Spirit. As we have emphasized before, this life cannot be attained by man's own efforts. But man must practice and follow the love connected with faith. Whatever is in conflict with love must be resisted. He must turn away from the striving after "self-conceit" which leads to envy (Gal. 5:26). He must constantly follow the consequences of the death from "the passions and desires" of the flesh (5:24) experienced in baptism, in that he puts to death "what is earthly in you: immorality, impurity, passion, evil desire, and covetousness, which is idolatry" (Col. 3:5), and also puts away "anger, wrath, malice, slander, and foul talk" and lying (Col. 3:8). Acceptance of the gospel meant that man had "put off the old nature with its practices" and had "put on the new nature, which is being renewed in knowledge after the image of its creator" (Col. 3:10; cf. Eph. 4:20ff.). The renewal, in which man's whole will is involved, is an inalienable part of the life of faith. The result of not growing "weary in well-doing" or losing heart, and of living in the life of the Spirit, was that in due season the Christian would reap the harvest of such a life (Gal. 6:9). At the return of Christ, when the promised age was to be revealed in the fulness of its meaning, the consequences of the work of both the flesh and the Spirit would appear. It would then be revealed both that the works of the Spirit led to eternal life and that life in the flesh inherently resulted in destruction and death (Gal. 6:8).

The proclamation of justification by faith and judgment according to works therefore belong together. But righteousness by works or righteousness by the law constitutes a selfish attitude and self-aggrandizement on the part of the pious. According to Paul there is perfect agreement between the fact that the gospel is a gift of that God who himself accomplishes all things, and that men who by faith have been incorporated into the life of the gospel must be admonished not to conduct themselves "according to the flesh."

b) Do good to all men (6:9-10)

The reiterated admonitions to do good to all men emphasize the necessity of practicing and manifesting the love which belongs with faith. The Galatians ought to understand that their factionalism and quarrels (5:15) show that their life was not the true life of the Spirit. Love to the neighbor was the fulfilment of the law. If this love was not active even among those with whom they were united in faith, the new life would prove to be false and fruitless. Love meant a delight in doing good to everyone in both a personal and a material sense. Those who received the gospel were united in the body of Christ. If the situation in the congregation became such as was described in 5:15, faith had been without fruit, and the mind of the flesh had driven out the mind of the Spirit.

Some have thought that these verses refer especially to the failings of the disciples in regard to their teachers, and would therefore be connected with what was said in vs. 6. This seems hardly probable, since the passage actually summarizes very sharply what has been said in the last part of the letter from 5:13 onward. On the contrary, however, vs. 6, which in itself appears interpolated in the context, may be connected with the previous and following sections in the sense that it emphasizes the demand for generosity, love, and a just recognition of the value of the instruction.

The Apostle's Summarizing Conclusion (6:11-18)

The Letter to the Galatians ends with a few final words in which Paul summarizes the matter of most importance in the letter, the rejection of the Judaizers' demand for circumcision.

The final section begins with a reference to the fact that Paul himself wrote with large letters to them. In Paul's day of course it was common to dictate letters and documents. On the basis of Rom. 16:22 (cf. II Thess. 3:17; I Cor. 16:21; Col. 4:18) it would appear that Paul generally dictated his letters, and that he sometimes added a greeting written by his own hand as a mark of authenticity. This seems to have been a common custom in antiquity. (Sometimes a secretary would write the letter on the basis of general instruction, and after reading it the author would add the greeting in his own hand).

The question has been discussed as to whether Paul's words here in Gal. 6:11 refer to his concluding remarks or to the whole letter. A third possibility would be that they refer to the final section which begins at 5:2; but there is hardly sufficient evidence for this view. It is not impossible in itself that the words refer to the whole letter. Since it was common, however, to add a few words in one's own handwriting to a dictated letter, it would seem safe to assume that Paul has done so here. In I Cor. 16:21; II Thess. 3:17; Col. 4:18, we find similar greetings which he claims to have written by his own hand. It seems natural also to understand the words as referring to the final section of the letter beginning at vs. 11.

Although the Greek text uses past tense (aorist, "I wrote"), the meaning is that to the *readers,* to whom Paul turns with the address, "See," the action was in past time. Other examples of this are found in I Cor. 9:15 and Philem. 19.

Some have thought that Paul's words about writing with large letters indicates that his penmanship was bad, possibly due to the ill-treatment he had endured. It is more natural, however, to assume that he wanted to emphasize his personal greeting concerning circumcision, as we may underscore a sentence. To call attention to an important matter in this way was not uncommon.

What Paul is especially concerned about in these concluding

remarks is the Galatians' relationship to circumcision. He wants to emphasize that the Judaizers' motive for advocating circumcision was not a serious moral zeal but something of a baser sort. They wanted to be highly esteemed. In the beginning of the letter Paul himself posed the question as to whether he was seeking the favor of men, and he adds that, if he were to please men, he would not be a servant of Christ (1:10). The Judaizers did not want to be subjected to the hatred and persecution which was the result of consistently following the Christian way of life. They were not servants of Christ. In the Judaistic interpretation and application the Christian faith would become a form of Judaism. Judaism was a legitimate religion in the Roman Empire. If a person preached circumcision and observance of the law, he could hope that his proclamation would be tolerated as a sect by the Jews. The intense hatred on the part of the Jews, which was the cause of many persecutions, became inevitable if a person proclaimed the gospel without making circumcision and the observance of the law conditions for salvation.

Paul saw clearly that the price for escaping hatred and persecution must never be paid, since in that case the truth of the gospel would be lost. The idea of righteousness by the law was inseparably connected with the circumcision of Gentiles. If they now demanded fulfilment of the law in the old sense, it would mean a corruption of faith in salvation through Christ.

That the Judaizers' zeal for circumcision was not geniune is evidenced, says Paul, by the fact that they themselves did not keep the law. As a Pharisee Paul had learned that the law was indivisible. To break *one* commandment was to break all (cf. 5:3). It was not possible to keep a part of the law and skip other parts. This was condemned even in Jewish interpretation. The Judaizers wanted to escape persecution and have the honor of being the leaders whom the Galatians followed and who had brought them back to circumcision. Paul is anxious to emphasize that it is not a question of a real keeping of the law. These Judaizers did not keep the law in the Jewish sense, and much less did they keep it in the deeper, Christian sense (cf. 5:14; Rom. 8:4). But they wanted to have the glory of having the Galatians show by their circumcision that they were their followers. Even though they were possibly Gentiles by birth, they carried on a zealous Jewish propaganda.

It would be quite proper to ask about Paul's own motives. He has stated them clearly. He does not seek glory for himself. His only glorying is in the cross of Christ. Through the cross he has been crucified to the world, and the world to him. What to the world was the greatest shame, the execution of Jesus on the cross, was to him the greatest glory. *To glory* in the cross was a strange paradox. But "the foolishness of God is wiser than men, and the weakness of God is stronger than men" (I Cor. 1:25). Circumcision and the law were the honor and glory of the Jews. But this was a glorying according to the common standard among men. There is another glory, that which comes from God. This was connected with the fulfilment of the law in the Spirit, and the condition for that was the cross of Christ. Thus the true circumcision took place. "He is a Jew who is one inwardly, and real circumcision is a matter of the heart, spiritual and not literal. His praise is not from men but from God" (Rom. 2:29). This praise Paul possessed. The new righteousness had come through the cross of Christ. Paul's statement in 6:14 is closely related to his words in 2:19. We might also say that I Cor. 1:18–2:16 elaborates what is referred to very briefly here (cf. also Deut. 10:16; 30:6; Jer. 4:4; 9:25-26).

Through the cross of Christ the world was dead to Paul. He was not bound by it, nor by the desire for recognition and honor connected with it. He had seen the life of God revealed through the cross, which to the world was the greatest shame. Circumcision, the pride of being a Jew, belonging to the chosen people, and being righteous through the law—all this was of the world. Paul had found the center of his life in a new life, and he was now dead to all the rest. He did not simply relinquish it. He was as separated from it as if he had died. Just as all this had lost its power to entice and influence him, so his attachment was to another world. Therefore he was no longer concerned with the things of this age. The statement that the world was dead to him and he to the world expresses the same idea from a different point of view. What he had found in Christ was his sole glory and boast. Here were the motives for everything in his life and work.

These ideas remind us of 2:19-20. Through the cross of Christ the whole world has been crucified to Paul. The whole world, as well as his own "self," the natural self connected with the world, has died through the cross of Christ. In the resurrection of Christ the powers and life of a new age had come. The self which was tied to the world, and the world which held this self in captivity, con-

stituted the reality of "the flesh," whose typical reaction and work
were described in 5:19ff., and which by nature belonged to death
(cf. 6:8). The Christian must not live after the flesh, as Paul
explains in Rom. 8:12-14. "For if you live according to the flesh
you will die, but if by the Spirit you put to death the deeds of the
body you will live. For all who are led by the Spirit of God are
sons of God."

The Spirit of Christ, the power and life of the promised new
age, became a reality when Jesus the Messiah came. Through
faith Christians participate in this reality even now before the
return of Christ. Someday the new life—perceived even now—
will be given to them. The cross of Christ was the boundary between the rule of the old and that of the new. Through the body
men continued to belong to "the present evil age" (1:4), and
consequently they also must die (Rom. 8:10). Since Christ
through his cross has taken away the curse of the law (3:13),
which constituted the power of sin (cf. I Cor. 15:56), "the evil
age" had been overcome. Those who had been incorporated into
the body of Christ and had been crucified with him were therefore free from the power of the present age. For the new man in
whom Christ lived, and who in this world lived by faith in Christ
(2:20), the ways of this age were something foreign. To him the
world was dead.

Paul therefore summarizes his point of view in the words: "For
neither circumcision counts for anything, nor uncircumcision, but
a new creation" (cf. 2:20). By these words he emphasizes what
he has said in the whole letter and especially in 5:6. To be a new
creature and to have a faith working through love, as he says in
5:6, is one and the same thing (cf. also Col. 3:11).

The same thought occurs in I Cor. 7:19. "Neither circumcision
counts for anything nor uncircumcision, but keeping the commandments of God." The Jews who had the law did not keep the
law even in its external sense (Rom. 2:17ff.) It was precisely those
who walked by the Spirit that kept the law in its proper sense.

Even though it can be said that, according to Paul, the commandments of God are fulfilled through faith, the meaning is not
that the Spirit or faith supplied the power to fulfil the commandments in the old, literal, Jewish sense. But what could not be done
through commandments and works of the law was accomplished
in the Spirit and in faith. The law was "weak through the flesh"
and could not produce life and righteousness. But in faith man did

not stand in the presence of commandments he wanted to realize in order to obtain his own righteousness. On the contrary, righteousness was given to him in faith. Love, too, was given in faith. To do God's will did not mean to keep certain definite commands through which man could attain to righteousness. God's will was done in faith, in which man had become a new creature.

The expression "a new creation" is known from rabbinical writings. Even if Paul has borrowed the expression from that source, he has at any rate given it a new meaning. He in whom Christ lives (2:20) is a new creature. In II Cor. 5:17 the expression "a new creation" occurs in a pregnant sense: "If any one is in Christ, he is a new creation; the old has passed away, behold, the new has come."

A new creation means not simply the reception of certain spiritual gifts, but participation in a new existence, in the new world that has come in Christ. The word creation (*ktisis*) does not refer primarily to the act of creation, but to the new state which has come in Christ. But this presupposes an act of creation. As we have pointed out in the exegesis of 1:15-17, Paul associates the light of faith in the heart with the action of God in the creation of the world in II Cor. 4:6: "For it is the God who said, 'Let light shine out of darkness,' who has shone in our hearts to give the light of the knowledge of the glory of God in the face of Christ." The same power of God that was active in creation had now been at work in and through Christ, and it was constantly active now in the gospel through which the Christian became a new creation. He explains in II Cor. 5:17ff. how the new creation is connected with the work of reconciliation: "All this is from God, who through Christ reconciled us to himself." That Christ had come and accomplished his work, that the reconciliation had taken place and Christ had risen again, was a new creative act of God. The work of reconciliation continues now in that it becomes continually valid for men through the ministry of reconciliation. Something new had come, a new creation, and man had been made a part of it. The divine act of justification continued. That the new could be said to be the fulfilment of the promise and the fulfilling of the law, and in this way was connected with God's previous work, does not make it any less new. Because the splendor of the ministration of the Spirit was boundless, what before had had splendor had no splendor at all (II Cor. 3:10).

In vss. 12-16 Paul has summarized briefly what to him was

most important in the letter. His point was that for circumcision to be given a decisive importance was to deny the revelation in Christ. This would mean hiding from oneself the persuasive, penetrating, and superlative significance of the gospel. If salvation were made dependent on law and circumcision, the new would be denied. It was a question of life and death, therefore, when the Judaizers, in order to avoid persecution and offense, wanted to transform the Messianic faith in the righteousness from God through Christ into something connected with the demand for circumcision. Even though they were willing to admit that the Messiah had come in Jesus, they denied by their demand for circumcision the faith that belonged to the Messianic time. Those who submitted to circumcision were severed from Christ and had fallen away from grace (5:4).

In connection with Paul's summary in these verses we may consider his most urgent concern in the whole letter: it was of vital importance to establish the fact that circumcision was not a condition for fellowship in the church. Uncertainty on that point could bring serious consequences. It was for this reason that Paul had clashed so sharply with Peter in Antioch. It was Paul's special task to clarify the meaning of the gospel at this point. He had been called for this purpose, and therefore he was conscious of having been chosen as the apostle to the Gentiles and a servant of the gospel. For this reason his proclamation had a special tone and a greater sharpness in regard to circumcision than the preaching of the other apostles. His gospel was not only *directed* to the Gentiles, but he had seen that, because of its very content, it could not be connected with a demand for circumcision. It was not so that the primary task was the conversion of the Jews, and then the Gentiles could be permitted to join the church of the Jewish Christians. The conversion of the Gentiles was now the primary task, and only through this development would the full number of the Jews adhere to the faith. But it was this very *gospel to the Gentiles* that presented the facts most clearly and in the right relationship to the law. Paul could therefore speak of *my* gospel, although there was only *one* gospel (1:7). He had been entrusted with the proclamation of the gospel in a special context and with a special connotation and clarity. He proclaimed the same reality as the other apostles, but he did so in an especially incisive and clear form.

According to Paul the work of the gospel was a continuation of

287

God's redemptive work in the Old Testament, but in a new form. The promised Messiah had come in Christ, and in the gospel concerning him God himself was present with salvation. In the gospel God bestowed salvation and life on those who accepted it. God himself had chosen Paul as a servant of the gospel. Through him it was to be brought to the Gentiles. This work was now in progress, and God's final election, anticipated in the time of the old covenant, was even now taking place. In this election in the last days the Gentiles were being received as fellow heirs with the Jews in the promised salvation. It was precisely this faith in securing life and righteousness through law, circumcision, and observance of commandments that had caused unrest, led the Galatians astray, and had compelled Paul to intervene with this letter. Now he hopes that he has restored the Galatians to the gospel, and that henceforth they will live in a faith working through love.

It has generally been held as beyond question that those who advocated circumcision in Galatia were Jewish Christians. There are many factors in favor of this view. They were of course contending for a Jewish-Christian point of view. A century ago the Tübingen School argued that they were Jewish Christians closely related to the Jerusalem apostles. Even since it became clear that the theories of the Tübingen School had to be modified, these Judaizers have generally been regarded as Jewish Christians.

As we have indicated in our exegesis of Galatians 2, the theory of a fundamental, theological conflict between Paul and the Jerusalem apostles is certainly false, even though there may have been divergences and minor differences in regard to the meaning of the gospel. The large work by Johannes Munck, *Paulus und die Heilsgeschichte*, presents a radical criticism not only of the Tübingen School but also of its persistent aftereffects. Munck points out especially (p. 79ff.) that the words which describe those who advocate circumcision in 6:13 indicate that they were Gentile Christians. The best attested text is "those who let themselves be circumcised" (*peritemnomenoi*), not "those who have been circumcised," or "the circumcised." This seems to imply that he is thinking of people who were not circumcised as children but are receiving it now. Even if this passage does not fully prove that they were Gentile Christians—the expression could designate the group in which circumcision regularly took place—it would seem most natural to interpret it as referring to those who were not yet circumcised, but who advocated this for themselves and for others. The common assumption that the Judaizers *must* have been Jewish Christians depends on the claim that has been reiterated over more than a century, that they were sent out from Jerusalem, and that the apostles there represented a point of view contrary to Paul. (Peter was certainly not a Judaizer. Cf. also Hirsch, *Zwei Fragen zu Galater 6*, [Z.N.W., 1939]) If we abandon that conception, it would seem natural to regard the Judaizers in Galatia mostly as Gentiles who had understood the gospel as a form of Judaism, and who in their eagerness to share in the righteousness spoken of in the Scriptures wanted to combine faith in Jesus as the Messiah with circumcision and observance of the law. They could have advocated circumcision both before and after their own submission to it.

We should also observe Paul's statement in 5:12: "I wish those who unsettle you would mutilate themselves." This sounds as if the troublemakers were not yet circumcised.

Even though the Galatians had heard Paul's instruction, they had never understood the whole meaning of the gospel, because it implied really a special interpretation of the Old Testament Scriptures. Paul did not make the Gentiles into Jewish proselytes, but he surely instructed them in the Old Testament. He interpreted the promises and guided them into the thinking found in Scripture. We must never forget that the Old Testament was the Bible of the Gentile Christians also and the holy document to which Paul referred them.

Possibly after these Gentile Christians no longer stood directly under Paul's influence and teaching, they began to interpret the Old Testament in a more Jewish sense. That Jews and Jewish Christians who retained the Jewish view of the law were active in this agitation is probable. Paul's interpretation was based on the revelation he had received. Those who had been converted but had not examined the Scriptures themselves from the new point of view could easily begin to interpret them in a rather superficial fashion. In this they would be encouraged by the traditional Jewish interpretation. There were synagogues and Jews near them, from whom they could learn to read the Old Testament from the Jewish point of view. It is not difficult to understand that they could readily accept the proclamation that Jesus was the Messiah, but for the rest were encouraged to follow the Jewish interpretation of the law and circumcision as requirements for salvation. Paul himself regarded Jerusalem as the center of Christianity. He gathered money for the poor in Jerusalem. The Jewish Christians were, of course, circumcised and in general adhered to the law. It is easy to understand how the Gentile Christians would be eager to conduct themselves as Jewish Christians, and that they would fail to see what appeared superficially as a paradox, that only freedom from the law in its Jewish interpretation could lead to a true obedience to the law in its real sense.

It is therefore easy to understand how the opinion could arise that it was proper to follow the law in certain external respects, and that this was a requirement for obtaining full righteousness. They may have argued that they ought to be circumcised and seek salvation *both* through the law *and* through faith in Jesus as the Messiah. What the Judaizers failed to see was that they were two different ways of salvation which could never be combined. They did not understand that faith in Christ absolutely *excluded* the way of salvation by means of the righteousness of the law. What they denied was exactly that which had been entrusted to Paul through revelation.

What complicates the question as to whether the Judaizers were Jewish or Gentile Christians is the fact that they may have been Gentile Christians who were about to submit to circumcision or already had done so. They accepted the Jewish Christians as a pattern in a false sense, and in doing so they were possibly encouraged by those who were unable to relinquish the Jewish conception of the law and Jewish exclusiveness. Other Jewish Christians apparently continued to observe the law, at least in part, without making it a requirement for righteousness. The Judaizers wanted to be similar to them in an external sense and accept circumcision, but in doing so they had to regard circumcision and the observance of the law (for example in regard to clean and unclean food and table fellowship) as requirements for righteousness and as something without which membership in the church could not be obtained. By accepting this false view they transformed the gospel into its opposite and made righteousness through faith in Christ a righteousness by the law. That certain of the circumcised still felt compelled to regard these requirements as necessary for membership in the church is probable, as we have said, and they thus encouraged the zeal of the Judaizing Gentile Christians. This was the cause of the conflict itself and the reason why Paul had to intervene as sharply as he does in the letter. For this reason he had to write such violent and desperate words as in 1:8-9; 4:19-20; and 5:12, since he had heard that the Galatians had permitted themselves to be enticed to a teaching which resembled the gospel but in reality was its exact opposite.

Finally Paul pronounces peace and mercy upon those who walk according to the rule he had indicated. They could not live according to that which was regarded as important in this age. Peace and mercy were the fruits of the Spirit, spiritual realities of the new life. Paul wishes that these may be given to the Galatians. His wish is meant as a gift he sends; a reality which he not only wishes for them, but bespeaks for them in such a way that they will actually receive it (cf. 1:3 above, and Matt. 10:12-13; Luke 10:5-6).

Those who had truly received the gospel constituted the new people of God, the true Israel, to which Scripture bore witness. The new people of God were related to the people of the old covenant in the same way as righteousness from God was related to the revelation through the law. The people of the old covenant had to prepare for and be a prototype of the new Israel. Through baptism into Christ, through faith in him, and through his Spirit this new people of God became the true circumcision according to the circumcision which is not made with hands (Phil. 3:3; Col. 2:11; Rom. 3:29-30), as Paul elsewhere expressed this same idea. God's Israel is therefore God's people in the eschatological sense. They belong to the last days and fulfil that which happened to the Israel of old. This Israel receives the fulfilment of the promises and realizes the law in its true sense, after its former external meaning and validity had been abrogated. That Israel of which Paul speaks especially in Rom. 9:6ff. is the Israel of promise. But the promise was fulfilled in Christ. All those who belonged to him were the children of promise. This Israel was to be completed when the fulness of the children of Israel according to the flesh would be incorporated into it. Thus the children of Israel according to the flesh were to find the way back to their election and to the promises given to them (Rom. 3:2).

Finally Paul expresses the hope that no one will cause him any further anxiety. He hopes that he has elucidated the meaning of the gospel and its relationship to circumcision so clearly in the letter that he will not need to worry any more about the attitude of the Galatians. He mentions as a special reason for this hope that he bears on his body "the marks (*stigmata*) of Jesus." This word "stigma" lies back of the expression "to stigmatize." The question has been asked whether Paul's words here imply that he had been stigmatized. There is, however, no report of his having been stigmatized at this time. It seems more natural to understand them as a reference to the marks he had on his body as a result of scourgings and torture for the sake of Christ (cf. II Cor. 11:23ff.). In II Cor. 4:10 he speaks of the marks of death: "always carrying in the body the death [Swedish version, "marks of death"] of Jesus, so that the life of Jesus may also be manifested in our bodies." In the ancient world a slave might be branded to show that he belonged to a specific master. In this way he was also protected against claims from others. It was a custom that the slaves of a temple received special signs which marked them for life as belonging to a diety. Paul speaks of himself as a bond-servant of Jesus Christ. Christian freedom consisted in being a slave to the neighbor in the service of love (5:13). We may compare I Cor. 7:22: "He who was called in the Lord as a slave is a freedman of the Lord. Likewise he who was free when called is a slave of Christ."

"The sufferings of Christ" which Paul had endured (II Cor. 1:5) had left their marks upon his body. These marked him as a slave of Christ. These gave him also the authority to speak as one who completely belonged to Christ. His authority as an apostle was confirmed by these marks of suffering. In reality an apostle is known through his sufferings for the sake of Christ (cf. II Cor. 1:5; 4:10ff.; Rom. 5:3; 8:17; Phil. 3:10-11; II Tim. 2:9ff.).

Contrary to his usual custom Paul did not end his letter with personal greetings but with a summary of his message. He ends with the apostolic benediction on the Galatian congregations. In spite of the severity of the letter he calls them here as in 1:11 and 4:12 his "brethren," and adds to it a confirmatory "Amen." The grace of Christ will guard them against turning away from faith in Christ and from righteousness in him, and it will preserve them as Paul's brethren in the church of Christ.

Concluding Review

The Letter to the Galatians is one of the oldest of the New Testament writings. It averted the great danger that the church might have become a Messianic sect within Judaism. In that case late Judaism's conception of salvation and the way of salvation would have been retained in principle, even though Jesus was acknowledged as the Messiah. His work would then have been that of a teacher and prophet who proclaimed a new morality, a deeper faith, and a law and manner of life valid for a small, exclusive group.

In our day through the celebrated discoveries in the Qumram Caves it becomes abundantly clear how easily the Christians under Jewish influence could have transformed the church into a Jewish, Messianic sect in one form or another. Paul's letters testify to the struggle against such dangers. The letters of Paul have always been regarded by the Jews as the most difficult to understand of the whole New Testament and have been most decisively rejected. It is more difficult to reinterpret them in the direction of a general idealism than for instance the Gospels. But in reality the proclamation of Paul is the same as that of Jesus, and his theology is closely related to the rest of the New Testament.

When Paul had come to the insight that the Messiah had come, and that this involved the fulfilment of both the law and the promise in the Old Testament Scriptures, he insisted that an entirely new situation had been created, which included the whole world. Paul did not conceive of the law as a static entity completed before Christ, but as an expression of the word and acts of the living God. The law had been carried to its conclusion, but this did not mean at all that it was set aside. On the contrary, now for the first time it could speak in the full sense. It represented for Israel a living tradition which determined the whole of life. According to Paul it had now attained to its final goal. Obviously this involved many changes. But it did not mean that the past was denied or was declared wrong. On the contrary, it was confirmed in being brought to fulfilment. Now the light shone over the whole of its truth. The gospel was the fulfilment and the purpose and inmost will of the law, through which everything was brought out fully and clearly.

The law could never be fulfilled by keeping the commandments in fear and hope of reward; it could be done only when the life the law represented was fully realized in freedom. This freedom was given through the Spirit who is present in the church now because Christ had fulfilled the law through his work. What the law had intended to accomplish could now be done through the Spirit without running the risk that these works became simply a keeping of certain precepts in order thereby to gain "righteousness" (cf. Rom. 8:3-4; 9:31-32; 10:3). Such a righteousness of the law was easily connected with the breaking of the most elementary commandments (cf. Mark 7:3-15). The gospel extended beyond what the Mosaic law had been able to prescribe, and what earlier had been found in it. The meaning of the gospel was not that it provided a power to keep such commandments as had previously been too heavy and difficult to do. Its central point was that reconciliation and righteousness had now become a reality in Christ.

The fulfilment of the law through Christ took place when on the cross he took its condemnation upon himself. The task of the law was of course to reveal and judge sin. When Christ took its condemnation upon himself the condemnation was removed. "There is therefore now no condemnation for those who are in Christ Jesus" (Rom. 8:1). It is natural, therefore, for Paul's whole theology to have its center in the proclamation of the cross (cf. e.g., I Cor. 1:17-18; 2:2). The church, the people of the new covenant, the children of promise, "the Jerusalem above" (Gal. 4:26), the Israel of God, had life because Christ was present among them. In the union with him in faith the Christian participated in Christ's fulfilment of the law. This meant that he lived both in freedom *from* condemnation and *from* the necessity of having to procure righteousness through works of the law, and in freedom *to do* the works and to show forth the love belonging to the new life in Christ. The fulfilment of the law appears in both aspects of this freedom (cf. Gal. 3:13-14; 5:14). Sharing in the righteousness of Christ involved the fact that the Christian was crucified with Christ and lived in the Spirit, whereby the demands of the law were fully met in him.

It was clear from the very beginning, therefore, that obedience and works could not be motivated by an endeavor to build up one's own righteousness. The gospel meant the diametrical opposite of righteousness by works and law. It came as a proclamation of righteousness by faith. But in it the completion and fulfilment of the law were assumed and its fulness was given in and through the Spirit, through whom the Christian was united with the living Christ and his fulfilment of the law. In the life in the Spirit there appeared continually new works, in which man did not seek his own righteousness, but which were inseparably connected with faith. The Spirit was the Spirit of Christ. He was the sign that the living Christ was present and active in the church, and that the individual participated in life and righteousness through faith. To believe meant to be united with Christ so that he became *one* with the believer (Gal. 2:20). In faith God was acknowledged as true. Man submitted and held fast to the God who had now fulfilled his promises to Abraham, and who had now brought the election and the redemptive acts, of which the Scriptures of the old covenant spoke, to their fulness and final goal.

The prophets, too, had condemned the false righteousness the people had provided for themselves in their unfaithfulness to God's election (cf., e.g., Isa. 57:12). Paul prevented the young church from adopting the conception of righteousness prevalent among the Pharisees and the rabbis. He elucidated the nature of the gospel, and showed thereby also that righteousness in life here on earth must have its foundation and goal in the righteousness which belongs to the age beyond the boundaries of this present age, and which has been revealed through the risen Christ.

The settlement with the Judaizers, therefore, involved a great deal more than a significant event in the history of religion through which the young church was set free from a Jewish religion limited by legal precepts and circumcision. In the conception of the New Testament the coming of the Messianic time and the death and resurrection of Jesus meant that the Spirit, the power of the promised age to come, had already become active (cf. John 7:39; Acts 2:16ff.). Christ was not the Messiah of the Jews alone. During his earthly ministry Jesus had addressed himself primarily to "the lost sheep of the house of Israel" (cf. Matt. 15:24), and declared that he was sent to them. But his whole proclamation and his work envisioned a kingdom of God which would include all peoples, and which extended beyond the limitation of this world and time into an eternal kingdom of righteousness. According to the Gospel of John he spoke also of "other sheep" who were not of this fold (John 10:16), but whom he must also draw to himself (John 12:32). In the resurrection all limitations were abrogated. He was of the house of David "according to the flesh"

(Rom. 1:3), and through the resurrection he was "designated Son of God in power" (Rom. 1:4). As the Son of God he was the Lord of the world. The Gospels apply to him the divine name of the Old Testament: *kurios,* Lord. After the resurrection it became clear to the disciples that he was the Son of God (cf. John 20:28). What they had at times surmised or understood (cf. Matt. 16:16) had now become fully clear. Jesus was Lord both of this world and of the age to come. He was the Son of God. He was exalted to divine glory and honor, and was made by God both Lord and Messiah (cf. Acts 2:29-36). Because this was so, the gospel had a message to the whole world, a message valid even beyond the limits of time. The Spirit in the church was the earnest of the life to come. Through the Spirit life was characterized by a righteousness which by nature did not belong to this present age (cf. p. 268 above, and John 7:38-39; 16:7-15). The gospel did not imply, therefore, a morality, a doctrine, or a piety for this life alone. It united life on earth with the righteousness for which man had been created. This righteousness will appear in its full consummation when once death also has been overcome and the eternal life which belongs with this righteousness shall have appeared.

Type used in this book:
 Body, 10 on 12 and 9 on 10 Times Roman.
 Display, Airport Semi-bold.

Paper: White Spring Grove E. F.

DATE DUE